Success
in the
Workplace

2nd Edition

Margaret Brand

Ann Olney Sparkes

Berne J. Neufeld

**A Copp Clark Pitman
Business Book**

Copp Clark Ltd.

ISBN 0-7730-5552-5

Editing/Sheila Fletcher, June Trusty
Text Design & Illustrations/Christine Gilham
Cover Design/Allan Moon
Typesetting/April Haisell
Printing and binding/Webcom Limited

A B C D E F –WC– 01 00 99 98 97 96

Canadian Cataloguing in Publication Data
Main entry under title:
Success in the Workplace

2nd ed.
ISBN 0-7730-5552-5

1. Success in business. 2. Vocational guidance.
I. Brand, Margaret. II. Olney Sparkes, Ann.
III. Neufeld, Berne J.

HF536.S5 1996   650.1 C86-930112-X

Printed and bound in Canada

Acknowledgments

The original *Work and Employability Skills* modules, on which the first edition of this textbook is based, were prepared by the Eastern Townships School Board with the encouragement, advice, and assistance of many individuals and groups. The following are particularly thanked for their contributions.

H. Auger	D. Farrell	J. Mulholland
R. Beasse	D. Fidler	M. Mildon
D. Belden	J. Garneau	D. Nixon
N. Bilodeau	G. Goddard	R. Orr
J. Boluk	P. Grant	J. Perry-Gore
S.P. Chadha	M. Anaka-Hogue	A. Quick
S. Cochrane	P. Marcoux	C. Rodger
G. Dallaire	T. Matthews	L. Roy
K. Danaher	R. McConnachie	I. Smith
L. Doyle	W. McGee	R. Stymiest
A. Edwards	L. Miller	M. Taylor

Appreciation is also expressed to Paulette Proulx, Assistant to the National Co-ordinator of Education, Canadian Federation of Labour, for reviewing Chapter 20, "Labour Unions."

The publisher gratefully acknowledges the following whose responses to our survey on *Success in the Workplace* have assisted us in developing the second edition.

Carmen Graham
Grant Park HS, Winnipeg, MB

Robert Greene
Athens DHS, Athens, ON

Andy McKerroll
Wiarton DHS, Wiarton, ON

Sheila B. Hynes
Academy Canada Career College,
    Corner Brook, NF

Kim Northcott
Academy Canada Career College,
    St. John's, NF

Marilyn Cornish
Central College of Applied Arts,
    Technology and Continuing
    Education, Gander, NF

Frank Ryan
Sentinel SS, Vancouver, BC

Margaret Selassie
Northern CI & VS, Sarnia, ON

Cathy Hortsing
G.A. Wheable Centre for Adult
    Education, London, ON

Leah Taylor
Northern Lights College, Tumberler
    Ridge, BC

Don Giles
St. Marys DC & VI, St. Mary's ON

Roger Howse
Frontier School Div. No. 48,
    Winnipeg, MB

Gemma Brooks
Chomedey HS (Commercial
    Education Centre), Laval, PQ

Jessi Zielke
West Vancouver SS, Vancouver, BC

Acknowledgments

As indicated in the Preface, many revisions were made in order to ensure that *Success in the Workplace* remained current and relevant to today's students.

As author of the second edition. I wish sincerely to thank the following for their enthusiastic support and guidance: Ms. Brenda L. Shuflita, Labour Market Analyst, Human Resources Development Canada, Saanich Human Resource Centre of Canada, Victoria, B.C., for providing the most current career and labour market information available; Ms. Kathy Stephens, Economist, Research and Analysis, British Columbia Ministry of Education, Skills and Training, for sharing *Making Career Sense of Labour Market Information* with me; Mrs. Donna Michaels, Superintendent of Schools, Greater Victoria School District, for her wise counsel and moral support, and Ms. Carrie Trumpy, Department Head at Lambrick Park Secondary School, for pointing me towards invaluable resources on portfolios.

Special thanks is also due to four very special people at Copp Clark Ltd.: Ms. Marion Elliot, Managing Editor, School, Business, and Special Projects, for her unfailing, steadying influence; Ms. Susan R. Cox, Product Development Manager, Business Studies, for tirelessly supplying needed research materials; Ms. Sheila Fletcher, my intrepid Senior Editor, Business Studies, for her invaluable assistance; and, Mr. Hank Luck, Sales Representative for Copp Clark Ltd. in British Columbia, for promoting education through the able representation of his company for over 20 years.

Berne J. Neufeld

To my wonderful husband, Leo who has given me support and help with my career, and who has enjoyed so many successes in his

and

to our beloved son, Jason who has been a constant source of comfort, patience and encouragement

Preface

The first edition of *Success in the Workplace* was compiled by Margaret Brand and Ann Olney Sparkes, based on modules prepared by the Eastern Townships School Board. I was privileged to pilot this text in my Business and Technology, Entrepreneurship, International Co-operative Education program at Lambrick Park Secondary School, Victoria, B.C., in 1990 and, based on this positive experience, adopted it as part of the curriculum of the Program. Thus, I felt very honoured when asked by Copp Clark Ltd. to revise and update sections of *Success in the Workplace*.

In *Success in the Workplace, 2/e*, Chapters 3 through 12 have been completely revised to reflect the recent, dramatic changes in the workplace environment. Chapters 13 through 20 have been partially modified to reflect these same changes, and Unit 6 has been incorporated throughout the revised text. Chapter 4, Enhancing Your Employability Skills and Portfolio of Employability Skills, is new to the second edition.

Reflective learning has become a very effective tool both in the classroom and in the workplace. Accordingly, reflective learning exercises have been included in each chapter. Also, optional Internet activities have been added to some chapters. Following these suggestions, your curiosity and ingenuity will undoubtedly find other ways in using this powerful resource–the information highway. The last question in most exercise sets is one that presents a challenge by demanding quality thinking skills.

Finally, the messages of *Success in the Workplace, 2/e* to work-seekers are that the world of work is constantly changing and that success requires rapid adaptation to these changes. Arm yourself with a portfolio of skills and knowledge, carry an upbeat attitude and be prepared quickly to adapt to change. Riding the waves of change will be exciting, liberating and invigorating. We are confident that *Success in the Workplace, 2/e*, will inspire the reader with the attitude and knowledge to be truly successful in the world of work, wherever it may be.

Berne J. Neufeld

Readers who wish to do so may contact the author at her e-mail address: bneufeld@pinc.com

Contents

UNIT 1

You and the World of Work

introduction

Unit I will assist you to assess your interests and personal qualities. Learning the relationship between personal values, decision making, and the setting of goals will help you to understand the importance of setting short- and long-term goals. The chapter on employability skills will help you to target those generic employability skills that are crucial for today's workplace. The chapter on changing trends in the world of work explains some of the ways in which the workplace is changing and further emphasizes the types of skills that employees and employers need now and will need in the future. Careful study of this unit will provide you with the tools to make choices for a winning future.

Chapter 1

Discovering Your Self-Concept

<table>
<tr><td>objectives</td><td>After completing this chapter you should be able to:

▶ Explain what you like and what you don't like about yourself.
▶ Appreciate your own achievements more.
▶ Define the characteristics you value in other people.
▶ Understand that many types of work require people with specific characteristics.
▶ Identify occupations that your characteristics might suit.</td></tr>
</table>

introduction

Who are you? You might answer this question with your name and some information about your family and school. Such information helps to identify you to others, but have you ever realized that you also need ways to identify and explain yourself to yourself?

The way you see yourself is called your *self-concept*. You begin to develop a self-concept early in life and keep revising and reassessing it as you continue to change and have different experiences.

Developing a self-concept is like looking in a mirror, because it depends so much on how you believe others see you. You imagine how you appear to other people, and your experience in a situation might confirm or deny that. If the experience doesn't confirm it, you might change your self-concept to match the experience. For example, perhaps you think of yourself as a bit of a "loner." Then someone persuades you to try bowling as a hobby and you find that you really enjoy being part of a team. The probable result is that you'll adjust your self-concept.

How does the idea of self-concept relate to the world of work? You've probably heard people say, "I'm a schoolteacher," "I'm an office manager," in describing their social roles. What you do in the world of work forms a large part of your self-concept as an adult. It's important, then, for you to explain yourself to yourself as well as possible. Then the person you truly are can identify occupations that will satisfy and reward you, and contribute most to your self-concept. The following exercises will help you to analyse how you see yourself.

ACTIVITY 1

Identifying Your Self-Concept

Answer the following questions and give examples that illustrate your answers.

1. How is it helpful for us to compare ourselves with other people?
2. Is it sometimes harmful to compare ourselves with others?

3. With whom do you compare yourself?
4. Whom do you admire most?
5. Why do you admire this person?
6. Do you try to be like this person?
7. What is a social role?
8. Describe your social roles.

ACTIVITY 2

Words That Describe Me

1. From the list of words that appears at the bottom of this page and the top of the next page, choose ten words that best describe you and write them in your notebook.
2. Which of the words you've chosen would you like to change? Think of, or find in the list, more positive words that could be substituted for the words you'd like to replace. The words you choose can be opposites, or antonyms, such as:

   nervous/calm   stubborn/adaptable   clumsy/graceful

   Or the words can be synonyms and have the same meaning but convey a more positive impression. Think about how behaviours and actions can be described with a positive tone when they're appropriate and with a negative tone when they're seen as unacceptable, as the following word sets illustrate.

   stubborn/persistent   distrustful/cautious
3. Choose ten words from the list that do *not* describe you well. Would you like to be able to use any of these words in a description of yourself in the future?
4. Make a list of ten words that describe the type of person you'd like to be.

Self-Descriptive Words

able	certain	devious
adaptable	cheerful	diligent
adventurous	clever	disagreeable
agitated	clumsy	distrustful
agreeable	cold	dogmatic
aggressive	communicative	domineering
alert	complex	easygoing
ambitious	compulsive	energetic
anxious	confident	enthusiastic
apathetic	conforming	expressive
assertive	congenial	flexible
authoritative	considerate	forgiving
belligerent	controlled	frustrated
bitter	co-operative	good friend
bold	courteous	graceful
bossy	cranky	grateful
calm	creative	greedy
capable	credible	gregarious
carefree	curious	grumpy
careless	dependable	hardworking
cautious	determined	honest

hospitable	orderly	sensitive
humble	outgoing	sincere
humorous	patient	social
imaginative	persistent	stubborn
independent	physically fit	sympathetic
initiator	polite	tactless
intelligent	proud	talkative
involved	pugnacious	tense
kind	punctual	thorough
likable	reflective	timid
logical	reliable	tolerant
lonely	responsible	touchy
loyal	risk-taking	unappreciated
modest	rude	vain
nervous	self-confident	versatile
optimistic	self-reliant	well-groomed

ACTIVITY 3

My Accomplishments and Satisfactions

What things have you done that gave you pleasure and pride? Which activities give you satisfaction? What recognition have others given your accomplishments?

In your notebook, set up a table using the column heads explained below. Then refer to the lists of possible categories that follow these heads for ideas on the types of items you should use to complete your table. In some cases, you might insert an entry in either the first or second column only but, in every case, fill in the two final columns.

1. *Activities*: Name the activities and give specific examples.
2. *Achievements*: Name events in which you've participated, prizes, club offices, or awards you've received. Also describe any personal improvements you've made, such as improving your work or study habits, helping out more at home, cutting down on junk food—anything that has made you feel good about yourself.
3. *Responses of Others*: Explain whether the person is a relative, friend, acquaintance, employer, teacher, etc., and describe how that person reacted to your accomplishment.
4. *Your Reaction*: How did you feel about the activity or achievement? Did you feel proud? more self-confident? eager to become even better?

Possible Categories

Home:
▶ Chores
▶ Family
▶ Activities
▶ Hobbies

School:
▶ Subjects
▶ Languages learned
▶ Clubs
▶ Sports
▶ Other extracurricular activities

Community:
▶ Volunteer activities
▶ Part-time work
▶ Hobbies
▶ Other

Adapted from Ontario Ministry of Education. One Step at a Time: Educational and Career Explorations, 1984, p. 25.

Last summer I needed money to buy a mountain bike. I didn't have a job but I had some things of my own I could sell if I could find someone to buy them. I decided it would be a good idea for my family to have a garage sale to sell all of the family's unwanted items. My parents agreed I could have half the profits of the sale if I did all the organizing and assumed all the costs of running it. We set a date three weeks away so we would have enough time to advertise our sale.

That weekend I went to some garage sales to get ideas about pricing and ways to set up the sale. During my research I discovered that there were more customers when several garage sales were set up on the same street.

I decided to ask all the neighbours if they'd like to take part in our garage sale. I explained that if we co-ordinated our efforts we would all benefit. We could share the cost of the advertising, have a lot more customers, and have extra traffic on the street for only one day. Nine of our neighbours decided they'd like to participate. I made and distributed the posters and wrote the advertisement we put in the local newspaper.

The garage sale was a huge success. I earned $190 for my mountain bike. My parents and neighbours got some extra money and everyone had a good time. I increased my self-confidence and realized that I enjoyed selling. Someone liked one of the posters I made so much that she's hiring me to make some posters for her. One of my neighbours' friends whom I met that day offered me a part-time job for the summer working in her mobile canteen.

Question

In your notebook, set up a table with the following column heads. Under each heading, list the skills the writer used to arrange and stage the garage sale.

1. *Skills with Information*: For example, researching sale methods, pricing of goods, etc.
2. *Skills with People*: For example, with parents, neighbours, sale customers, etc.
3. *Skills with Things*: For example, with posters, merchandise, etc.

ACTIVITY 4　My Success Story

Choose one of the accomplishments that you included in Activity 3 on page 4, selecting one in which you played a principal role. In three or four paragraphs explain what you did, how you did it, your reward, and how you felt. Make sure that you give yourself full credit for your accomplishment. Write in the first person and use plenty of specific verbs to help identify the skills you used.

ACTIVITY 5

A Thinking Assignment

Pick six of the following ten questions and answer them in short paragraphs in your notebook.

1. It's the year 2025. The Governor General awards you the Order of Canada, one of the country's most distinguished awards. For what important contribution to Canada have you been honoured?
2. What qualities make you a reliable person?
3. What would you do if you had to spend the rest of your life in a wheel chair?
4. If you could be an animal, what would you be?
5. What do you like best about yourself?
6. You are a successful writer. What was the subject of your latest article or book?
7. What would you be willing to risk your life for? Why?
8. What well-known person are you like? In what ways?
9. You have one year to live. Someone gives you unlimited funds for a one-month vacation. Your health is still good. Where would you go?
10. Two of your best friends aren't speaking to each other because they've had a disagreement. Each wants you to take his or her side in the dispute. What do you do?

ACTIVITY 6

Dark Side/Light Side

Everyone is a mixture of things. Everyone is unique. Everyone has both strengths and weaknesses. In your notebook:

1. List at least five qualities that you *like* about yourself.
2. List at least five qualities that you *dislike* about yourself.
3. Then list which of these qualities apply to each of the following categories.

a) A friend would like
b) A friend would dislike
c) Would help you to live with others
d) Would make it hard to live with others
e) Would make you a good co-worker
f) Would make you a difficult co-worker
g) Would make you a good leader
h) Would make you a poor leader
i) Would make you a good employee
j) Would make you a difficult employee

ACTIVITY 7

What If?

1. You've moved to a distant, strange city that has a different custom to enable newcomers to meet new friends: you are required to make a poster that describes you and post it on a special bulletin board in a public place. Prepare such a poster.

2. You have a new pen pal, the same gender as you, who lives in another part of Canada. Write your first letter to him or her, describing yourself.

3. You attend university in a distant city. You have a large apartment and need someone to share the expenses. Make a list of characteristics you'd want in a room-mate. Then make a list of ten questions that you would ask a potential candidate to determine if she or he had the characteristics you'd like in a room-mate.

4. You need someone to stay with your teenage children this summer while you and your spouse are on vacation. What would the person you chose be like? Write a letter of application from the successful candidate in which the person describes herself or himself.

ACTIVITY 8 — People Who Work

1. In your notebook, write down the letters of the following items and then supply the names of three occupations that each of the descriptions fits.

a) Those who sometimes work at night
b) Those who work with numbers
c) Those who work with textual information
d) Those who design
e) Those who work alone
f) Those who evaluate
g) Those who work on the telephone
h) Those who work at home
i) Those with seasonal employment
j) Those who organize events

k) Those who operate machines
l) Those who work toward deadlines
m) Those who work outdoors
n) Those who do repetitive tasks
o) Those who work with nature
p) Those who work on teams
q) Those who repair items
r) Those who work on computers

2. Pick five of the occupations you listed that you would like to do.
3. Pick five of the occupations you listed that you would not like to do.

ACTIVITY 9 — Your Work Preferences

In your notebook, indicate your work preferences by putting the applicable letter next to the number of each of the items on the following page, using the key provided, When you've finished, look at your "Yes" answers and name three occupations that you think would suit these preferences. Then take into account your "Maybe" answers and add three more possible occupations.

Y = Yes	M = Maybe	N = No

1. Work with numbers
2. Work with computers
3. Perform a variety of duties
4. Work with nature
5. Work on a team
6. Perform repetitive, easy tasks
7. Travel frequently
8. Make presentations
9. Work outdoors
10. Use initiative
11. Have to meet deadline
12. Attend to details
13. Respond to emergencies
14. Organize events
15. Frequently work on the telephone
16. Work with information
17. Operate machinery
18. Look after customers
19. Have to dress up
20. Work at night
21. Communicate in writing

22. Repair equipment or machinery
23. Deal with people in a crisis
24. Be exposed to danger
25. Solve problems
26. Supervise other workers
27. Attend university
28. Provide a service
29. Work for a large organization
30. Work part-time
31. Work with ideas
32. Set my own priorities
33. Work with different age groups
34. Be required to use many skills
35. Have prestige
36. Work hard physically
37. Design a project
38. Work alone
39. Be required to do light physical work
40. Be closely supervised

 **ACTIVITY 10**

Appealing and Unappealing Work

Name three types of work that appeal to you and write a paragraph explaining the appeal of each. Then think of three types of work that *do not* appeal to you. Do those three have anything in common? Write a paragraph explaining why you feel they wouldn't suit you.

Chapter Summary Exercises

1 Write the following statements in your notebook, inserting the missing words that are indicated by the blanks.

   a) I feel angry when ____.
   b) The most important thing I've learned from my family is ____.
   c) The nicest thing I ever did for someone was ____.
   d) The biggest project I ever undertook was ____.
   e) I can't wait until I ____.
   f) I'd like to be able to ____.
   g) I like my friend ____ because ____.
   h) My friends think I'm special because I make a great effort to ____.
   i) I want to learn about ____.
   j) I feel competitive when ____.

k) If I had a million dollars to give to charity, I'd give it to ____.
l) If I could change my name I'd call myself ____ because then I ____.
m) I feel optimistic about ____.
n) My biggest hero/heroine is ____ because ____.
o) I sometimes find it hard to decide ____.
p) I'd like to change the way I always ____.
q) A perfect day for me would be ____.
r) I almost never ____.
s) I feel most independent when ____.
t) I'd like to try to ____ again.
u) I dream of the day when ____.
v) ____ has/have always fascinated me because ____.
w) I often get impatient with ____ because ____.
x) I'm happiest when ____.

2. Reassess your personal characteristics and relate them to a desired career option. Education and experience do not have to be considered for this exercise

3. In a 250-word essay, explain why you are (or are not) a good friend to have.

Reflective Journal

Respond to these statements in your journal

1. Imagine that you have five photographs taken of you, each one showing a different you. Describe the pictures.
2. What is the most difficult thing that you have ever done?
3. What is your greatest fear?
4. What is your greatest hope?
5. What is one way you would like to make a contribution to society?

Chapter 2

Defining Your Values

objectives

After completing this chapter you should be able to:

▶ Define the meaning and importance of values.
▶ Explain the relationship between values and decision making.
▶ Understand that values can change.
▶ Analyse your own values and those of people who are important to you.
▶ Realize how values apply to work situations.

introduction

Your values are your private, personal beliefs about what is most important to you, and about what is right or wrong, good or bad. Values are basic to decision making. Every day we make choices and decisions, choosing certain courses of action rather than others, using values as our guides. If a person achieves a goal but, in order to do so, violates his or her own belief about what is right or wrong, unhappiness results.

People have different values because every one of us experiences the world in a unique way. Your values might be right for you but completely wrong for someone else. Everyone has different concerns.

By understanding what your own values are and where they come from, you are better able to make decisions that are right for you. You get the most you can from life when you are careful about the choices you make.

To truly grow, change, and prosper, you need to become consciously aware of the rules you have for yourself and for others. When choosing a career, you really need to know what is important to you. Otherwise, how will you be able to measure your success or failure?

Values change when you change goals or your self-image. Different things become important when you have different goals. By understanding what your values are and where they come from, you're better able to make decisions that are right for you. The following exercises will help you to do this.

ACTIVITY 1

Where Are Values Learned?

Values are learned. How you perceive what is good and bad, worthy and unworthy, is based on your own experiences. Some things that seem right to you might seem wrong to others. In your notebook, make a list of where you think values are learned and explain how they are learned in each case.

Preferred Options

Rate from I to 4 your choices of answers for the following statements, with 4 indicating your first choice. If there's a choice you wouldn't make, indicate this with a zero.

1. I like to use my leisure time to:
    a) Complete personal projects.
    b) Visit friends.
    c) Do extra work.
    d) (Add another.)
2. If I had a party, I would:
    a) Invite as many people as I could.
    b) Just invite close friends.
    c) Plan every detail.
    d) Have high expectations.
3. If I could choose where I lived, it would be:
    a) In the country.
    b) In a downtown condominium.
    c) In a small town.
    d) In the suburbs.
4. After I turn sixty-five I want to:
    a) Travel.
    b) Do volunteer work.
    c) Continue at whatever job I've been doing.
    d) (Add another.)
5. If I had a house, it would have:
    a) Lots of private spaces.
    b) A large kitchen.
    c) Lots of furniture and keepsakes.
    d) Easy-maintenance features.
6. My favourite things are:
    a) Items that help me to do things.
    b) Books.
    c) Clothes.
    d) Animals.
7. I'd like to have:
    a) A group to hang around with.
    b) Several close friends.
    c) Many acquaintances.
    d) A best friend.
8. If a co-worker was abrupt with me, I'd:
    a) Choose to ignore her or him.
    b) Ask her or him if I've caused a problem.
    c) Ask if I could help.
    d) Ask other workers for advice on how to deal with the problem.

Value Statements

Write the following statements in your notebook, inserting the word or phrase that best expresses your values.

1. I'd like to participate on a team that ____.
2. I'd like to support ____.
3. I'd like to produce ____.
4. Children are really ____.
5. I think pets are ____.
6. I'd like to sell ____.
7. If I could change what school was like, I'd ____.
8. If I could meet one famous person, I'd choose ____.
9. My favourite season is ____.
10. I feel blue when ____.
11. I want to become skilled at ____.
12. I think I'm the best ____.
13. My favourite time of day is ____.
14. I get my best ideas ____.
15. I'd like to start ____.
16. I'd like to stop ____.
17. I'd like to tell the leaders of this country to stop ____.
18. I think children should ____.
19. The most important thing I learned in school was ____.
20. If I had unlimited funds, I'd go on a trip to ____.
21. ____ really makes me laugh.
22. My family likes to ____.
23. I feel really alive when I ____.
24. I feel confident about my ____.
25. I become angry when my friend ____.

Values Chart

How important are the following things To you? To your family? To your friends? Use a copy of the following chart provided by your teacher and check the appropriate boxes for each group. You'll then see at a glance if you think your values are different from those of the other important people in your life.

Values Chart

Value	Person	Very Important	Somewhat Important	Less Important	Not Important
Ambition: desire for success	Me				
	Parent or Guardian				
	Best Friend				
Beauty in both art and nature	Me				
	Parent or Guardian				
	Best Friend				
Benevolence: humanitarianism, generosity	Me				
	Parent or Guardian				
	Best Friend				
Compassion: kindliness, sympathy, concern for others	Me				
	Parent or Guardian				
	Best Friend				
Competence: skillfulness, capability, efficiency	Me				
	Parent or Guardian				
	Best Friend				
Creativity: ingeniousness, innovation, originality	Me				
	Parent or Guardian				
	Best Friend				
Emotional Health: mental well-being	Me				
	Parent or Guardian				
	Best Friend				

Value	Person	Very Important	Somewhat Important	Less Important	Not Important
Ethics: principles, moral standards	Me				
	Parent or Guardian				
	Best Friend				
Equality: belief in equal opportunity for others	Me				
	Parent or Guardian				
	Best Friend				
Honesty: truthfulness, frankness	Me				
	Parent or Guardian				
	Best Friend				
Honour: integrity, having a good name	Me				
	Parent or Guardian				
	Best Friend				
Influence: control or power over events or people	Me				
	Parent or Guardian				
	Best Friend				
Knowledge: information, learning, instruction	Me				
	Parent or Guardian				
	Best Friend				
Leisure: free or spare time	Me				
	Parent or Guardian				
	Best Friend				

Value	Person	Very Important	Somewhat Important	Less Important	Not Important
Love: affection, devotion, attachment to others	Me				
	Parent or Guardian				
	Best Friend				
Peace: absence of conflict or hostilities	Me				
	Parent or Guardian				
	Best Friend				
Physical Health: physical well-being	Me				
	Parent or Guardian				
	Best Friend				
Popularity: acclaim, regard, well-liked	Me				
	Parent or Guardian				
	Best Friend				
Prestige: good reputation, influence, social status	Me				
	Parent or Guardian				
	Best Friend				
Religious Faith: belief, conviction	Me				
	Parent or Guardian				
	Best Friend				
Security: safety, stability, confidence	Me				
	Parent or Guardian				
	Best Friend				

Value	Person	Very Important	Somewhat Important	Less Important	Not Important
Self-Sufficiency: self-reliance, independence	Me				
	Parent or Guardian				
	Best Friend				
Sincerity: earnest, honest, truthful	Me				
	Parent or Guardian				
	Best Friend				
Success: attainment, accomplishment	Me				
	Parent or Guardian				
	Best Friend				
Tolerance: open-mindedness, patience, acceptance	Me				
	Parent or Guardian				
	Best Friend				

In your notebook, answer the following questions.

1. Look at the check marks you inserted in the values chart. If the values were different for each group, why do you think they were different? Which values would you like to share with more people in your life?
2. Do you think that you can have seemingly conflicting values at the same time? For example, equality and prestige? Explain your answer.
3. If you had your dream career, which values of those listed in the chart would become more important to you?
4. How do members of the general population tell the government what they think is important? What are some of the government policies that demonstrate to us what politicians think is important?
5. Which of the values listed in the chart do you think might be important to people in the following occupations?

   a) Department store buyer
   b) Newspaper editor
   c) Personnel officer
   d) Nurse
   e) Social worker
   f) Architect
   g) Banker
   h) Farmer

Chapter Summary Exercises

1. Which values do you think are most important to you in a work situation? In your notebook, rank your answers to the following questions, using the letters in the key.

   Y = Yes   M = Maybe   No = No   N = Neutral

   a) Is a pleasing physical environment important to you?
   b) Do you want work that offers opportunity for advancement?
   c) Would you mind getting dirty at work?
   d) Would you like to dress up every day?
   e) Do you want to be able to use a skill that you have developed?
   f) Do you want to be able to use your creative abilities?
   g) Would you like to have work that you could forget about at the end of the day?
   h) Would it bother you if you disagreed with the moral conduct of the company for which you were working?
   i) Would you mind having less money but more leisure time?
   j) Do you want prestige from your occupation?
   k) Would you be willing to risk your physical health at your workplace?
   l) Would working with a team be important to you?
   m) Would you like to work alone?
   n) Would you be willing to sacrifice change for security?
   o) Would you like to influence decisions in your workplace?

2. Look back at Activity 10 on page 8. Using the above exercise as a guide, assess and analyse your personal values as they relate to three different areas of work that would suit you.

Reflective Journal

1. What is the greatest value that guides your life?
2. Explain what the following mean to you: ethics, love.
3. "Every day we make choices and decisions, choosing certain course of action rather than others, using values as our guides. If a person achieves a goal but, in order to do so, violates his or her own belief about what is right or wrong, unhappiness results" (page 10). Write about an incident from your own experience to which this statement could apply. The incident could have involved yourself or someone you know.
4. Would you accept a well-paying position that was destructive to the environment?

Internet Activity

To help focus your career search, use various search engines to seek out career counselling services online. Before completing career counselling activities on the Internet, assess them just as carefully as you would assess any other career counselling service.

Chapter 3

Targeting Your Future

objectives

After completing this chapter you should be able to:

▶ Explain the importance of setting short- and long-term goals.
▶ Identify possible career goals that are realistic.
▶ Use self-talk to develop affirmations leading to positive results.
▶ Find and follow the routes to learning for workplace success.
▶ Describe various methods of improving employability.

introduction

Goals are the aims, purposes, intentions, aspirations, ambitions, ideals, and destinations that give direction and meaning to our lives. In your life you will set many goals for yourself and spend much of your time trying to attain them

Perhaps you know people who'd like to tell you how to run your life. Their experience, knowledge, and ideas might be useful, but ultimately it is you who must decide which goals are important for you to pursue. The goals you choose should be reflective of who you are, your strengths, your weaknesses, and your values. As you change, your goals will change.

Becoming committed to achieving your goals involves thinking about what you want your future to be like and what type of person you want to be. We can't predict the future, but we *can* set goals and then work toward achieving them. Setting goals might sound like a big step, like a win or lose situation, like too big a commitment. But treat the future as your friend; be prepared for its arrival. Opportunities open up for those who are prepared.

Don't wait around for life to happen to you. If you see yourself as a passive participant in your life, a victim at the mercy of "the system," you're ducking responsibility for your life. Remember, we're all disadvantaged in some way and have to overcome obstacles.

People who achieve their goals start out by believing that they *can* achieve those goals (See *Self-Talk and Affirmations*, page 19). Take charge of the part of your life that you can control. Decide what you want. Remember, if you think you can or if you think you can't, you're *always* right. Think your goals through, obtain as much information as you can, and have faith in your belief that you *can* achieve your goals.

Goal Setting

Goals are the vehicle that take you in your chosen direction in life. With goals you become what you want; without them, you become what you were. The most important thing to remember about setting goals is that they belong to *you*—not to your parents, your friends, your teachers, or your boss.

This section will help you to learn how to set short- and long-term goals and how to take steps toward reaching these goals.

Self-Talk and Affirmations

What is self-talk? Self-talk is simply the continuous silent chatter to ourselves that goes on (a) when we are not engaged in conversation with others and (b) when we are not concentrating on some activity. It has been established through brain-wave readings that everyone self-talks silently from 150–300 words per minute. Most people average between 45 000 to 50 000 thoughts per day.

Why is self-talk important and what does it have to do with goals? The unconscious stores all memories and eventually expresses most self-suggestion in some fashion, finding ways of realizing the suggestions given it. What are the recurring themes in your talk? "I can't do math—I always forget names—I can't get along with others—Things never work out for me—" Or are they themes like, "I'm a capable person"—"I'm quick to learn"—"I work well with others"—"I know how to make the best of things"?

Self-talk can be a positive force that is helpful in achieving goals or it can be a negative and powerful form of self-sabotage.

How does self-talk work? Self-talk works very much on the same principle as a computer. As you use words, mental pictures, and feelings to program new information into your "software" or mind, you develop and strengthen new attitudes through repetition. This in turn leads to new behaviour.

Self-talk has been working for you all your life. What you imagine, desire, expect (positive or negative) is reinforced by self-talk and thereby prepares different levels of your mind to act accordingly.

What is an affirmation, and how does it relate to self-talk? An affirmation is a statement or belief (positive or negative) that tends to lead you to the end result you expect. So, in goal setting your positive self-talk will lead you to positive results. How can you word your affirmations so that they will work most effectively for you?

1. Always state an affirmation for a goal in the positive, *"I am now an excellent student,"* not *"I wish I were an excellent student."*
2. State goal affirmations in specific terms as if they have already happened, *"I am increasingly successful in my business and am earning "x" dollars a year,"* not *"I will be successful in my business."*

3. Make your goal affirmations personal; use "I" rather than "we."
4. Associate your affirmations with strong, positive feelings, e.g., *"I am enthusiastically increasing my successes as a student."*
5. Use action words where possible, e.g., *"I enjoy creating success in all areas of my life"* versus *"I am successful."*
6. Keep your affirmations simple.
7. Vary your affirmations, that is, have at least three affirmations for each goal.

For example:

> *I am consciously and joyously creating success in all areas of my life.*
>
> *I enjoy creating success easily and effortlessly.*
>
> *I desire success, I deserve success, I expect success.*

Three Steps to Creating New Habit Patterns

Many of us have developed some negative habits through constant negative self-talk. How can you create some positive new habit patterns?

Step 1   There must be a desire or need, such as setting specific goals.

Step 2   Program goal-setting data input through words, mental pictures and feelings.

Step 3   Reinforce goal setting by repetition through self-talk.

Confidence and Self-Esteem

Self-esteem, or your self-estimate, is the most important factor in achieving goals or personal growth. It is the hub of your personal wheel of success. If your self-esteem is low, you feel unworthy of success and are in danger of sabotaging everything you try to achieve. On the other hand, a feeling of self-worth contributes to your positive outlook and affects the way others regard you. Self-esteem is learned through early conditioning and can be changed or modified. Do you see yourself in either of these two lists?

Low Self-Worth	High Self-Worth
1. Martyrhood (struggle and sacrifice)	1. Has goals and purpose
2. Victimhood (blame others)	2. Has positive expectations, hopefulness
3. Compares self to others	3. Uses positive self-talk
4. Uses guilt to control and punish	4. Determined to succeed

5. Dishonest with self	5. Altruistic
6. Lives unconsciously	6. Has inner awareness
7. Feels undeserving of success	7. Has humility

suggestions for goal setting

1. The goal must be your *own* desire.
2. Always write your goal down, always in the present tense as already achieved.
3. Be specific about your goal-setting.
4. Set goals for yourself, not for others.
5. Whenever possible don't put time limits on goals.
6. Keep your personal goals to yourself.
7. Establish the benefits you will gain by achieving your goals.
8. Affirm no more than 15 goals at a time.

▶ After you have defined your goals, identify the skills you already have that will help you achieve those goals. Do some research for the skills you will need if you are not sure. Teachers and library and career resource centres can help you identify the skills needed.

▶ Identify the barriers to achieving your goals. Lack of money? Time? Your attitude? Write down the barriers and problem solve ways to overcome them.

▶ Do not let a major, long-term goal overwhelm you. Break it down into short-term, do-able goals.

▶ Goals exist to serve *you*. If your goal is something you no longer want, you can change it.

time sequencing of goals

Write your goals out in the following sequence:
Areas: spiritual, mental, emotional, physical, social/community, financial, career, fun and recreation.

Write out your:

1. Six-month goal
2. Twelve-month goal
3. 24-month goal
4. Five-year goal
5. Ten-year Ideal Goal
6. Three- to six-month goal
   a) Three-month goal
   b) Four-month goal
   c) Five-month goal.

Goal Board

Purpose: Focusing on your goals.

Cut out a number of pictures representing your end goals in different areas of your life. Create a collage of these pictures on your goal board. In this way you can "see" all your goals as a constant stimulus and reminder for your unconscious. Post your goal board where only you can see it, unless you want to share it.

Marco volunteered to prepare a quarterly newsletter for a charity organization. Preparing the first one made him realize how little he knew about computers and software. He decided to learn as much as he could about the software while at the same time improving his inputting skills.

Step 1: **Long-term goal:** I am enthusiastically learning how to use a word processing package and to improve my inputting skills.

Step 2: **Immediate goal:** Research manuals that I can use as resources.
Intermediate goal: I will key all my assignments and personal correspondence, learning how to highlight, using boldface, italics, bullets, and boxes, and learning how to print envelopes.
Three-month goal: I'll learn one new element of the software every weekday, starting with the formats and skills I feel I'm most likely to need. In three months, I will be capable of producing an excellent newsletter, and my work skills will continue to improve.

Step 3: **Identify any obstacles or barriers:** I have no computer at home, so how can I practise?

Step 4: **Overcome obstacles or plan around them:** I'll talk to the computer teacher about coming in early or staying late to practise on the school computers. I'll look into the cost of renting a computer and software. I'll also look into the cost of buying some secondhand equipment since I can't afford a new system.

Step 5: **Evaluate your progress.** Last time I went to the newsletter office, I knew exactly how to select a font and outline caps for the masthead, drop caps for the beginnings of articles, italics for authors' names, boldface for important dates, columns for varied reading, and boxes for important announcements. I can now prepare a more attractive newsletter, and I have improved my work skills as well.

The Routes to Learning for Career Success

Aside from working at your self-esteem and doing some careful goal-setting, how can you prepare for the future? One important way is through education and training. By the year 2005, 40 percent of work opportunities will require a university degree and the other 60 percent will require at least high school graduation. Never has it

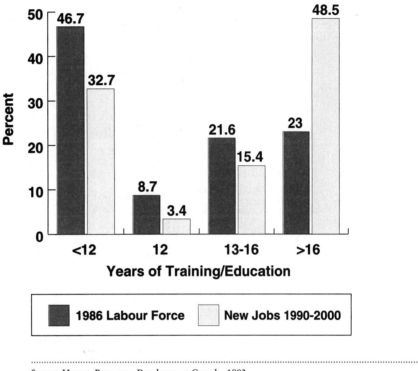

Source: Human Resources Development Canada, 1992

Figure 3.1 Changing Occupational Skill Requirements

been more critical for students to stay in school! Generally, if work is available to high school dropouts, it will be at the most menial level and will probably be paid accordingly. And don't count on fast-food outlets for work. Laser cookers and robotic technology will enable customers to order food just the way they like it by pressing buttons on a machine dispenser—the food will taste better and cost less, too! It is said almost 80 percent of fast-food jobs will disappear. Since the fast-food industry is Canada's largest employer, thousands will be out of work. The positive spin to this, however, is that people with computer skills to run the new equipment and to repair it, will be in demand.

Career Gateways to the Future

So how and where do you fit into the workplace of the 21st century? You are at the beginning of an exciting career journey. Let's examine the range of possibilities open to you.

Your journey begins with *you*. You are standing in an airport. Ahead are the Career Gateways to different career destinations. Think about the following areas and then check the questions with each Career Gateway on pages 26 and 27 and figure out which career is right for you. Now get ready to take off to your new Career Destination.

The kind of person you are—*your qualities equal great beginnings*

Each of us begins life with our own unique personality and temperament. These qualities help us decide what we want to do with our lives. For example, are you:

- persistent?
- conscientious?
- orderly?
- practical?

- social?
- compassionate?
- co-operative?

Your qualities are the starting point for your choices about the future.

What you do—*your personal best equals great opportunities*

Each of us is born with unique talents that help us excel at different tasks. For example, do you have:

- an eye for detail?
- a great imagination?
- a gift for numbers?
- the ability to get along with people?
- a special fondness for animals?
- an understanding about how things work?

Your unique talents may send you in new and interesting career directions.

"Gateways" and "Career Destination" information from: Your Career Passport. Career Planning: Your Passport to the Future, 1995/1996. Human Resources Development Canada.

Your education and training — *learning equals many choices*

A career journey does not necessarily have only one destination. There may be many stops along the way, and new goals and challenges to make you head off in new directions. Remember that lifelong learning will help you acquire new skills that may make your journey more interesting and challenging. For example, you add on:

- ▶ a high school diploma
- ▶ a community college or CÉGEP diploma
- ▶ a university diploma
- ▶ apprenticeship training
- ▶ on-the-job training
- ▶ a certificate from a specialized training program.

Diplomas, certificates, licences—they are all tools that give you greater career opportunities and expand your choice of destinations.

ACTIVITY 2

Gateways to Success

Write Gateway 1, Gateway 2, up to Gateway 8 on every second line in your notebook. Then read the introduction and the questions in each "Gateway" on the following pages. Under the appropriate Gateway number in your notebook, put a check mark for each question to which your answer would be "Yes." (You might not want to read the material in *every* Gateway. If you are sure that that Gateway doesn't interest you at all, proceed to one that does.) When you have worked through all the Gateways that interest you, add up the check marks in each Gateway. Proceed to the pages where you will find the Career Destination in which the number of check marks show you have the greatest interest.

Gateway 1

Careers in Math, Science, and Engineering

Scientific and technical knowledge is expanding at an enormously rapid rate with new discoveries almost every day. This is a terrific career journey for those people who combine great analytical skills and lots of curiosity.

- ❏ Are you good at analysing and solving problems?
- ❏ Do you like figuring out how things work?
- ❏ Are you challenged by experiments and discovering new things?
- ❏ Is math a turn-on for you?
- ❏ Do equipment and technical instruments interest you?

Travel to your Career Destination on page 28.

Gateway 2

Careers in Health and Medicine

People in health and medicine have a real knack for caring about others and wanting to improve people's lives. This is an exciting career journey with many possibilities from promoting wellness to developing new drugs or therapies to combat disease.

- ❏ Are you curious about the way the human body works?
- ❏ Do you wonder what causes diseases and why?
- ❏ Do you like to help people when they are sick or upset?
- ❏ Are you interested in equipment and technical instruments?

Travel to your Career Destination on page 29.

Gateway 9

Careers in Arts, Culture and Entertainment

Books, articles, plays, movies, music, dance, art—the only limit to creation is the boundary of the human mind and spirit. Take this exciting career journey and you could be heading into the unknown.

- ❏ Are you imaginative and creative?
- ❏ Do you have a particular artistic talent such as writing, drawing or singing?
- ❏ Are you a natural performer?
- ❏ Do you like investigating things and reporting on them?
- ❏ Do you like to make things using your own ideas?

Travel to your Career Destination on page 36

Gateway 8

Careers in Computers and Software

yourcareer@future.scene—as computer and software specialists continue to journey into cyberspace, their discoveries are changing the way people work and live. Hop on this career journey and the ride could be wild and challenging.

- ❏ Do you have ideas for great computer games?
- ❏ Do you like to do mathematical calculations?
- ❏ Are you good at explaining how computers work?
- ❏ Can you think of new ways to use computers and software?
- ❏ Do you like doing work that requires precision and attention to detail?

Travel to your Career Destination on page 35.

Gateway 7

Careers in Sports and Recreation

People in sports and recreation work in thousands of different careers from training athletes to selling sports equipment to winning gold medals. This is a terrific career journey for high-energy people.

- ❏ Are you a fitness freak?
- ❏ Are you competitive and willing to work hard?
- ❏ Do you like the idea of adventures?
- ❏ Do you like helping people train and practise their sport?
- ❏ Are you interested in the medical or psychological aspect of sports activities?

Travel to your Career Destination on page 34.

Gateway 3
Careers in Education, Social Services, and Religion

Canada is undergoing rapid social and economic changes that are affecting many people. This fulfilling career journey may be right for you if you like to help and support others.

- ❏ Are you interested in other people's lives?
- ❏ Can you handle people who are upset and worried?
- ❏ Are you comforting and compassionate?
- ❏ Are you curious about what makes people tick?
- ❏ Do you want to help people find more meaning in their lives?

Travel to your Career Destination on page 30.

Gateway 4
Careers in Law Enforcement, Government and Social Sciences

Canada is now part of the global community and therefore a more culturally diverse nation. People who choose this exciting career journey bring their ideas and solutions to the challenge we face as a society.

- ❏ Are you curious about how society works?
- ❏ Do you like to read about trends and attitudes?
- ❏ Are you interested in protecting people?
- ❏ Do you want to find ways to make a more just society?
- ❏ Do you enjoy assisting people when they need help?

Travel to your Career Destination on page 31.

Gateway 6
Careers in Business, Finance and Sales

Our global community is a huge marketplace with people buying and selling every product and service imaginable. This is a great career journey with thousands of exciting occupations for a person with a head for business.

- ❏ Are you good with numbers and calculations?
- ❏ Are you sociable and outgoing?
- ❏ Do you have the ability to convince people about things?
- ❏ Do you have a lot of ideas and initiative?
- ❏ Are you interested in running your own business some day?

Travel to your Career Destination on page 33.

Gateway 5
Careers involving Machines and Equipment

A telephone, bus, CD, sneakers—everything we use reflects the work of skilled people in construction, transportation, electronics, utilities, manufacturing and natural resources. This is a great career journey if you're a hands-on person with a curiosity about how things work.

- ❏ Do you like making, assembling, and repairing things?
- ❏ Do you like driving and operating big machines?
- ❏ Are you the kind of person who enjoys a steady pace of work?
- ❏ Are you interested in how computers and machines work together?
- ❏ Are you an active person who enjoys working outdoors?

Travel to your Career Destination on page 32.

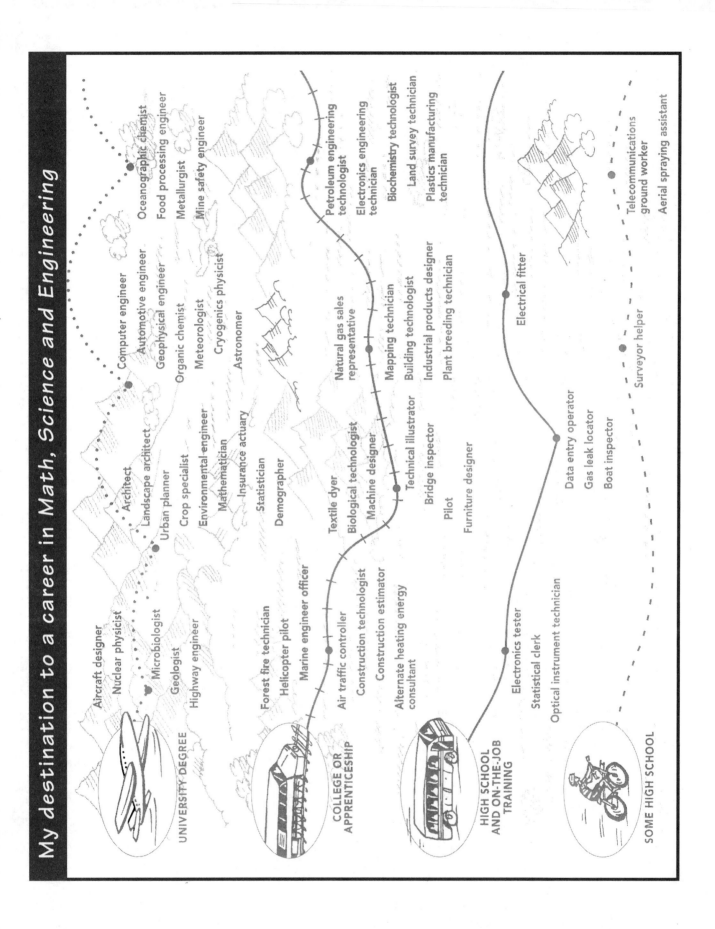

My destination to a career in Math, Science and Engineering

UNIVERSITY DEGREE

Aircraft designer
Nuclear physicist
Microbiologist
Geologist
Highway engineer
Computer engineer
Architect
Landscape architect
Urban planner
Automotive engineer
Geophysical engineer
Organic chemist
Crop specialist
Environmental engineer
Mathematician
Insurance actuary
Meteorologist
Cryogenics physicist
Astronomer
Statistician
Demographer
Oceanographic chemist
Food processing engineer
Metallurgist
Mine safety engineer

COLLEGE OR APPRENTICESHIP

Forest fire technician
Helicopter pilot
Marine engineer officer
Air traffic controller
Construction technologist
Construction estimator
Alternate heating energy consultant
Textile dyer
Biological technologist
Machine designer
Technical illustrator
Bridge inspector
Pilot
Furniture designer
Natural gas sales representative
Mapping technician
Building technologist
Industrial products designer
Plant breeding technician
Petroleum engineering technologist
Electronics engineering technician
Biochemistry technologist
Land survey technician
Plastics manufacturing technician

HIGH SCHOOL AND ON-THE-JOB TRAINING

Electronics tester
Statistical clerk
Optical instrument technician
Data entry operator
Gas leak locator
Boat inspector
Electrical fitter
Surveyor helper

SOME HIGH SCHOOL

Telecommunications ground worker
Aerial spraying assistant

My destination to a career in Health and Medicine

UNIVERSITY DEGREE

Dietitian
Patient care co-ordinator
Head nurse
Hospital administrator
Professor of medicine
Pediatrician
Community health nurse

Family physician
Occupational therapist
Psychiatrist
Physiotherapist

Pharmacist
Cardiology nurse technician
Foot specialist

Plastic surgeon
Obstetrician
Chiropractor
Audiologist

Language pathologist
Optometrist
Dentist

Naturopathic physician
Health care consultant
Veterinarian

Medical laboratory assistant
Respiratory therapist

Prosthetist
Nuclear medicine technologist

X-ray technician
Optician
Cardiac stress technologist

COLLEGE OR APPRENTICESHIP

Acupuncturist
Midwife

Herbologist
Paramedic
Ambulance service supervisor
Mental health worker

Hypnotherapist
Dental hygienist
Medical secretary
Animal health technician

Operating room technician
Dental laboratory technician

HIGH SCHOOL AND ON-THE-JOB TRAINING

Neuropsychiatric aide
Weight loss consultant
Assistant nurse

Nursing home attendant
Patient care aide
Acupuncture assistant
Morgue attendant

Medical receptionist
Pharmacy technician
Surgical assistant

Optical technician
Ceramic dental-moulder
Pharmacy assistant
Orthopedic assistant

SOME HIGH SCHOOL

Chiropractic aide

Physiotherapy assistant
Optometrist assistant

Hospital dietary aide
Blood donor clinic assistant
Clinic laboratory helper

Radiology aide
Medical clinic assistant

My destination to a career in Education, Social Services and Religion

University professor
School principal
Minister of religion
Social work director
Flight simulator instructor
Psychologist
Family social worker

UNIVERSITY DEGREE

Guidance counsellor
Vocational training school teacher
Computer training instructor
Company trainer
Commercial art instructor

Librarian
Training and development consultant
School counsellor

Education statistician
University laboratory assistant
Education research officer

Physical training instructor
Student activities advisor
Rehabilitation worker
Early childhood educator
Relocation consultant

Native outreach worker
Sign language instructor
Firefighter trainer
Teacher of physically disabled persons

Firefighter chief
Fire inspector
Life skills coach

COLLEGE OR APPRENTICESHIP

Youth worker
Special education teacher

Driving instructor
Guidance services technician
Teacher of the blind

Nanny
Pre-school helper
Public speaking consultant

Training clerk
Audio-visual materials assistant

HIGH SCHOOL AND ON-THE-JOB TRAINING

Live-in caregiver
Home support worker

Religious education worker
Special education assistant
Foster parent

Educational resource assistant

SOME HIGH SCHOOL

My destination to a career in Law, Enforcement, And Social Sciences

UNIVERSITY DEGREE

Family court judge
Criminal lawyer
Human rights officer
City councillor
Historian

Elections officer
Forensic pathologist
Conservator
Economist

Child welfare policy researcher
Market research analyst
Law professor
Law reporter

Geographer
Archaeologist

Sociologist
Probation officer
Human resources manager

COLLEGE OR APPRENTICESHIP

Postal Chief
Police Chief
Court administrator
Customs inspector
Immigration agent
Police officer

Highway construction inspector
Legal researcher
Police scuba diver
Library technician
Forensic photographer

Historical technician
Air traffic controller

Employment counsellor
Paralegal
Museum guide

Security consultant
Postal counter clerk

Liquor licence inspector
Courtroom clerk
Mail sorter
House detective
Election enumerator
Letter carrier

HIGH SCHOOL AND ON-THE-JOB TRAINING

Prison guard
Animal control officer

Human resources clerk
Survey interviewer

SOME HIGH SCHOOL

Gate attendant
Airport security guard

My destination to a career in Machines and Equipment

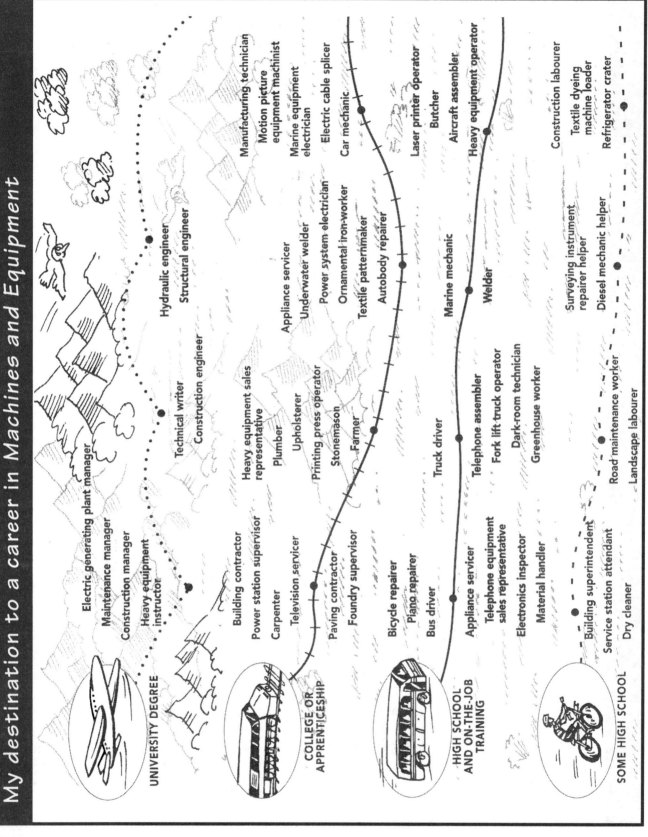

UNIVERSITY DEGREE

Electric generating plant manager
Maintenance manager
Construction manager
Heavy equipment instructor

Hydraulic engineer
Structural engineer

Technical writer
Construction engineer

Manufacturing technician
Motion picture equipment machinist
Marine equipment electrician
Electric cable splicer
Car mechanic

COLLEGE OR APPRENTICESHIP

Building contractor
Power station supervisor
Carpenter
Television servicer

Heavy equipment sales representative
Plumber
Upholsterer
Printing press operator
Stonemason
Farmer

Appliance servicer
Underwater welder
Power system electrician
Ornamental iron-worker
Textile patternmaker
Autobody repairer

Laser printer operator
Butcher
Aircraft assembler
Heavy equipment operator

Paving contractor
Foundry supervisor

Marine mechanic
Welder

HIGH SCHOOL AND ON-THE-JOB TRAINING

Bicycle repairer
Piano repairer
Bus driver

Appliance servicer
Telephone equipment sales representative
Electronics inspector
Material handler

Truck driver

Telephone assembler
Fork lift truck operator
Dark-room technician
Greenhouse worker

Construction labourer
Textile dyeing machine loader
Refrigerator crater

Surveying instrument repairer helper
Diesel mechanic helper

SOME HIGH SCHOOL

Building superintendent
Service station attendant
Dry cleaner

Road maintenance worker
Landscape labourer

My destination to a career in Business, Finance and Sales

UNIVERSITY DEGREE

Financial manager
Purchasing director
Bank manager
Business consultant
Stockbroker
Financial planner

Mortgage broker
Investment dealer
Sales manager
Investment counsellor
Advertising director

Media relations manager
Employee relations officer
Personnel director

Union representative
Accountant
Money market analyst

COLLEGE OR APPRENTICESHIP

Property administrator
Office manager
Executive housekeeper

Trade show planner
Hotel supervisor

Personnel recruiter
Insurance agent

Conference planner
Hairstylist

Chef
Barber
Baker

Insurance adjuster
Bookkeeper
Head cashier

Shipper/receiver
Insurance clerk
Tax return preparer

Telephone operator
Cosmetician
Image consultant

HIGH SCHOOL AND ON-THE-JOB TRAINING

Skin care specialist
Fashion consultant
Dog trainer

Flight attendant
Banquet server

Wedding consultant

Car salesperson
Customer service clerk

Taxi driver

Price checker
Fast-food preparer
Janitor
Bartender helper

Carpet cleaner
Grocery packer
Home cleaner

SOME HIGH SCHOOL

Newspaper vendor
Telemarketer

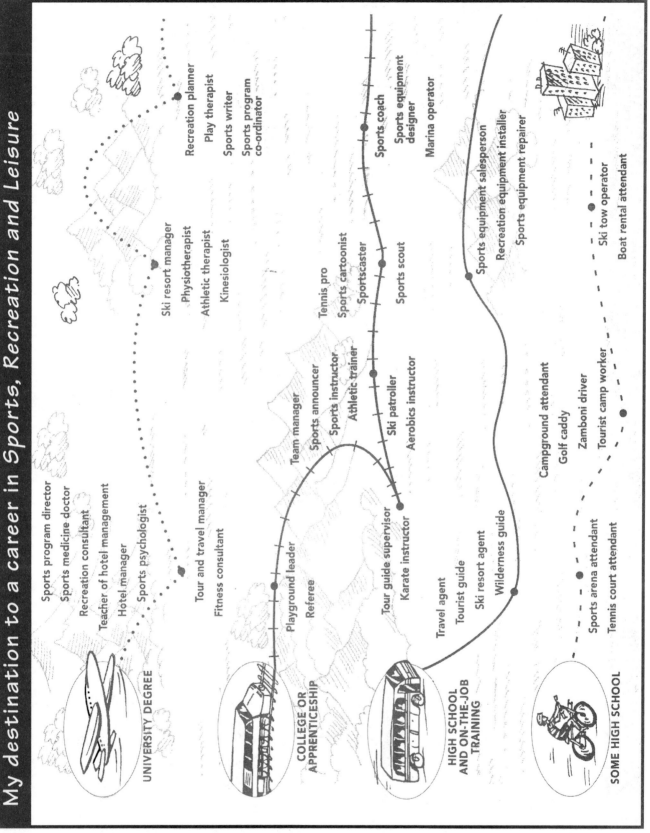

My destination to a career in Sports, Recreation and Leisure

UNIVERSITY DEGREE

Sports program director
Sports medicine doctor
Recreation consultant
Teacher of hotel management
Hotel manager
Sports psychologist

Tour and travel manager

Fitness consultant

Ski resort manager
Physiotherapist
Athletic therapist
Kinesiologist

Recreation planner
Play therapist
Sports writer
Sports program
co-ordinator

Sports coach
Sports equipment
designer

Marina operator

COLLEGE OR APPRENTICESHIP

Playground leader
Referee

Team manager
Sports announcer
Sports instructor
Athletic trainer

Tennis pro
Sports cartoonist
Sportscaster

Sports scout

Tour guide supervisor
Karate instructor

Ski patroller
Aerobics instructor

Sports equipment salesperson
Recreation equipment installer
Sports equipment repairer

HIGH SCHOOL AND ON-THE-JOB TRAINING

Travel agent
Tourist guide
Ski resort agent
Wilderness guide

Campground attendant
Golf caddy
Zamboni driver
Tourist camp worker

SOME HIGH SCHOOL

Sports arena attendant
Tennis court attendant

Ski tow operator
Boat rental attendant

My destination to a career in *Computers and Software*

UNIVERSITY DEGREE

- Information systems manager
- Professor of computer science
- Computer consultant
- Data centre manager
- Software training instructor
- Human-computer interface specialist
- Multimedia software designer
- Game designer
- Software engineer
- Graphics specialist
- Computer magazine editor
- Computer engineer
- User support analyst
- Computer search librarian
- Computer-assisted drafting instructor
- Hardware engineer
- Telecommunications specialist
- Systems analyst
- Scientific programmer
- Software analyst
- Database designer
- Operating systems developer
- Business systems specialist

COLLEGE OR APPRENTICESHIP

- Technical training specialist
- Computer operator supervisor
- Word processing supervisor
- Network controller
- Software sales representative
- User support specialist
- Customer support representative
- Computer-aided design technologist
- Hardware specialist
- Magnetic tape operator
- Documentation specialist
- Hardware technologist
- Computer-assisted machinist
- Computer-assisted design technician
- Computer equipment repairer
- Communications technician
- Field service technician
- Inspector/tester

HIGH SCHOOL AND ON-THE-JOB TRAINING

- Data administrator
- Data processing co-ordinator
- Computer store manager
- Tape librarian
- Integrated circuit assembler
- Systems security specialist
- Desktop publishing operator
- Computer salesperson
- Help desk representative
- Internet service provider
- Console operator
- Local area network administrator
- Computer peripheral equipment operator
- Systems operator

STOP

SOME HIGH SCHOOL

My destination to a career in Arts, Culture and Entertainment

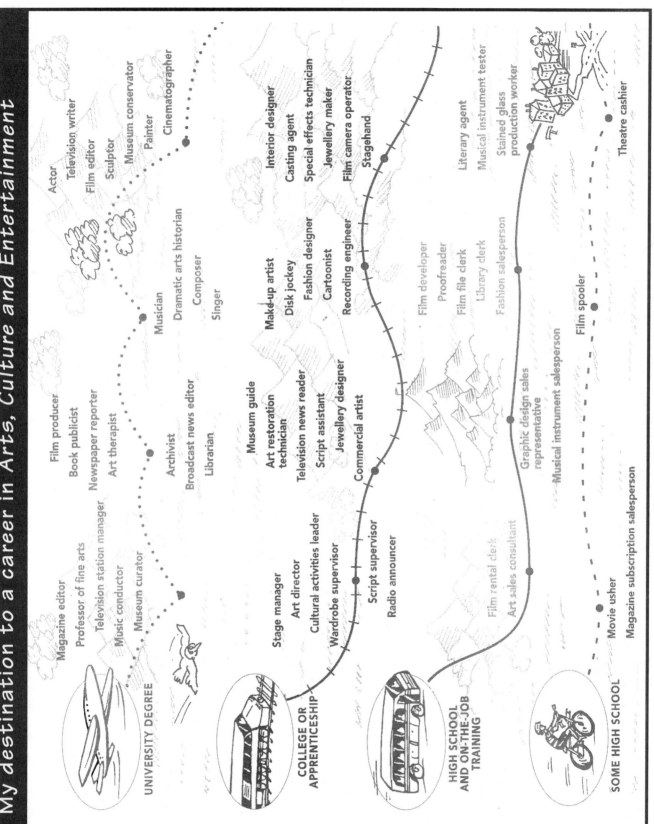

UNIVERSITY DEGREE

Magazine editor
Professor of fine arts
Television station manager
Music conductor
Museum curator

Film producer
Book publicist
Newspaper reporter
Art therapist

Musician

Archivist
Broadcast news editor
Librarian

Dramatic arts historian
Composer
Singer

Actor
Television writer
Film editor
Sculptor
Museum conservator
Painter
Cinematographer

COLLEGE OR APPRENTICESHIP

Stage manager
Art director
Cultural activities leader
Wardrobe supervisor

Script supervisor
Radio announcer

Museum guide
Art restoration technician
Television news reader
Script assistant
Jewellery designer
Commercial artist

Make-up artist
Disk jockey
Fashion designer
Cartoonist
Recording engineer

Interior designer
Casting agent
Special effects technician
Jewellery maker
Film camera operator
Stagehand

HIGH SCHOOL AND ON-THE-JOB TRAINING

Film rental clerk
Art sales consultant

Graphic design sales representative
Musical instrument salesperson

Film developer
Proofreader
Film file clerk
Library clerk
Fashion salesperson

Literary agent
Musical instrument tester
Stained glass production worker

SOME HIGH SCHOOL

Movie usher
Magazine subscription salesperson

Film spooler

Theatre cashier

Directing Your Interests

What career destination(s) interested you? Now take a look at Frank Feather's list of 120 Best Growth Careers to 2005. Frank Feather is an author whose book, *Careers for the Future*, describes the workplace workers can expect to find over the next few years. His "120 Best Growth Careers to 2005" appear on pages 38 to 41.

The section below explains the categories Feather has used and shows you how to interpret his rankings.

If none of your career destination choices fall into a high growth type of work, don't worry. All indications at this stage are that all the types of work mentioned will continue to exist and many will grow, albeit not as rapidly as the "high growth" ones. The important thing is to identify your values, interests, and abilities and then to target the best, most effective route to the type of work you want to do.

The Tables Explained

All jobs are ranked according to their projected percentage growth between 1994 and 2005. Also shown in the rankings are the following pieces of information:

▶ The percent (%) of each job type that will be held by women in 2005. Comparisons are not shown with 1994 but women will gain in almost every occupation.

▶ The percent (%) of each job category that will be part-time. With a leisure society evolving, more and more jobs will become part-time in most categories. There are some exceptions where part-time jobs are becoming full-time in order to keep up with demand but, by and large, we are becoming a nation of part-time workers. These percentages will help guide those who prefer part-time work.

▶ The approximate comparative salary levels of each career is shown in the "Earnings" column; the more "$" signs, the higher the earnings level vis-a-vis other jobs.

▶ An assessment of the stress level of the job as shown by the symbol "!"; the more exclamation marks, the higher the stress level!

▶ Minimum education requirements for entry level positions are indicated as follows:

High = High School Diploma;
Coll = Community College or Vocational/Apprenticeship Diploma;
Univ = University Undergraduate Degree or higher.

▶ Where on-the-job travel is involved, whether to worksites or by car or airplane, this is shown by the letter "T"; the more "Ts," the more travel-intensive the job.

From Canada's BEST CAREERS Guide, Revised 2nd Edition, *Copyright © 1995. Frank Feather.*

The 120 Best Growth Careers to 2005

(Ranked by % growth, 1994–2005)

The "Top 30"

Growth Rank #	Type of Occupation	%Inc over 1994	% Fe- male	% Part- Time	Earn- ings ($)	Stress Level (!)	Edu- ca- tion	Job Travel (T)
1	Physician/Surgeon	71	40	15	$$$$	!!!	Univ	
2	Psychiatrist/-ologist	66	50	20	$$$$	!!	Univ	
3	Pharmacist	64	70	30	$$$	!	Univ	
4	Lawyer	62	40	5	$$$$	!!	Univ	TT
5	Nurse	62	90	60	$$	!!!!	Univ	T
6	Vocational Teacher	62	60	25	$$	!	Univ	
7	Osteopath/Chiropractr	61	40	10	$$$$	!	Univ	
8	Nursing Assistant	61	90	70	$	!	Coll	
9	Accountant/Auditor	58	60	25	$$$$	!!	Univ	TT
10	Health Manager	58	60	5	$$$	!!!	Coll	
11	Dispensing Optician	56	70	10	$$	!	Coll	
12	Guidance Counsellor	55	75	20	$$$	!	Univ	T
13	Computer Programr	54	40	15	$$$	!!	Coll	
14	Audio/Physiotherpst	54	90	40	$$	!	Univ	
15	Food/Drink Server	53	90	80	$	!!!!!	High	
16	Radiology Technician	50	90	40	$	!!	Coll	
17	Hospital Orderly	49	80	60	$	!!!	High	
18	Air Pilot/Navigator	49	10	5	$$$$	!!!!	Coll	TTT
19	Food/Drink Sprvsr	49	70	35	$$	!!	Coll	
20	Socio-Anthropologist	48	55	30	$$$$	!	Univ	
21	Dentist/Orthodontist	47	25	10	$$$$	!!	Univ	
22	Dietician/Nutritionist	47	90	40	$$	!	Univ	T
23	Personnel Officer	46	70	15	$$	!	Univ	TT
24	Executive/Snr Offcl	45	40	5	$$$$	!!!!	Univ	TTT
25	Optometrist	44	60	10	$$$$	!	Univ	
26	Veterinarian	44	40	20	$$$$	!!	Univ	TT
27	Denturist/Hygienist	44	95	40	$	!!	Coll	
28	Bus/Transit Driver	44	50	40	$	!!	–	TTT
29	University Professor	43	50	25	$$$$	!	Univ	T
30	Biologist/Bioscientist	43	40	10	$$$	!	Univ	T

The 120 Best Growth Careers to 2005

(Ranked by % growth, 1994–2005)

"Next-Best 30"

Growth Rank #	Type of Occupation	%Inc over 1994	% Fe-male	% Part-Time	Earn-ings ($)	Stress Level (!)	Edu-ca-tion	Job Travel (T)
31	Telecom Installer	42	10	20	$$	!	Coll	TTT
32	Services Manager	42	45	10	$$	!!	Coll	
33	Product/Intrr Designer	42	90	50	$$	!	Coll	TT
34	Community Planner	41	10	10	$$$	!	Univ	TT
35	Stockbroker/Trader	40	35	10	$$$$	!!!!!	Univ	
36	Special Ed Teacher	40	80	25	$$	!!	Univ	T
37	Travel Attendant	40	80	20	TT	!!!!!	High	TTT
38	Audio-Video Techncn	40	20	15	$	!!!	Coll	
39	Sports/Recrtn. Trainer	38	40	50	$	!!!	Coll	TTT
40	Social Worker	37	70	30	$$	!!!	Univ	TT
41	Medical Lab Techncn	36	90	30	$	!!	Coll	
42	Cleaner/Homecare Aid	36	50	50	R	!!!	–	T
43	Social Service Worker	34	70	30	$	!!!!!	Coll	TT
44	Personnel Manager	33	50	5	$$$$	!!!	Univ	TT
45	Aerospace Engineer	32	10	5	$$$	!	Univ	T
46	TV/Radio/Film Prodcr	32	40	15	$$	!!!!!	Coll	TTT
47	Social Science Mngr	32	60	15	$$	!	Univ	
48	Radio/TV Announcer	32	40	40	$$	!!	Coll	T
49	Sales Supervisor	31	50	15	$$$	!!	Coll	TTT
50	Painter/Paperhanger	31	5	40	$	!	–	T
51	Financial Comptroller	30	50	5	$$$$	!!	Univ	T
52	Transportation Mgr	30	10	5	$$$$	!!	Coll	TT
53	Secondy Schl Teacher	30	55	25	$$	!!!	Univ	T
54	PR Officer/Agent	30	60	20	$$	!!!!	Univ	TTT
55	Librarian/Curator	30	60	25	$	!	Univ	
56	Photographer/Grip	30	30	40	$	!!	High	TT
57	Garden/Nursery Staff	30	30	40	$	!	High	TTT
58	Salesperson	29	70	60	$	!!	High	
59	Radio/TV Stn Techncn	28	30	20	$	!!	High	T
60	Air Traffic Controller	28	10	5	$$$$	!!!!!	High	

The 120 Best Growth Careers to 2005

(Ranked by % growth, 1994–2005)

"Third-Best 30"

Growth Rank #	Type of Occupation	%Inc over 1994	% Fe-male	% Part-Time	Earn-ings ($)	Stress Level (!)	Edu-ca-tion	Job Travel (T)
61	Translator/Interpreter	27	60	40	$$	!!!!!	Univ	TTT
62	Techncl Sales/Advisor	26	15	10	$$$	!!	Coll	TT
63	EDP Operator	26	80	10	$$	!!!	High	
64	Artist/Illustrator	26	40	30	$	!!	Coll	T
65	Musician/Singer	26	35	40	$	!!!	Coll	TT
66	Education Managers	25	35	10	$$$	!!	Univ	T
67	Police Offcr/Detective	25	20	10	$$	!!!	Coll	TTT
68	Security Guard	26	30	50	$	!!	–	TT
69	Photograph Processor	25	70	25	$	!	Coll	
70	Actor/Actress	25	50	60	$	!!!!!	Coll	TTT
71	Receptnst/Info Clerk	24	95	50	$	!!	High	
72	Writer/Editor	24	50	60	$	!!!	Univ	TT
73	Secretary/Steno	24	99	40	$	!!!!!	Coll	
74	K-7 Elementy Teacher	23	90	25	$$	!!!	Univ	T
75	Insurance Salesperson	21	20	30	$$	!!!	Coll	T
76	Chef/Cook	21	40	70	$	!!!!	Coll	
77	Advertising Manager	20	30	10	$$$	!!	Coll	TT
78	Advertsg/Sales Expert	20	60	20	$$	!!	Coll	T
79	Inspector (Govt.)	20	5	5	$$	!	Coll	TT
80	Forester/Eco-Scientist	20	20	5	$$	!	Coll	T
81	Choreographer/Dancer	20	80	40	$	!!!!	Coll	TT
82	Sales Supervisor	19	40	10	$$$	!!	Coll	TT
83	Archivist/Conservator	19	75	40	$$	!!	Univ	
84	Travel Agent/Clerk	18	80	40	$$	!!!!	High	TTT
85	Realty Salesperson	18	60	40	$$	!!	High	TT
86	Drafter/Designer	18	30	10	$$	!	Coll	T
87	Physicist	17	15	5	$$$	!	Univ	T
88	Architect	17	10	10	$$$	!	Univ	TT
89	Construction Manager	15	1	5	$$$	!!	Coll	TT
90	Geologist	15	5	5	$$$	!	Univ	TTT

The 120 Best Growth Careers to 2005

(Ranked by % growth, 1994–2005)

30 "So-So" Jobs

Growth Rank #	Type of Occupation	%Inc over 1994	% Fe-male	% Part-Time	Earn-ings ($)	Stress Level (!)	Edu-ca-tion	Job Travel (T)
91	Electrical Engineer	15	5	10	$$$	!!	Univ	T
92	Forestry Technician	15	25	5	$$	!	Coll	TTT
93	Business Servicer	15	50	20	$$	!!	Coll	TTT
94	Equipment Installer	15	20	20	$	!!	Coll	TTT
95	Civil Engineer	14	5	5	$$$	!	Univ	TT
96	Inspector (non-Govt)	14	5	10	$$	!	Coll	TTT
97	Insurance Adjuster	14	20	25	$$	!	High	TTT
98	Comment Traveller	13	15	15	$$$	!!!	Coll	TTT
99	Science Manager	12	5	5	$$$	!	Univ	
100	EDP Supervisor	11	40	10	$$	!!!	Coll	
101	Equipment Tester	11	10	10	$$	!!	Coll	T
102	Fire-Fighter	10	–	20	$$	!!	High	TT
103	Funeral Director	10	5	10	$$	!	Coll	T
104	Metals Tester	8	–	10	$	!	Coll	
105	Auto Mechanic	8	5	25	$	!	Coll	
106	Brick/Tile Layer	8	–	10	$	!	High	TT
107	Concrete Finisher	7	–	10	$	!	–	TT
108	Plasterer/Dry-Waller	5	–	25	$	!	–	TT
109	Roofer/Waterproofer	6	–	30	$	!!!	–	TT
110	Industrial Engineer	5	–	5	$$	!	Univ	TT
111	Architect Techncn	5	–	–	$	!	Coll	TT
112	Glazier	3	–	20	$	!!!	–	TT
113	Carpenter/Woodwrkr	3	–	10	$	!	Coll	TT
114	Chemist	3	30	–	$$$	!	Univ	
115	Economist	3	40	–	$$$	!	Univ	
116	Production Manager	2	5	10	$$	!!	Coll	
117	Hairstyler/Beauticn	2	80	65	$	!	High	
118	General Office Clerk	2	80	80	$	!	High	
119	Cashier/Teller	1	90	70	$	!!!	High	
120	Typist/Clerk-Typist	1	95	70	$	!!!!	High	

The Routes to Learning

Today's labour market is going through many changes, and will continue to do so for some years to come. The positions with good wages and benefits are going increasingly to people with higher education and skill levels.

How can you prepare for the future? Continue your education and training. Further education can widen your range of career options, prepare you for more challenging work, and enrich your personal life.

Canada's schools and learning institutions provide a wide variety of programs designed to teach you what you need or want to know.

route 1 University

Universities offer courses of study—full-time, part-time or co-op—that will broaden your knowledge and develop your analytical and thinking skills. Some programs such as engineering provide career-oriented, specialized training with an academic component.

Universities offer many programs, including:

Architecture
Business administration
Dentistry
Economics
Geology
History
Law
Mathematics
Medicine
Political Science

route 2 College/CÉGEP

Colleges and CÉGEP's (Collèges d'enseignement général et professionel) offer two- to-three-year programs that combine academic learning with hands-on training and lead to a diploma or certificate.

Colleges and CÉGEP's offer a variety of programs. Some examples:

Accounting	Dental lab technology
Advertising	Fashion merchandising
Ambulance and emergency care	Food service management
Computer systems	Heavy duty equipment mechanics
Correctional work	Journalism

route 3 Private Vocational, Technical and Trade Schools

Privately owned vocational, technical and trade schools provide short, career-oriented training courses. Classroom study can be full- or part-time and may be combined with on-the-job training. Some schools also supervise programs for the government and other institutions.

Vocational, technical and trade schools offer many courses which lead to careers such as:

Accountant	Clothing designer	Pharmacy assistant
Bookkeeper	Dental office assistant	Secretary
Business assistant administrator	Draftsperson	Truck driver
	Locksmith	

route 4 Apprenticeship

Apprenticeship is a special kind of training required for many occupations in trades and technologies. It combines classroom instruction at a college or CÉGEP as well as on-the-job, paid training. See pages xx to xx.

route 5 Professional and Vocational Associations

Regulated Associations: These associations offer training and certification in an area of specialization, and people who want to work in that area must be certified. The associations' training usually requires work in the field, attendance at seminars and passing of examinations. Occupations that require such certification include real estate brokers, massage therapists, insurance brokers, chartered accountants and stockbrokers.

Non-regulated Associations: These associations offer training and certification in an area of specialization, but membership, training and certification are not requirements for employment. However, many people find that the courses provided by non-regulated associations are important routes to finding work in their chosen field. There are many occupations handled by non-regulated associations, including gemologists, bankers, administrators, managers and direct marketers.

route 6 Other Specialized Educational Institutions

There are many schools and institutes, some private and some publicly funded, that provide practical, non-academic training in specific areas of study. These schools offer a wide variety of courses in such areas as fine and performing arts, driver education, cooking, aviation, modelling, hairstyling, languages and financial management.

route 7 Company Training

Many companies today provide employees with in-house training or offer support if employees want to take courses outside the workplace. If you're interested in your company's training programs, check with the human resources or personnel department at your workplace.

route 8 Community Groups and Other Non-Profit Organizations

Many community groups, neighbourhood organizations and non-profit institutions such as the YMCA offer training in a variety of subjects. These programs are often designed for people in transition who need to upgrade their employment skills.

Remember, too, that learning continues throughout your life. You can take night-school courses or distance-learning courses in many subjects.

Adapted from Career Information Partnership Canada, Canada Prospects, 1994 Human Resources Development Canada.

Trades/Apprenticeships

An entry into the labour market overlooked by most students is apprenticeship to the trades. It is a system of training, incorporating on-the-job learning with short periods of formal or in-school learning, leading to certification or licensing in the trades. Formal exams are required at several levels throughout the training process.

In general, trades across Canada are regulated by the apprenticeship branch of each provincial government. Each province and territory has its own "designated trades" which it regulates. These designated trades are classified as either voluntary or compulsory. *Voluntary* means a person can train and work in the field without certification or can choose to write the exam and obtain certification. *Compulsory* means that it is against the law to work in the trade without proper certification. Since certification is a legal prerequisite to working in compulsory trades, it is like a licensing process.

Even though certification in a trade may not be compulsory, the industry can create a standard requiring certification for employment through unions or employer preferences. Therefore, although apprentices may not be required by law to write the exams, they may not find employment until they are certified. It is important to investigate this through the trade councils, apprenticeship branches, and unions.

General entry into an apprenticeship program is based on the completion of a provincially set grade level and employment in the trade. Community colleges in nine provinces provide the in-school portion of training for apprenticeship, while Québec provides its training through the secondary school system. Some community colleges also provide pre-program preparation for a trade that can give the student enough knowledge and experience to encourage an employer to take him or her on as an apprentice.

The Interprovincial Standards Program

The apprenticeship system developed separately in each province and territory. This has resulted in different systems of training and certification and even different classifications (designations) of what is a trade. In order to provide greater mobility across Canada for skilled workers, interprovincial standards and exams have been developed for some trades. They are called Red Seal trades, and the bearer of the certificate is recognized as qualified across Canada. An Interprovincial Standards Red Seal can be obtained through the following routes:

- by graduating from a recognized provincial or territorial apprenticeship training program or by obtaining a journeyperson-level certificate from a province or territory; and
- by passing the Interprovincial Standards Examination for that trade.

The Red Seal is attached to the Journeyperson Certificate. Its holder can work and move freely from part of Canada to another. The following table shows the Red Seal trades.

Red Seal Trades

Baker	Industrial Mechanic (Millwright)
Boilermaker	Lineman
Bricklayer	Machinist
Cabinetmaker	Motor Vehicle Body Repairer (Metal and Paint)
Carpenter	Motor Vehicle Mechanic
Construction Electrician	Oil Burner Mechanic - Residential
Cook	Painter and Decorator
Electronic Technician - Consumer Products	Plumber
Floor Covering Installer	Refrigeration and Air Conditioning Mechanic
Glazier	Roofer
Hairstyling	Sheet Metal Worker
Heavy Duty Equipment Mechanic	Sprinkler System Installer
Industrial Electrician	Truck and Transport Mechanic
Industrial Instrument Mechanic	Welder

Studies show that students who become involved in apprenticeship show higher satisfaction than those who pursue other programs. Among groups of students surveyed after completion of college, university and apprenticeship programs, a significantly higher number of apprenticeship participants would select the same program again. The salaries for people with apprenticeship training can reach the range of some people with professional training.

In order to promote trades in high school, individual trades are producing videos and posters for schools. Government is supporting women's access projects. Women in Trades and Technology (WITT), a national non-profit advocacy group, is active in the encouragement, training and promotion of women in trades and technologies.

If you are considering trade apprentices, it is recommended that you contact the trade council, apprenticeship branch or union. WITT can provide information, speakers and mentors for women considering trades.

From Making Career Sense of Labour Market Information *by Elaine O'Reilly and Diane Alfred. Published by © Canadian Guidance and Counselling Foundation, 1995*

Chapter Summary Exercises

1. In your notebook write the following statements, supplying the word or phrase that best completes each sentence.

   a) The skills that I want to continue to develop are ____.
   b) The new skills that I want to acquire are ____.
   c) In my first year of work, I hope to ____.
   d) To ensure that I remain technically competent, I plan to ____.
   e) To ensure that I remain physically fit and in good health, I plan to ____.
   f) My immediate career goal is ____.
   g) An alternative career goal is ____.

2. Identify problems that interfere with attaining career goals. Identify personal goals that may be satisfied through a combination of work, community, social, and family roles.

Reflective Journal

1. State three things that you could do to help you prepare for the future.
2. When you consider possible careers, do you need to earn some type of certification to reach your goals? List the types of certification. Is it possible for you to use skills you have learned in school to help you fulfil your goals? List these skills.
3. "Learning is for life." Explain what this statement means to you.

Internet Activity

You can find both provincial and national career development products and labour market information on the Internet. Surf the Net for these career resources, beginning with your provincial government Internet sources.

Bookmark and catalogue the career resource addresses with a brief description of what each contains. Continue to add to this excellent career reference resource list as you discover more fascinating and informative Web sites.

Chapter 4

Enhancing Your Employability Skills

objectives

After completing this chapter you should be able to:

- ▶ Identify what employability skills are.
- ▶ Document your employability skills.
- ▶ Develop your employability skills.
- ▶ Prepare and customize your employability skills portfolio.
- ▶ Understand what makes a portfolio worker.

introduction

In 1991, a group of leading Canadian corporations participated in a round table discussion sponsored by the Conference Board of Canada. The purpose of the discussion was to identify the general skills that every student and worker should have, not only for entry-level work but for work at all levels. The result was the *Employability Skills Profile*. This Profile presents the critical skills required of the Canadian workforce as documented by the Conference Board of Canada from these round table meetings. In the remainder of the chapter and the book, we will clarify these skills and show you how best to acquire and use them.

In today's work search, a prospective employer must be convinced of your versatility. Although the work may vary a great deal, the basic skills the employer requires do not. A versatile employee is top-notch in the generic skills, attitudes, and behaviours described in the *Profile* and can demonstrate to a prospective employer that he or she can transfer those skills, attitudes, and behaviours to any type of work.

An invaluable aid in discovering, documenting and developing your employability skills is a *portfolio*. Your personal portfolio will contain evidence of your attainment in academic, personal management and teamwork skills, as outlined in the *Employability Skills Profile* on page 48. Many employers today are biased toward the work seeker who presents an accurate, up-to-date portfolio displaying his or her accomplishments.

The basic premise of the employability skills portfolio is that learning is a lifelong process. It enables students and workers to recognize successes, identify gaps in skills, and find ways to fill them and gain confidence for preparing for work. It identifies you as a *portfolio worker*, a person whose skills and experience make you the ideal worker in today's workplace. Students and workers should continuously upgrade their portfolio as they develop new skills or enhance existing ones.

EMPLOYABILITY SKILLS PROFILE

The Critical Skills Required of the Canadian Work Force

Academic Skills
Those skills that provide the basic foundation to get, keep, and progress on a job and to achieve the best results

Personal Management Skills
The combination of skills, attitudes, and behaviours required to get, keep, and progress on a job and to achieve the best results

Teamwork Skills
Those skills needed to work with others on a job and to achieve the best results

---

Canadian employers need a person who can:

Communicate
- Understand and speak the languages in which business is conducted
- Listen to understand and learn
- Read, comprehend, and use written materials, including graphs, charts, and displays
- Write effectively in the languages in which business is conducted

Think
- Think critically and act logically to evaluate situations, solve problems, and make decisions
- Understand and solve problems involving mathematics and use the results
- Use technology, instruments, tools, and information systems effectively
- Access and apply specialized knowledge from various fields (e.g., skilled trades, technology, physical sciences, arts, and social sciences)

Learn
Continue to learn for life

Canadian employers need a person who can demonstrate:

Positive Attitudes and Behaviours
- Self-esteem and confidence
- Honesty, integrity, and personal ethics
- A positive attitude toward learning, growth, and personal health
- Initiative, energy, and persistence to get the job done

Responsibility
- The ability to set goals and priorities in work and personal life
- The ability to plan and manage time, money, and other resources to achieve goals
- Accountability for actions taken

Adaptability
- A positive attitude toward change
- Recognition of and respect for people's diversity and individual differences
- The ability to identify and suggest new ideas to get the job done—creativity

Canadian employers need a person who can:

Work with Others
- Understand and contribute to the organization's goals
- Understand and work within the culture of the group
- Plan and make decisions with others and support the outcomes
- Respect the thoughts and opinions of others in the group
- Exercise "give and take" to achieve group results
- Seek a team approach as appropriate
- Lead when appropriate, mobilizing the group for high performance

From, *Employability Skills Profile: What Are Employers Looking For?* Brochure 1992 E (Ottawa: The Conference Board of Canada, 1992).

Employability Skills Profile

The Conference Board of Canada *Employability Skills Profile* lists 26 skills considered necessary for success in the workplace. The *Profile* presents these skills in very abstract terms in order to recognize every niche of the workforce. As a practical aid to students and work seekers, the Conference Board of Canada's *Profile* contents are interpreted in this chapter for better understanding. The chapter provides students and work seekers with practical suggestions for their own career development and performance. See how your skills and attitudes match up with what employers are looking for, and find out ways to fill in the blanks of your personal employability skills profile: The combination of skills, attitudes, and behaviours required to obtain, keep, and progress at work and to achieve the best results is the combination sought by Canadian employers.

I. Academic Skills or *How You Think*

Communicate

- ▶ speak clearly, write well and understand ideas, including proper use of technical terminology
- ▶ read and understand written materials; including proper use of technical terminology
- ▶ listen to instructions to understand and to learn

Think

- ▶ think critically to solve problems and make decisions
- ▶ learn how to use the technology and make appropriate decisions while using it

Learn

- ▶ learn new things and demonstrate a positive attitude toward lifelong learning

II. Personal Management Skills or *How You Act*

Positive Attitudes and Behaviours

- ▶ faith in their ability to do a job well; and capacity to handle constructive criticism; self-esteem and confidence
- ▶ honesty, integrity, and confidentiality consistent with the values of the workplace
- ▶ an ability to begin new tasks when appropriate, and energy and persistence to get the job done

Responsibility

- ▶ responsibility for actions taken and effective handling of any consequences
- ▶ an ability to set professional and personal goals and to plan and manage time, money, and other resources to achieve these goals

Adaptability

▶ a positive attitude to change by being flexible and adaptable
▶ respect for others' diversity and individual differences
▶ new or innovative ideas to get the job done with an enterprising or entrepreneurial spirit—creativity

III. Teamwork Skills or *How You Work With Others*

Work with Others

▶ understand and work within the group—(teamwork)
▶ contribute to common goals of the organization
▶ exercise "give and take" to achieve group results
▶ recognize when to lead and when to follow for high performance

Employability Skills Portfolio

Portfolios have long been used by artists, interior decorators, writers, and others to show the range and quality of work they are capable of doing. Similarly, in school, portfolios are being used by students to measure and report where they are in their learning. What better means, then, than an *employability skills portfolio* to highlight your capabilities for a potential employer. In an *employability skills portfolio* students and workers can record and evaluate their employability skills both for themselves in planning their futures and for prospective employers.

In the rest of this chapter and throughout the book, suggestions will be made on ways to document your successes, capabilities, and expanding skills and accomplishments as applied to particular work environments. In so doing you will be able to give a realistic, substantiated description of *you* in the context of the world of work. When complete it does what no résumé can; it shows the quality and variety of work of which you are capable. Start saving and documenting your portfolio samples NOW.

What to Include in Your Employability Skills Portfolio

1. Include *only the very best that you can do*; if it isn't your best don't include it.
2. Prepare photographs or drawings (black and white or colour copies) of your best work.
3. Use videotapes, computer disks, CD-ROMS—whichever medium best reflects the character of the sample displaying your skills.
4. Limit the number of samples for each presentation; up to **twelve** is probably ideal.

5. As your portfolio grows, continually replace existing samples with better ones.
6. To stand out in the crowd, make your creative approach to the portfolio unique, not just the samples. If you are strong in a particular area, stress it in your portfolio.
7. Gear your portfolio to each interview by tailoring the samples toward what the interviewer likely would want to see for that position. If you have it, show it!
8. Be prepared to discuss each sample with the interviewer and be able to explain its evolution.

What to Omit from Your Employability Skills Portfolio

1. Leave out everything that is not your **very** best work.
2. Omit or redo any work that is not "clean." Do not include classroom material containing corrections or comments. Crisp, neat, clean, clear samples are what interviewers want to see—they show neatness, organization, and professionalism.
3. Never let an error of any kind stay—spelling, punctuation, or syntax. Make sure someone with good grammatical, spelling and punctuation skills has proofread all your samples.
4. Omit samples not implicitly related to the work for which you have applied.
5. Omit samples that might be considered in poor or questionable taste.
6. Limit the number of samples demonstrating the same skill.
7. Omit anything that looks like bragging or boasting.

highlighting your employability skills

Suggestions for your portfolio that demonstrate *academic skills*.

▶ Foreign language(s) you can speak and/or write.
▶ Trade skills (computer drafting, mechanics, sewing).
▶ Special work skills (efficiency, punctuality, enthusiasm).
▶ Computer skills (software and/or programming proficiencies; hardware expertise).
▶ Licence to operate specialized equipment and machinery, vehicles of different sizes.
▶ Scholarships, transcripts, awards.
▶ Video or CD-ROM you developed.
▶ Poem, short story, or essay you have written.

Suggestions for your portfolio that demonstrate *personal management skills*:

▶ Evaluations from work experience or paid work.
▶ Recognition Awards (citizenship, effort, scholarship etc.).
▶ Extra-curricular courses taken out of school (music, first aid, CPR, etc.).
▶ Self-directed volunteer work (hospitals, canvassing, charity fund-raiser, etc.).
▶ Letters of commendation or recommendations from employers and teachers.

Suggestions for your portfolio that demonstrate *teamwork skills*:

- ▶ Membership in Student Council or School Annual Staff.
- ▶ Certificates (effort, honour roll, citizenship, etc.).
- ▶ In-school and out of school club memberships.
- ▶ In-school and out of school sports teams.
- ▶ Letters of recommendation
- ▶ Letters of commendation
- ▶ Examples of peer counselling, student tutoring

Add other samples under each of these three categories that really make the portfolio a first-class representation of you and what you have accomplished.

Putting Your Employability Skills Portfolio Together

- ▶ To make the best possible impression assemble your samples in a neat, professional-looking binder.
- ▶ Place the samples in protective acetate leaves which open on three sides like a book.
- ▶ Personalize your cover page to reflect your areas of expertise.
- ▶ Consider ease of presentation to an employer.
- ▶ Put photocopies only (not the originals) of certificates, awards, letters of recommendation, etc., in your portfolio.
- ▶ Reproduce coloured samples in **colour**.
- ▶ Design your portfolio to reflect your own uniqueness and creativity.
- ▶ Select samples that highlight quality learning, change, or growth.
- ▶ Be truthful, informed, and straight with your samples; don't be "gimmicky" or "cute."

Ways to Use Your Employability Skills Portfolio

1. Defining your career plans.
2. Obtaining work: part-time, full-time, volunteer.
3. Applying for a scholarship or bursary.
4. Getting entrance to university, college, technical school, and/or apprenticeships.
5. Supporting application for advanced placement to an instructional institution.
6. Demonstrating prior knowledge of a subject in order to challenge courses.
7. Evaluating and building on employability skills.
8. Becoming a portfolio worker.

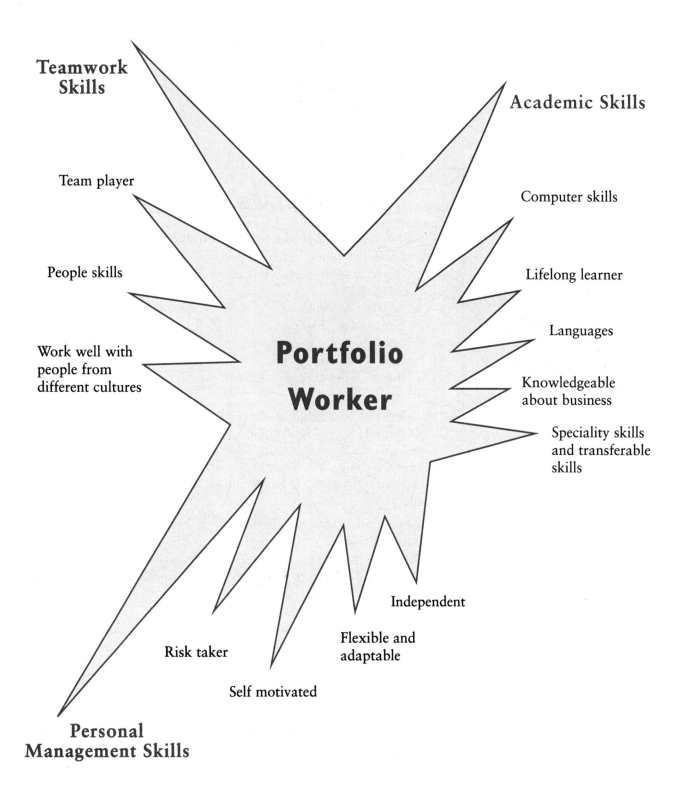

Teamwork
Skills

Team player

People skills

Work well with
people from
different cultures

**Portfolio
Worker**

Academic Skills

Computer skills

Lifelong learner

Languages

Knowledgeable
about business

Speciality skills
and transferable
skills

Independent

Risk taker

Flexible and
adaptable

Self motivated

Personal
Management Skills

Figure 4.1 Are you an "employability skills" person?

Custom-Tailoring Your Portfolio

You will probably be attending interviews for various types of work. The advantage that your portfolio gives you is that it is fluid, not static. You can add to, remove, or replace any of its contents in order to target an interview and a position effectively.

A Champion's Checklist

▶ Focus your employability skills portfolio for the specific situation for which you are applying.

▶ Be careful not to include too many samples; aim for quality not quantity.

▶ Bring your portfolio with you to the interview unless asked to drop it off ahead of time.

▶ Practise your portfolio presentation on your friends, family, or teacher before the interview. They may suggest additions or deletions to the portfolio as well as help you smooth your presentation.

▶ Custom-tailor your employability skills portfolio to the work for which you are applying:

For example, as a computer graphic artist these are some of the things you might include in your employability skills portfolio for the interview:

- A portfolio cover page that demonstrates your skills as a graphic artist.
- Quality samples of your work in the graphics area—print-outs, computer disk and/or CD-ROM, if appropriate.
- Certificates and awards related to attendance, work habits, citizenship.
- Other carefully selected works that show your creativity and artistic talent.

Chapter Summary Exercises

1. What will your work do for you? If you make the wrong choice, your work might not do much for you—in fact, it might make you very unhappy. That's why, when making work choices, it's very important to take into consideration the things you've learned about yourself.

   Your work should make you feel like "somebody." Work gives many people a sense of identity; it makes them feel as though they have something to offer. At the same time, work should provide you with something interesting to do and with the money to buy things you need and want.

Below is a list of expectations that many people have about work. Decide the importance of each to you and rank them in your notebook, using the following key.

A = Most Important   B = Very Important
C = Somewhat Important   D = Least Important

i	Good pay	*vii*	Feedback from supervisor
ii	Job security	*viii*	Full appreciation for efforts
iii	Promotion possibilities	*ix*	Sympathetic help with
iv	Good working conditions		personal problems
v	Interesting work	*x*	Feeling of being "in" on
vi	Company loyalty to		things
	employees		

2. Obtain definitions of work from ten of your classmates. Then prepare a report summarizing the results of your interviews. Do most of them have the same attitude or did each give a different definition? How does the definition given by the majority of your classmates compare with your definition of work?
3. List the criteria you should keep in mind for any work samples that you plan to include in your portfolio.
4. Identify effective portfolio presentation skills, and work in small groups demonstrating and critiquing each other's skills.

Reflective Journal

1. Using the Employability Skills Profile (page 48), rate yourself as an employee. Use a scale of 1 to 10, with 10 representing a perfect score.
2. From your response to the above, select the employability skills for which you gave yourself a low score and describe how you could improve each skill.

Internet Activity

Go to the Career Resource Home Page (by Rensselaer) (http://www.rpi.edu/dept/cdc/)

and the Monster Board Search (Job Listing) (http://www.monster.com/b/search/sesid=30293058,513d&func=scroll).

Surf through the databases, noting the employability skills that are frequently repeated. Note their similarity to generic employability skills discussed in this chapter.

Chapter 5

Changing Trends in the World of Work

objectives	After completing this chapter you should be able to:

- ▶ Discuss the employment factors in Canada that are changing the job market.
- ▶ Explain why people should be prepared to change careers.
- ▶ Understand why it is important to obtain as much education as possible.
- ▶ List some jobs and skills that are predicted to be in demand in the future.

introduction

Students and workers not only ask "What would I like to do? What occupations would match my interests and aptitudes?" but are also asking "Will there be work in this field when I'm finished the training? What should I train in to get work? Are there many openings in this type of work?" The numbers and types of jobs and careers available in the '90s and beyond will be the result of many forces of change in Canadian society. Because labour market information can change so rapidly, and does, it is important students and workers choose carefully sources of labour market information to help answer these questions and to always keep updated on the latest information. The workplace is changing. What does that mean for workers of today? It means new challenges that require new skills and a different attitude toward work.

A: Change Factors

Four major factors are causing the dramatic changes in the way we work:

1. **New technologies** are evident all around us. Many more people are doing many more tasks at a faster pace by means of personal computers and fax machines. Robots can do many repetitive jobs, and computers are greatly reducing the turnaround time on production and specialized tasks.

Implications for the way we work:

▶ New equipment makes it possible for you to work at home where the overhead is low and where you can work as needed.

▶ Electronic mail and cellular telephones help keep you up to date and in touch wherever you are.

▶ New technologies require new and different skills from today's workers. You must be prepared to continually update your skills throughout your working life.

2. **The changing workplace structure** means that in order to be more efficient and profitable, companies are cutting back by reducing the number of employees. This process is referred to as downsizing, rightsizing or restructuring. Sudden lay-offs make us feel that we have less control over our work and our lives than in the past. Choosing self-employment can be a way of trying to regain some of that control or a way of supplementing our income. As you saw in the previous chapter, you need many skills for today's workplace. All of these skills, along with your work experiences, combine to define you as a **portfolio worker**.

career options for today's winner: the portfolio worker

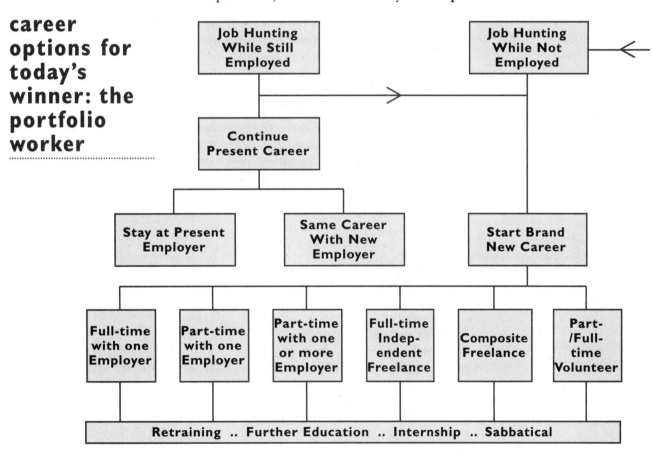

Figure 5.1 Career options for the 21st century: full or part-time, with the same or several new employers, or totally freelance. Such career paths will also involve periods of further education and retraining, perhaps an internship with another organization, and even a sabbatical.

Source: Canada's BEST CAREERS Guide, Revised 2nd Edition, Copyright © 1995. Frank Feather.

Think of your career path as combining and switching some or all of the following:

Part-time work: As companies downsize much permanent, full-time work has disappeared and more part-time than full-time work is created today. Part-time work is defined by Statistics Canada as under 30 hours per week. Permanent part-time workers are considered regular employees with the same benefits, job security and salaries as full-time employees. However, other types of part-time workers are considered casual workers and do not have the same protection as the permanent part-time workers do. A portfolio worker can use part-time work to gain industry experience and skills. It is possible, in this scenario, to have more than one part-time job.

Temporary work: Companies, usually through employment agencies, are bringing in full-time temporary workers for times when they are very busy, and letting them go when business slackens. They also use "temps" to cover for people on leave or extended absence. Temp work can give a wide variety of on-the-job experiences with many opportunities to learn new skills. For a portfolio worker it is another way "to get a foot in the door."

Contract work: Contracted work is usually not essential to the basic service or commodity of the business. For example, a computer software company might contract out the editing of a software package since its core workers are programmers, not editors. "Employers" become "clients" and portfolio workers as contract workers must be adept at marketing their expertise to prospective clients along with the skills of their specific field. They also must have excellent management skills, work as many hours as it takes to get the job done and always be on the lookout for potential work opportunities.

Project-based employment: Workers are hired to form a project team and when the project is over, so is the work. An example would be putting a team together to create a Home Page on the World Wide Web on the Internet for a business. When the work is completed the individuals go on to projects with other companies.

Consulting/Freelance: Companies hire, on an "as need" basis, specialists with professional or technical expertise. Hiring outside experts is less expensive than hiring and training employees. A portfolio worker might work for a consulting firm that brings together people with a range of skills and services. Consultants sometimes subcontract parts of a large project to other freelance consultants.

Entrepreneurship: Workers set up their own small business, usually but not always home-based. The service sector such as food services, personal care services, business services, knowledge and information services, and financial services, to name a few, are the fastest growing sector of the economy. There is almost no limit to the range of opportunities for self-employment for a portfolio worker.

3. **Changing demographics,** such as a decline in the birth rate and an aging population, have an impact on everyone. Women are having fewer babies than a generation ago. More women in two-career or single parent families are working outside the home. The average life expectancy for Canadian men is 78 years and for women about 83. The bulk of Canadian workers are moving into middle age, and more people are retiring at 55 instead of 65. All these factors will create a shortage of younger workers. Futurists predict that there will be an increased demand for skilled workers and more opportunities for youth, people with disabilities, aboriginals, and visible minorities. The government will continue to encourage immigration to increase the number of skilled workers.

4. **The shift to a service economy** (from an economy based on natural resources and agriculture) has increased the number of part-time job openings. As a result there are more opportunities for entrepreneurs to start up specialty businesses to fill new needs. Competition both locally and from around the world increases the need for quality and excellent service. Companies are making use of temporary employees to increase their workforce at peak periods and hiring consultants or external experts to work on special projects.

Minding Your Own Business (Entrepreneurship)

A growing number of Canadians are starting their own businesses. By the year 2000, the home business sector will be 20 percent of the labour force.

Do you have to be born an entrepreneur or can you learn and develop the necessary skills? Answer the following ten questions. If the answer to at least seven out of ten is yes, you at least have the potential and inclination for entrepreneurship. If you didn't answer yes to at least seven, you might need to develop some additional skills.

1. Do you enjoy working by yourself and being independent?
2. Do you have the confidence to make decisions and take calculated risks?
3. Are you willing to work hard, 10–12 hours a day, seven days a week to achieve your goal?
4. Do you have support from family members to help you cope with the enormous pressures and problems you will face?
5. Do you have an inner drive to succeed at what you start and follow it through to completion?
6. Can you fight back no matter how many times you are told "no," or even come back from failure?
7. Do you have confidence in yourself and in your ability to succeed?
8. Do you possess self-discipline, leadership abilities and organizational skills?
9. Are you equally good at sales and collecting money as you are in accounting or making things?
10. Are you willing to retrain yourself in new areas on an ongoing basis?

If you are not sure that starting your own business is for you, go through the questions again with a friend or someone you can trust. Ask for his or her opinion and compare with your own answers.

If you answered mostly in the affirmative and there is a definite potential, you will need to acquire more training, a business plan, proper financing and a mentor to help you on your way. To find out more before you start up your business, research and plan carefully. There are many places you can find this information. Here are a few:

- **Instructional Materials and Courses**

Many high schools, as well as colleges and universities, offer courses in entrepreneurship. These may be full- or part-time programs on starting your own business or small business management. Why not take a course while in high school, "just in case"?

- **Business Development Bank of Canada (BDC)**

The Business Development Bank of Canada (formerly the Federal Business Development Bank) offers a wide range of financial services, especially to small- and medium-sized businesses. It provides training, financial and strategic planning services and extensive counselling and business mentoring. For example, its Counselling Assistance to Small Enterprises (CASE) provides counselling and advice at a very reasonable cost and BDC's Special Initiatives are designed to meet the particular needs of certain entrepreneurs—women, aboriginal groups, young people and members of the ethnocultural communities. The Business Development Bank of Canada also provides a wide range of publications such as brochures, handbooks and do-it-yourself kits. For information, contact the branch nearest you or call, toll free, 1-800-361-2126.

- **Canada Business Service Centres**

Canada Business Service Centres are located in most metropolitan areas. They provide an entry point to the full range of business-related programs and services available from federal, provincial and municipal government departments and agencies. Consult the government pages of your local telephone directory and call for further information. Ask for the "home page" address of their World Wide Web (WWW) site on the Internet and explore.

- **Human Resources Centres of Canada (HRCC)**

A Human Resources Centre of Canada is able to advise on a number of business-related programs. One is its Self-Employment Assistance (SEA) program that provides income support, training and technical advice, for up to one year, to Employment Insurance claimants interested in starting their own business. The HRCC also works closely with local organizations and can refer you to other services available. A useful publication of theirs on entrepreneurship is a booklet called "Minding Your Own Business." You will find HRCC in the government pages of your telephone directory. Be sure to ask for their website when you call.

- **Libraries**

Check your school and local library or the library of a nearby college or university for recent listings on small business. The librarian is a very knowledgeable resource and can help and guide you on the use of the library as well as recommend specific books, periodicals, government documents, research studies, newspaper clippings, magazines and directories.

- **Financial Institutions**

Financial institutions such as banks, trust companies, credit unions, and caisses populaires provide financial support and have publications on starting a small business.

Some financial institutions have excellent resources on starting your own business using interactive software designed to help you create a winning business plan. Two software packages available free of charge are the Royal Bank of Canada's *The Big Idea for Small Business* and Toronto-Dominion's *TD Business Planner*. Your free copy can be obtained by calling the bank's Business Banking Centre. Check out the trust companies, credit unions and caisses populaires for their software packages on starting your own business and for the address of their WWW sites on the Internet.

> ## Implications for the way we work:
>
> ▶ There are more part-time, temporary and contract work opportunities.
> ▶ People who want to start up their own businesses need to assess the opportunities.
>
> They can begin this process by identifying unmet needs or problems in the market place.

To think about:

1. How have you been influenced by the changes mentioned here?
2. Do you know people who have been laid off because of downsizing or restructuring? What have they done? How have they been successful?
3. How have the new technologies impacted on your life?
4. Are you aware of the changing demographics in your community?
5. What new services or small businesses have you noticed around you?

B: Changing Attitudes

The changes in the economy and the workforce are accompanied by changes in our attitudes.

Lifestyle choices. In response to changes in the workplace, people are taking more control over their lives and making lifestyle decisions that impact their work. For many people, permanent and long-term jobs are a thing of the past. Workers now realize that they have to be prepared to make frequent work and career changes.

Search for meaning. Having satisfying work motivates people to do a good job. Depending on the stage you are at in your life, you will have different expectations of work. At one stage you may work simply to meet your basic needs and later you may want opportunities for more responsibility. At some point in your career you may find that you want more out of work than just a routine job. You reach a "plateau" in your career and begin to look for change and new challenges. Sometimes that means going beyond the company or the types of work you have been doing.

As people reach middle age, they often ask themselves questions like "Is this all there is to life?" or "Is this how I want to live my life?" Such soul-searching can lead to renewed awareness that can push people to examine what is really important to them and to make changes in their work and personal lives.

Combining study and work. Lifelong learning has become a familiar concept to most people. The education system and the wide variety of post-secondary educational programs make it possible for people of all ages to continue studying. Many high school students are employed part-time while attending school. You or someone you know may have returned to school to upgrade education and acquire new skills. Distance learning programs offer the opportunity to take recognized training at home using a combination of correspondence materials, telephone, television and computer link-ups. Another learning option is to take non-credit, continuing education courses that schools and community groups offer on every topic imaginable.

Employers recognize the need for training on the job but they also realize that people can benefit from further classroom training. Some companies provide the space and equipment for their employees to take training in the workplace after work hours. Others permit their employees to take an educational leave or pay for part of their educational expenses.

Retirement and longer life span. Sixty-five used to be the customary age for retirement. Now some companies are encouraging employees to take early retirement at age 55. This gives people the opportunity to begin something new—different jobs, businesses of their own, for example. For this reason people may "retire" several times in their careers.

At the age of 55 or 65, many people still need some income and want to continue contributing to society. A life of full-time leisure may not appeal to them. That is why a recent poll showed nearly 55 percent of people of retirement age work for reasons other than money.

To think about:

1. What lifestyle choices have you made in the past?
2. What lifestyle choices are you considering making?
3. Do you know any adults who have gone back to school?
4. Who do you know who has made a mid-career change?
5. Do you know anyone who has taken early retirement or who combines retirement and paid work?

C: Changing Definitions

Definitions of work, security, and success have to keep up with changes too.

A new definition of work. The traditional image of work is what people do when they leave the house at a regular time five days a week to go to offices or plants and put in eight to ten hours with scheduled times for coffee breaks and lunch. For this they receive regular paycheques with deductions taken off for benefits.

We need to broaden our definition of work to include a wide range of options. Does "being out of work" only mean not having a regular, full-time, paid job? What about volunteer work? Homemakers have known for a long time that unpaid or volunteer work tends not to have the same status as paid work. However this is changing; the value of volunteer work is receiving more recognition now as an option to paid work and an important contribution to our society.

Work occurs wherever people are involved in activities where they make things, provide services, and contribute to society.

A new definition of security. Security means feeling safe. It once meant having a steady job for as long as you wanted with a company that valued you as a permanent part of the corporate family.

The new definition of security is more personal. It means feeling safe because you have skills you can transfer from one company or industry to another as so-called permanent jobs continue to decrease due to changes in ownership, restructuring, or technological change. It means keeping up with the times and continually learning. Being adaptable and being able to handle changes can give a person a sense of security. The new security lies in your confidence in your own skills, and ability rather than in a job.

A new definition of success. Success is obtaining a favourable result from something you do. In work, success has often been defined by promotions, pay raises, prestige, and recognition. Traditionally, success has meant moving up the career ladder in a company; the higher up you get, the better. In contrast, a new definition of success may mean taking a lateral transfer to a position at your present level (or even below it) that would be more personally rewarding for you.

The new definition of success means proving your worth based on your *own* standards and expectations rather than on those of others. Success, in your own terms, will be based on *your* personal values and beliefs. It does not need to be confined to work, but can include achievements related to family, leisure activities, and community activities. For many people a successful life means being able to balance all parts of life, rather than overemphasizing work.

The challenge for you is to define success for yourself rather than rely on a traditional definition of the word. Personal resourcefulness calls for people to be creative, confident, and independent. Many people are already very successful in many types of work. You can get encouragement, support and new ideas by finding people doing the kinds of things you are interested in. They can act as role models for you as you create your own definition of success.

To think about:

1. What does the word "work" mean to you?
2. What is your personal definition of security?
3. How do you define success for yourself?

Change Factors, pages 56-64, adapted from: *Change Work of All Sorts*, Learning Resources Distributing Centre, Ministry of Advanced Education and Career Development, Edmonton, AB, © 1993.

what the numbers mean

Job Openings and Growth Rates*

Recall that, in Chapter 3, we discussed the top "growth careers" but suggested that you shouldn't worry unduly if your choice of work wasn't on the list. Here's why. There are different kinds of growth and different meanings that might surprise you. What produces job openings? Increases in the total number of job openings projected by the Canadian Occupational Projection System (COPS) is based on two factors:

1. *Economic growth* powers the expansion of many work fields.
2. The *need to replace workers* who retire, die, return to school, or return to the household or change jobs (attrition).

In many jobs there will be as many or more job openings due to replacement needs rather than economic growth. What this means is that even occupational fields that are not growing or even projected to experience job loss, can still produce job openings because of attrition.

What does *growth rates* mean? The projected growth of an occupation from COPS is usually reported as an average annual percent change, with an occupation described as having an above or below average growth rate as determined by the size of the existing workforce in the occupation. A high or above average rate of growth in a small occupation does not necessarily mean that the growing field will offer a large number of jobs. Despite the higher than average projected growth for "knowledge workers" such as computer programmers, the number of jobs produced by these small fields will be much lower in number than the "low tech" jobs in sales and service. What this means is that large occupational fields with below average growth can still produce more job openings than small occupational fields with high growth.

While increases in the total number of job openings is probably the most useful number for career planning, it is important to be aware that a high growth rate is often a signal of new emerging fields that will sustain growth for many years to come.

---

* *This section to the end of the chapter adapted from* Making Career Sense of Labour Market Information *by Elaine O'Reilly and Diane Alfred. Published by © Canadian Guidance and Counselling Foundation, 1995.*

Top Jobs in the Canadian Economy 1994–2005

Typical Top Jobs by Growth Rate

- Taxi and Limo Drivers and Chauffeurs
- Hotel Front Desk Clerks
- Food and Beverage Servers
- Managers d'Hôtel
- Restaurant and Food Service Managers
- Bartenders
- Actors
- Chefs
- Accommodation Service Managers
- Athletes
- Food Service Counter Attendants
- Support and Assisting Occupations in Motion Pictures, Broadcasting and the Performing Arts
- Bus Drivers and Other Transportation Operators
- Shoe Repairers and Shoemakers
- Other Technical Occupations in Motion Pictures, Broadcasting and the Performing Arts
- Attendants in Amusement and Recreation

Typical Top Jobs by Total Number of Job Openings

- Retail Salespersons
- Secretaries
- Retail Trade Managers
- Food and Beverage Servers
- Accounting and Related Clerks
- Janitors and Building Supervisors
- Cooks
- Registered Nurses
- Light Duty Cleaners
- Farmers and Farm Managers
- Cashiers
- General Office Clerks
- Truck Drivers
- Restaurant and Food Service Managers
- Kitchen and Food Service Managers
- Elementary and Kindergarten Teachers
- Receptionists
- Food Service Counter Attendants
- Sales Representatives, Wholesale Trade (Non-technical)
- Babysitters and Nannies

Typical Top Jobs by Earnings

- Specialist Physicians
- Judges
- General Practitioners and Family Physicians
- Dentists
- Senior Managers: Finance, Communications and Business Services
- Senior Managers in Goods Production
- Lawyers and Quebec Notaries
- Senior Managers: Trade and Broadcasting
- Optometrists
- Chiropractors
- Air Pilots, Flight Engineers and Flying Instructors
- Primary Production Managers (Except Agriculture)
- Engineering, Science and Architectural Managers
- University Professors
- Petroleum Engineers

Other Factors To Consider When Making Your Own List of Top Jobs

- Shortage or oversupply of qualified workers in the field.
- Geographic location (does the job require relocation).
- Job security (some occupations are highly susceptible to recessionary or seasonal pressures).
- Opportunity for full-time or part-time employment.
- Education level required.
- Commitment of employers in the occupational field to employment equity.

Keys To Your Future

By now, you have probably realized that *you* are the major key to your future! The onus is on you to prepare yourself, to find work, and to update your skills and your goals. Following are eight keys you can use to help prepare yourself for today's workplace.

Key: 1: All the components making up the labour market serve to affect one bottom line for the work seeker—supply and demand.

Tips/Research Suggestions
Use information sources to gather supply and demand information before making a decision. These sources could include:

- the education or training institution being considered;
- the regional economist publications;
- unions and associations;
- CEC counsellors;
- local service groups who are willing to share information on the occupations of their members;
- Chamber of Commerce.

Key: 2: Sources of information are everywhere. Only a lack of creative investigation limits the number of sources.

Tips/Research Suggestions
Ask, ask, ask! Don't be afraid to ask anyone for help or suggestions. Ask your neighbours, former teachers, association receptionists, relatives and anyone you meet on the job, for example, the TV repairer or computer technician who installs your printer. Always ask the person who gives you some information for another name for you to contact.

Key: 3: Using labour market information in career planning is a process that has to be learned and practised.

Tips/Research Suggestions
Read the business section of the newspaper. Practise asking labour market questions about what you read. Study the want ads and ask yourself what you can learn from the types and numbers of job descriptions, the salaries, etc. Check your interpretations with your friends or people in business.

Key: 4: Technology has an impact on virtually every occupation and on the training and education that any member of the labour force will have.

Tips/Research Suggestions
Check first with employers or associations and unions for what high-tech skills are in demand and what advanced equipment is being used, and then make sure that the training program or institution you choose is up-to-date enough to give you these skills and knowledge.

Key: 5: Computer skills have become generic, transferable skills, in demand in every occupation.

Tips/Research Suggestions

Make sure you have computer skills. Check the program of study to see if it includes computer training. If not, take extra training at night or during school breaks or after you finish the program.

Key: 6: Multi-skilling is more and more required in the new economy.

Tips/Research Suggestions
- Take note of what to train in, if you want to be an effective supervisor in the new economy.
- No matter what your technical expertise, study management skills.
- No matter what your management expertise, study technological developments.

Key: 7: The components of the labour market are interwoven to such a degree that discussion of each one necessarily involves reintroduction of the others.

Tips/Research Suggestions
- As you investigate occupations, ask what extra skill training is of added value to the new entrant in the field. Ask what kinds of jobs are being phased out or what layoffs occurred. Find out what skills are involved that have to be picked up by the remaining workers and train yourself in these areas.
- Expect that any information you receive will change. Check several sources of information and ask about different labour market influences to get a whole picture. Change in any component may cause a chain reaction that will influence your original sources of information.

Key: 8: In newspapers, journals, books, reports, studies and brochures aimed at youth, employers, employees, practitioners, students and teachers, the same message recurs: the growth area will be in services; expect less job security; and many people will be self-employed.

Tips/Research Suggestions

Think creatively about your options and ways of linking your expertise with growth areas of the economy. For example, consider preparing yourself with expertise in a field that includes small business management. If science is not your area, think about a service you might offer to those involved in the field. If international marketing is out of your range, figure out a service you can offer those involved in that field. If every business needs the benefit of programmers and analysts, and it is not in your realm, how could you fit into that market, for example, a matching service, providing technical people for contract positions with firms?

The new Canadian economy calls for efficient use of the information that is readily available to the population. By learning to locate and use easily accessible data, counsellors, teachers and their clients or students become integral parts of the labour market system, enabling individuals to develop career paths that suit their abilities and the changing needs of the labour market.

A Champion's Checklist

▶ Try not to limit your expectations by what you did in the past. Focus on what you can do now and in the future.

▶ Re-think who you are and what you can do.

▶ Take stock of your transferable skills. You may be able to use the same skills in a different career or in another industry.

▶ Assess yourself. Write down your strengths and weaknesses. Make a list of your goals and dreams.

▶ Be flexible and open. You might be surprised at what interests you.

▶ Network—talk to people about ideas, opportunities, and work.

▶ Expand your contacts through volunteer work and joining organizations.

▶ Think about starting a business.

▶ Consider getting more schooling or retraining to develop new skills or enhance the ones you have already.

▶ If you have a career goal in mind, develop your skills by volunteering or finding paid work that gives you experience in that career field.

Chapter Summary Exercises

1. Why is it important to have math skills for today's workplace?
2. What four major factors are causing the dramatic changes in the way we work?
3. Why should people be prepared to change careers?
4. List five guidelines for work success.
5. Explain what is meant by "job openings" as compared to "job growth rates."
6. You have low-paying, unskilled work. List five steps that you could take to obtain employment in a higher-paying, skilled area.
7. Discuss the changing requirements of the workplace and how they impact career changes.
8. Using *Keys to Your Future* on pages 67 and 68 as a guide, outline how you would prepare yourself for the workplace.

Reflective Journal Entries

1. Write a short description of how a changing population has affected work opportunities in Canada. What, if anything, does the "baby boom" mean for you and your work opportunities?
2. Briefly explain why you should welcome and embrace change.

Internet Activity

Complete at least one of the eight *Keys to Your Future* Tips/Research Suggestions as outlined on pages 67 and 68, using the Internet as your information source. Carefully record this information and present it in report format.

UNIT 2

The Work Search

introduction

In today's work environment you need an edge. It is not enough to have the skills and qualifications for the work you want to do—you need to be able to find and convince employers that you should be hired. Unit 2 will take you step by step through the work-search process: locating work prospects, gathering personal information, preparing résumés, writing cover letters, and having interviews.

Chapter 6

Preparing for the Work Search

introduction

Effective preparation for your work search involves gathering together the items and information that you will need. If you are well prepared, you will save time and be ready to take advantage of opportunities that you might otherwise miss. The following are some important preparations that you should make.

1. Time Management

Time is a resource that never can be regained and managing it well is a skill. You want to organize your time to maximize productivity and efficiency and reduce stress. To organize your time effectively do some of the following:

1. Carry a day planner, pocket-sized or larger, computerized or not, to record all your personal and business time commitments. Be sure your day planner is very businesslike and professional in appearance reflecting the no-nonsense image you wish to project.
2. Prioritize your daily tasks in your day planner with colour coding, alphabetically or numerically. At the end of the day cross off those tasks completed and put those not completed on the next day's list.
3. Think ahead; use time efficiently. Do the things you don't like first. They won't be hanging over your head and they are more likely to get done. Save the best tasks to the last. Do not procrastinate by putting things off until another time. It will prevent you from achieving your goals.
4. Carry your day planner into the interview for instant referral—"Are you free next Monday?" You check your day planner. "Yes, I am." A potential employer is impressed, inferring that you are a

person who can be relied upon to be on time and to complete tasks on time.

5. Give yourself time for fun; celebrate your successes. It will refresh you and renew your energy.

2. How to Get Your Social Insurance Number (SIN)

You need a Social Insurance Number (SIN) for most work in Canada.

1. Find your original birth certificate.
2. Apply at your local Human Resources Centre of Canada (formerly called the Canada Employment Centre) and complete a SIN form similar to the one on page 73. Check the Government of Canada section in the telephone book for the address.
3. Present your original birth certificate (not a photocopy) with your completed SIN form at the front office.
4. While you are waiting for your SIN card to arrive, you still can apply for work. The HRCC will give you a receipt to show employers. It could take up to *six weeks* for your SIN card to arrive. Within three days after having received your Social Insurance Number submit it to your employer.
5. Your SIN card is free. If you lose your card, however, you will need to re-apply (again with original birth certificate) and pay a service charge for a replacement card.
6. Your Social Insurance Number is yours *for life*; when you die the number dies with you. Guard your number carefully. For government and employment purposes, this is your identity. Do not give it out freely and never put it on your résumé.

3. Collecting Personal Information

To be well prepared for your work search, you need all of your personal information. You can use this information in preparing your résumé, completing application forms, and answering questions during interviews.

The best way to collect this information is to write everything down on a personal information form. For your convenience you may wish to use the *Personal Information Form* provided in the teacher's manual.

4. Identify the type of work you are looking for. (Refer to Chapter 3)

5. Obtain references:

Contact people whose names you might want to use as references. These are people whom the employer could contact to vouch for your character and ability. Naturally, you want references who will speak favourably of you. Prepare a record of their names, titles, full addresses (including postal codes), and telephone numbers. Do not use close friends or relatives as references.

Human Resources Development Canada   Développement des ressources humaines Canada

PROTECTED WHEN COMPLETED - A

APPLICATION FOR A :

☐ FIRST SOCIAL INSURANCE NUMBER CARD

☐ REPLACEMENT CARD (fee of $ 10.00 must be paid)

☐ CHANGE OF NAME(S) ON CARD

☐ CHANGE OF STATUS

☐ OTHER CHANGES (no card will be issued)

DO NOT WRITE IN THIS AREA

> YOUR APPLICATION WILL BE RETURNED IF NOT ACCOMPANIED BY THE REQUIRED DOCUMENTS (see instruction sheet for details)

INFORMATION CONCERNING THE APPLICANT. PLEASE PRINT CLEARLY.

1   NAME TO BE SHOWN ON CARD ▸   FIRST NAME   MIDDLE NAME (if wanted on card)   FAMILY NAME

2   DATE OF BIRTH ▸   D   M   Y   **3**   SEX ▸ ☐ MALE   ☐ FEMALE   ☐ CHECK BLOCK IF YOU ARE A TWIN

4   MOTHER'S FULL NAME AT HER BIRTH   **5**   FATHER'S FULL NAME AT HIS BIRTH

6   APPLICANT'S PLACE OF BIRTH ▸   CITY, TOWN OR VILLAGE   PROVINCE   COUNTRY

7   FAMILY NAME AT BIRTH   **8**   OTHER FAMILY NAME(S) PREVIOUSLY USED

9   HAVE YOU EVER HAD A SOCIAL INSURANCE NUMBER ▸ ☐ NO   ☐ YES   **10**   IF "YES", WRITE YOUR NUMBER HERE ▸

11   STATUS IN CANADA ▸ ☐ CANADIAN CITIZEN   ☐ REGISTERED INDIAN   ☐ PERMANENT RESIDENT   ☐ OTHER   **12**   AREA CODE   TELEPHONE NO.

13   ADDRESS WHERE YOU WANT YOUR SIN CARD TO BE MAILED   NUMBER AND STREET   APARTMENT NO.   CITY, TOWN OR VILLAGE   PROVINCE   POSTAL CODE

> IT IS AN OFFENCE TO KNOWINGLY APPLY FOR MORE THAN ONE SOCIAL INSURANCE NUMBER. YOU ARE NOT PERMITTED TO GIVE OR LEND YOUR CARD TO ANYONE.

14   (IF YOU ARE UNDER 12 YEARS OF AGE, YOUR PARENT/GUARDIAN MUST SIGN AND INDICATE HIS/HER RELATIONSHIP. IF "X" IS USED AS A SIGNATURE, HAVE TWO WITNESSES SIGN HERE)

APPLICANT'S SIGNATURE ▸   DATE ▸

INFORMATION COLLECTED ON THIS FORM IS USED FOR THE PURPOSE OF ISSUING SOCIAL INSURANCE NUMBERS. ITS COLLECTION IS AUTHORIZED BY THE UNEMPLOYMENT INSURANCE ACT. FOR MORE DETAILS ON THE USES AND RIGHTS CONCERNING INSPECTION AND CORRECTION OF THE INFORMATION, REFER TO THE PUBLICATION INFO SOURCE, BANK NO. EIC PPU 390, AVAILABLE IN CANADA EMPLOYMENT CENTRES AND MAJOR PUBLIC LIBRAIRIES.

DO NOT WRITE BELOW, FOR LOCAL OFFICE USE ONLY

A   ALL NAMES AS SHOWN ON PRIMARY DOC. ▸   GIVEN NAMES   FAMILY NAME

B   DATE OF BIRTH AS SHOWN ON PRIMARY DOC.   D   M   Y   **C**   PRIMARY DOCUMENT SEEN (ABBR.)   (SERIAL / REG. NO.)   SUPPORTING DOCUMENT SEEN (ABBR.)

D   PRIORITY SIN REASON   CEC FAX NO. ( )   GEMDES CODE

E   FEE PAID IF REPLACEMENT CARD   AMOUNT $ RECEIPT NO.   CERTIFICATION STAMP

REMARKS

F

NAS 2120 (04-94) B

(FRANÇAIS AU VERSO)

Canada

Figure 6.1 SIN card application form

PREPARING FOR THE WORK SEARCH   CHAPTER 6   **73**

6. Appearance:

Being well groomed is essential when meeting prospective employers. Remember, you are the product, so package yourself appropriately. Are your clothes suitable? Do you need a haircut? (Refer to Chapter 11)

7. Maintain records:

Maintain records of contacts you make with prospective employers so that you can take appropriate follow-up action. (Refer to Chapter 10).

8. Work search techniques:

You must know where and how to look for work. This chapter will give you many suggestions for locating work.

9. Positive attitude:

Maintain a positive attitude. If you *expect* to find work, your chances of finding it improve.

Locating Work*

The work market today is tough whether you are looking for full-time, part-time, or contract work. There are often many applicants for the same position, and often opportunities for work are not advertised in the newspapers or posted at employment centres.

Work searchers today need to be information specialists, constantly digging for more information about their area of interest and expertise. They need to find out about trends in their industry, what training is required, and who is hiring and firing.

Many people search out work at *Human Resources Centres of Canada*, their provincial career counselling centres, and through their schools. You need to use every resource available to find work. Here are some other resources for your work search.

1. Networking

Networking is a process of connecting with others as a means to finding work. Although at first glance, a person may seem to be an unlikely candidate for your network, you never know who is in his or her circle of friends and acquaintances. It's the *connection*, the web of contacts you set in motion and develop, that is important. Get used to telling people you are looking for work. Tell you friends, your friends' parents, your relatives, your neighbours, all the people you can think of, that you need work and that you are a hard worker. To refresh their memory on your skills and work experience, give them copies of your résumé for reference.

Circle of Contacts

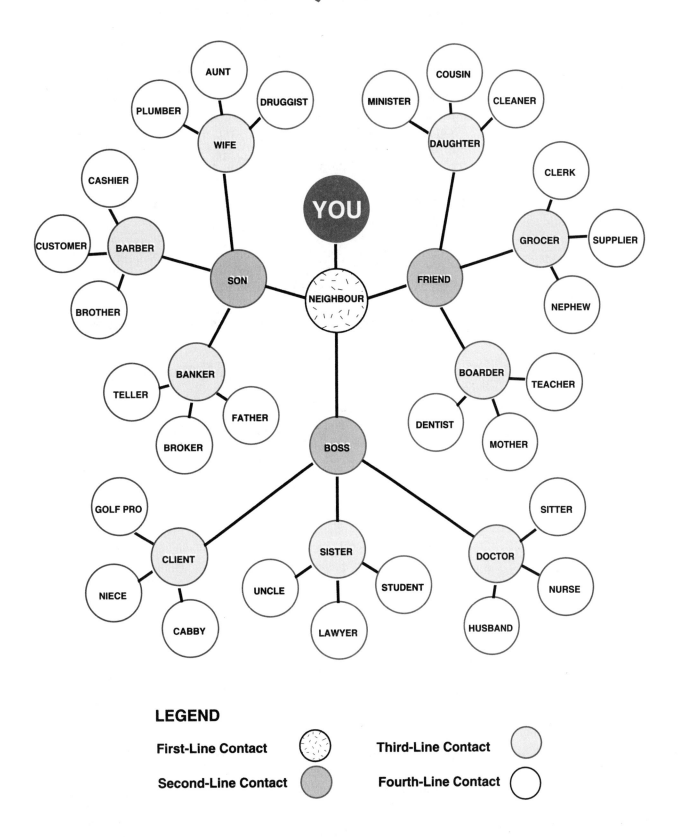

Figure 6.2 A network web

When the network begins to work for you and the leads start coming in, keep careful track of the information on work lead forms or cards. (See example below. Your teacher will give you blank copies of the forms.)

2. Libraries

Use the library to find out about trends in the labour market and the economy. Business magazines, newspaper articles, placement annuals, occupational monographs, and industrial directories are filled with information about different industries. Also, many industries have trade magazines containing information and employment ads.

3. Unions and Professional and Trade Associations

These organizations have information about their specific industry. Some publish newsletters for members that may include information on education, training, and work opportunities.

4. Workshops, Conventions, and Work Fairs

Watch for and attend events held by schools, trade associations, and industries in your community. Such events offer useful opportunities to gain information and make contacts.

Work Lead Form

Network Contact: _____ Date: _____

Type of Work: _____

Name or Organization: _____ Phone: _____

Street Address: _____

Room Number: _____

Travel Directions: _____

Date of Interview: _____ Time: _____

Name of Interviewer: _____

Title of Interviewer: _____

Materials to Bring: _____

Results of Interview: _____

Next Steps: _____

Figure 6.3 Work lead form

5. The Media

Television, radio, and newspapers carry up-to-the-minute information about current trends in the economy and their effects on the labour market.

6. The Internet and the Information Highway

Today work searchers have a new resource—the information highway. Think of it as a library that is so new, the information it contains is not yet organized on shelves or in a card catalogue.

Just as an intercity highway takes you at high speed straight to your choice of destinations, the information highway takes you speedily to information about your choice of subjects. This worldwide computer network includes community networks, thousands of interest groups, databases, and on-line news services.

How can you use this uncharted highway to search for work opportunities? You will need access to a computer with a modem and communications software package. This could be your own equipment or one at a school, library or career centre.

The computer must be hooked to a telephone line and a service such as your Schoolnet, your local community network, a commercial on-line service or a commercial Internet service provider, all of which provide access to the information highway.

From this point, where you head on the information highway is up to you. There are many different directions you can go on a work search:

▶ Search on your local community network for work bulletin boards.
▶ Look for on-line newspapers that carry classified ads.
▶ Read news services and databases that provide information about industries and the labour market.
▶ Join interest groups devoted to work opportunities, entrepreneurship, and home-based businesses.

Remember, when you are cruising the information highway, it is up to you to find out what is on it and what is useful. There are no road guides or maps for users, just your own curiosity and ingenuity.

7. Classified Ads

Study classifieds. Although only about five percent of work is obtained through classified ads, they can give you information on the specific education and experience required for particular kinds of work. An overview of the classifieds can also give you a general idea about industries that are expanding and looking for workers.

*Adapted from Canada Prospects, 1995/1996, Canada's Guide to Career Planning, MP43-01-2-1995E.

ACTIVITY 1

Understanding Advertisement Abbreviations for Work

Many newspapers use abbreviations to save space in their work-offer ads. Below is a list of abbreviations that are often used. In your notebook, write down each abbreviation and then supply the definition of it.

1.	appt.	9.	eqpt.	17.	mgr.
2.	apt.	10.	exp.	18.	min.
3.	ASAP	11.	ext.	19.	p.t.
4.	asst.	12.	hqtrs.	20.	refs.
5.	bldg.	13.	hrly.	21.	rep.
6.	const.	14.	hvy.	22.	temp.
7.	c.v.	15.	inf.	23.	trnee.
8.	dept.	16.	K	24.	wk.

Figure 6.4 Samples of help-wanted ads

Bilingual Person Friday

Distribution centre seeking someone energetic and well organized to work in conjunction with sales department and warehouse.

Requirements:
Bilingual (excellent English and French grammar), word processing (WordPerfect), knowledge of inventory control.

Remuneration based on exp.

Fringe benefits. Send résumé to

C.G. Industrial Products,
564 Boulevard Felix, Montreal,
PQ H4L 1J5.

Shop Foreperson

Dynamic automobile dealership requires an enthusiastic leader and motivator of people.
Applicants must be able to diagnose electronic components and must have a thorough knowledge of EFI/fuel systems.

Salary 35K plus bonus and company car. Refs. required. Send c.v. to:
The Star,
Dept 274. P.O. Box 2000,
Dominion Place, Hamilton, ON L3V 5A8

Opportunity available with prominent retail store chain. Many p.t. positions open for present & future stores.

For appt., please call Michele, 854-7831.

• Data Entry •

Experienced individual needed for data entry in order-processing department of modern textile operation. Conscientiousness and intelligence are prime assets. Send résumé (including inputting speed) to:

Dorcas Creations,
654 Leonard St.,
Winnipeg, MB R4H 3H8,
Attention: Mr. G. Santori.

Exp. dependable person responsible for cleaning team in large office bldg., east end, night shift. Good hrly rate. 243-0770.

Warehouse Worker

Person needed for general work in distribution warehouse. Must have exp. Some hvy work. Apply 766 Industrial Drive from 8-11 a.m.

Intermediate Accountant required immediately. Duties will include assisting the accountant in the preparation of monthly financial statements and reports, budgeting, job costing, accounts rec., accounts payable, payroll, etc. applicant must be exp. and should possess a 2 yr., business administration diploma or 3rd level CGA/CMA. Position also requires applicant to have good communication skills and be a team player.
Please send résumé with salary expectations to:

Reddislab Structures Inc.
8 Portugal Cove Road
St. John's NF A1B 4J2
709-555-7766.
Attention: J. Funamoto

LARCO, a leading worldwide manufacturer of pressure relief and explosion protection products, requires a bilingual (French/English), dynamic, sales-oriented individual to handle customer service inquiries, quotations, and order processing at its hqtrs.

The ideal candidate for this entry-level position will have excellent communication skills, computer word processing/order entry experience and preferably some technical (Mechanical Engineering) post-secondary education.

Excellent benefits. Remuneration commensurate with experience. Forward your résumé in confidence to:

Larco Canada, Inc.
1684 Jasper Av.
Edmonton AB
T5J 3B5
Attention: General Mngr
No phone calls please

The following is a newly created position at *Northland Publishing.*

Title: **Production/Editorial Assistant**

Required Skills
- Must be computer literate and have the desire to work in a highly technical environment.
- The ability to work with a team of people and manage the required workload independently.
- Excellent communication skills.
- A keen appreciation for detail and quality is necessary for both print publications and CD-ROMs.
- Strong organizational and time management skills.

Education/Experience

A post-secondary level education and at least one year related experience.

All interested applicants should reply to Elena de Souza, Editorial Director, General Delivery, Keno City, YT Y0B 2G1 Fax 403 555-2722

Analysing the Work Advertisements

Answer the following questions about work advertisements in Figure 6.4.

1. Which advertisements would you answer with a letter?
2. Which advertisements would you answer with a fax?
3. Which work requires the use of more than one language?
4. Which work requires knowledge of several software packages?
5. What kind of work would *definitely* require working nights? What kind of work would *probably* require working nights?
6. Do any of the ads imply that heavy physical work would be required?
7. What work ads ask for the most education?
8. What work ads do not ask for experience?
9. If all of the work was in your region, what work would you apply for?

Extracting Information from Work Advertisements

Consult one of your local newspapers to find an advertisement for work that fits each of the following categories. Write the name of each category in your notebook and then use the information in the advertisement to answer the questions that follow the list of categories.

- ▶ Office and Sales (secretary, administrative assistant, clerk, computer operator, salesclerk, sales representative)
- ▶ Mechanical and Industrial Services (mechanic, shop foreperson, engineer)
- ▶ Medical and Food Services (nurse, nursing assistant, doctor, X-ray or lab personnel, cashier, server)
- ▶ Personal Services (counsellor, lawyer, teacher)

1. What is the position title?
2. What qualifications does the work require?
3. Whom are you supposed to contact regarding the position?
4. How does the prospective employer wish to be contacted (in person, by telephone, by letter, etc.)?

(You might want to carry out this activity on the Internet.)

Chapter Summary Exercises

1. List five important items you should attend to before beginning your work search and explain why each is important.
2. Complete a personal information form (provided by your teacher).
3. Name four career and work information resources currently available on the information highway?
4. Identify a network of people to assist you in securing work. Use the *Circle of Contacts* network web on page 75 as a model.

Reflective Journal

1. "Time is a resource that never can be regained." What does this mean to you?
2. Analyse your network of personal and professional contacts. How can they help you in your work search?
3. How did you get your current or last part-time work? Describe the steps you had to go through. What did you learn about looking for work?
4. Describe any volunteer work that you have done. What skills or knowledge did you acquire from this experience that could be used in future work?
5. Why is it important to maintain a positive attitude when looking for work? What are some things you can do, by yourself or with friends, to keep thinking positively?

Internet Activity

Research and write a report on the Social Insurance Number. Check out your local *Human Resources Centre of Canada Home Page* on the Internet for this information. The Internet Home Page address is available from your local Human Resources Centre.

or

Making work contacts online via discussion groups and newsgroups in your field of interest is an excellent way (40 percent success rate) to find work. Use keywords to search for contacts, then e-mail your questions about work in your area of interest, organizations, people to contact who are hiring. *Someone* will answer. Give it a try!

Chapter 7

Power Résumés

| objectives | After completing this chapter you should be able to: |

objectives

After completing this chapter you should be able to:

▶ List and explain various parts of a power résumé.
▶ Short list "do's" and "don'ts" in résumé preparation.
▶ Prepare a one- or two-page power résumé.

introduction

As indicated in Chapter 5, *Changing Trends in the World of Work*, the job market in the late 90s and into the 21st century will be very difficult to enter simply because the jobs will not be there. The competition for work that is available will be fierce and only the individuals who work hard and pay attention to detail when hunting for work will prevail. Follow carefully the suggestions in the next four chapters and your chances of being a winner in your work search increase at least fourfold. You can do it!

Beating the Odds

A résumé has one very specific function: to get the interview. An employer who is deluged with résumés needs to devise a short-listing technique to quickly bring the number of résumés down from the hundreds received in response to an advertisement to a manageable number. How is this done efficiently and quickly? One very quick and easy way employers use is to give each résumé a cursory glance, five seconds at most, looking for reasons NOT to keep it. Handwritten? *Definitely a no.* Corners curled, paper wrinkled? *Into the basket!* Smudges, coffee stains etc.? *Not a chance.* Design difficult to read? *Haven't the time!* and so it goes until about fifteen or twenty résumés are left for closer scrutiny. Now the employer reads more carefully. Oops, here's a spelling error: *Pitch this one.* No postal codes, no telephone numbers? *It's a loser.* Grammatical error? *Not wanted here.* (A candidate making these kinds of errors does not appear to have the necessary skills). Now having brought the number of "winning" résumés down to six or eight, the employer is ready to call individuals in for an interview.

Making the Short List

The name of the game, therefore, is to prepare a résumé so powerful it will survive the short-listing techniques the employer uses. These are controllables—you can do this! Here are some ways to be sure to be short-listed.

First, buy good quality paper (bond with a watermark you can see when you hold the paper up to the light). Remember the employer is going to "feel" your résumé first. The touch of fine paper will automatically cause the person to look at what is being held. Now you've got the recipient's attention! What he or she will see first is the colour of your bond paper: white, off-white, ivory, light blue, cream, light brown—whatever looks quietly elegant. You want your résumé to stand out, not look as if it came off an assembly line. Be sure, therefore, to print each résumé separately, laser print if possible. If you are using a typewriter, be sure to use a plastic, one-time use carbon ribbon. A power résumé should never be photocopied; however, if you need to save money, a laser printed or plastic one-time use carbon ribbon-printed master, copied on equipment that produces a clear, sharp copy, on top-grade paper, is the next best thing. If you *really* want the interview, though, don't photocopy!

Grabbing the Advantage

You survived the first and second cut! How can you *keep* the reader's attention? When glancing at a résumé the reader's eyes automatically look about one-third of the way down a page, so grab the attention right away by leading with your big guns: What do you have to offer that will make you irresistible to the employer? Is it your work history? Education? Special skills? Once you have decided on your most impressive attribute for this particular job, lead with it, then follow with your next most impressive attribute, and so on. Always put the least interesting (to an employer) information about yourself, such as personal information, at the end of the résumé. However, in *that* personal information, include something about yourself that is unique. (For example: *Have lived on five continents, speak fluent Mandarin, Portuguese, and English.*) This too is an attention grabber and may become the focus of discussion during the interview. Above all, keep your résumé brief with lots of white space. Someone should be able to read it in seconds since that may be all the time you get! NOW, let's get started on your winning power résumé.

Parts of the Power Résumé

✓ **Name:** Give your first and last name only (no nicknames). Highlight your name so that it stands out. You could box it, boldface it, increase the font size, print it in a different (but highly legible) font. If it has fewer than 15 letters, you could spreadcentre your name by putting one space between each letter and three spaces between each name to make it stand out. By doing this you are saying to the employer, "This is *me*—I am proud of me!"

| Jamilah Fazal |

✓ **Address:** Give your complete address. Never abbreviate in the address other than the two capitalized letters for the provinces/territories (e.g., ON, PQ, YK). Always put the postal code on a line by itself.

2389 Castle Drive
Victoria, BC
B8N 5G7

✓ **Telephone/Fax Number:** Always include the area code with your telephone/fax number. Two acceptable styles for area codes are:

(604) 555-1234 or 604/555-1234

✓ **E-mail address:** If you have one, include it. You thereby give the message that you are computer literate and familiar with the information highway, almost certainly a required skill for the 21st century. Besides it might just be the winning edge!

E-mail: fazal@uvictoria.bc.ca

✓ **Objective or Career Profile:** An objective gives focus, direction and support to the body of the résumé. It is an attention grabber if it is right on target with the position advertised. Use an objective only if it makes sense; otherwise use the cover letter to inform the employer of your specific or broad career goals.

When you are "shopping" for work, you might use instead a *Career Profile*, usually written in broad statements that focus on skills, achievements, and outstanding character attributes, verified by the content of the résumé.

✓ **Education:** If you are looking for your first full-time work, the education section becomes very important. List your most recent education first, including your major areas of study (not necessarily a degree). Include the name of the school and dates of attendance. If you are in the process of completing your post-secondary training, mention the year and area of specialized study. If you have begun your post-secondary education, omit your high school education; mentioning it could focus more attention on it than you want. Additional training courses and certificates should be included.

✓ **Work Experience:** If your work history matches the work description, you may want to lead with it. List your most recent work experience first and work backwards, in other words, reverse chronological order. Include job title, employer, city, province/territories (use two letter abbreviations, e.g., MB, NF, AB), job responsibilities and accomplishments, and the dates of employment. Try to think like an employer; what would you want to see as reader of your résumé?

Use active verbs to briefly tell what you have done, what you accomplished, and what the benefits were to your employer.

If you are just out of school, include school work experience programs, summer and part-time employment, and volunteer work. With paid work becoming increasingly more difficult for young people to find, volunteer work becomes immensely important. Excellent work experience and references can be obtained as easily in unpaid as in paid work.

✓ **Awards and Activities:** List scholarships, academic honours, or certificates you received. Be sure to stress your extra-curricular activities and special achievements in sports, clubs, or other school activities, often evidence to employers of leadership, dedication, and initiative. Your awards and school activities will play a lesser role in your résumé as you gain more work experience and over time you will likely refer only to degree attained and major awards.

✓ **Special Skills and Attitudes:** Highlight in this section the skills you have that relate directly to the position for which you are applying. These may include specific computer applications, fluency in a foreign language, or special abilities you possess that are not necessarily part of your formal education. Highlight, as well, such attributes as honesty, enthusiasm, and maturity, qualities that make you indispensable in the work place.

✓ **References:** There is usually not enough room to list references on a one-page power résumé. This does not mean, however, that you do not include them. Under the reference section on your résumé write, "References attached." On paper identical to that used in your résumé give three or four references—never less than two. Include name, title, company, address and phone/fax numbers (e-mail address if applicable). Prior permission to use any individual's name as a reference is a *must* and as a courtesy inform your references that they may be contacted. The résumés that say "References available on request" risk delay or rejection; employers in a hurry want their task made simple, so they will likely favour people whose references are attached to the résumé. Furthermore, the employer may recognize one of your references and be favourably impressed. Thus, your résumé stands out from the others.

A Winning Power Résumé

Layout:

▶ One inch (2.5 cm) border margin.
▶ Only one typeface such as Times (Roman), serif or Helvetica, sans-serif. Font size 10, 11 or 12 pt.

- ▶ Short, snappy sentences.
- ▶ Two- to three-line spaces between sections.
- ▶ Consistency and caution when using the following **power tools for** emphasis and highlighting:
  boldfacing, <u>underlining,</u> *italicizing,* - dashes, • bullets.
- ▶ One page in length—two pages are the absolute limit.

Paper:

- - Size 8 1/2 by 11, designated weight between 16 and 25 lbs.
- - Textured bond, Classic Laid; or linen, Howard Linen White, printed on side with watermark face and right side up.
- - Prime choice of colour—white, off-white, ivory, or cream.

Content:

- - Keep brief but market your skills.
- - Stay focused and precise.
- - Use power words (action verbs).
- - Include relevant character traits and attributes.
- - Ensure that it's readable at a glance, has lots of white space.

Do *not* include:

- - age/birthdate
- - race
- - religion
- - marital status
- - sexual preference
- - Social Insurance Number

Now, go for the perfect power résumé. Proofread! Proofread! **Proofread!**

A Champion's Checklist:

- ▶ Is the setup easy to read and pleasing to look at?
- ▶ Are there any typo (spelling) errors or punctuation errors?
- ▶ Have the power tools (bullets, underline, bold, italics, dashes) been used consistently and with restraint?
- ▶ If more than one page, did you:

  1. Make sure your name and phone number are on page 2?
  2. Paginate your résumé ("1 of 2" at the bottom of the first page and "2 of 2" at the bottom of the second page)?
  3. Staple the pages together with one staple in the top left corner?

- ▶ Is your cover letter written on paper that matches your résumé?
- ▶ Did you sign your cover letter with your legal signature, in ink?
- ▶ Did you include your business card? (See Chapter 9.)
- ▶ Did you enclose your power résumé package in a 9 x 12 white envelope?

Action Power Words

To create succinct, dynamic writing in your résumé, use action-packed power words at the beginning of sentences. Power words highlight your qualities and show strength, impressing employers. Following are some power words to choose from:

achieved	directed	led	reversed
administered	distributed	maintained	reviewed
advanced	drafted	managed	revised
advised	edited	marketed	saved
analysed	eliminated	motivated	scheduled
assisted	enabled	negotiated	screened
authored	encouraged	operated	set
balanced	established	organized	shaped
budgeted	expanded	oversaw	skilled
built	expedited	participated	sold
calculated	focused	performed	solved
coached	forecasted	planned	streamlined
collected	founded	prepared	strengthened
compiled	gathered	presented	structured
completed	generated	processed	supervised
computed	guided	programmed	supported
conducted	handled	promoted	tabulated
contracted	headed up	proposed	taught
coordinated	identified	provided	tested
counseled	implemented	published	trained
created	improved	purchased	travelled
cut	increased	recommended	trimmed
decreased	initiated	reduced	unified
delegated	innovated	reinforced	upgraded
demonstrated	installed	reorganized	validated
designed	instituted	researched	worked
developed	introduced	resolved	wrote
devised	launched	restructured	

Character/Attitude Power Word List

Include some outstanding characteristics and work attitudes from this list to help market your skills and add punch to your pitch. Choose those most suitable for you and be able to defend them during an interview.

Able to advance	Flexible
Able to take criticism well	Friendly
Adaptable	Good communicator
Adhere to traditional values	Honest
Courteous	Mature
Creative	Motivated
Determined	Neat
Emotionally stable	Objective
Enthusiastic	Organized
Ethical	Persevere

Problem-solver   Risk-taker
Prompt   Self-motivated
Reliable   Sincere
Respectful   Tolerant

ACTIVITY 1

All About Power Résumés

Write the following sentences in your notebook, inserting the missing words or phrases.

1. A résumé's specific function is _____.
2. A résumé usually consists of _____ sections. They are _____.
3. Personal information usually not included in the résumé is _____.
4. A career objective gives _____ to your résumé if _____.
5. Six reasons an employer may reject your résumé are _____.
6. Ten champion checks for a power résumé are _____.
7. I feel my best work attitudes are _____.

Jamilah Fazal

2389 Castle Drive
Victoria, BC
V8N 5G7

E-mail: fazal@uvictoria.bc.ca   Telephone/Fax: (604) 555-1234

Seeking a position in a PC environment where computer technical skills would be utilized.

Technical Experience

MS-DOS • Windows 95 • O/S 2 • Macintosh • Amiga

- *Programming Experience:*
  Fluent in BASIC, MS Quick Basic, MS Visual Basic for Windows, MS C, Turbo C++; familiar with SAS/C - Amiga and Turbo Pascal.

- *Software Experience:*
  Proven abilities in the following application programs:
  3 Dimensional Modeling in Autodesk 3-D Studio Rev. 3, Ray Tracing Software—POV-RAY, TrueSpace, Corel Draw, Adobe Photoshop, Deluxe Paint II and more, Procomm Plus for Windows, Telix and other communication software, MS Word, MS Works and Aldus Pagemaker (DOS & MAC).

- *Hardware Experience:*
  Skilled in installing memory, expansion cards, disk drives, CD-ROM drives, printers, video and sound cards, modems.

Work Experience

Sanctuary Woods Multimedia Corporation   Victoria, BC
  Modelled in 3D using 3-D Studio, producing clear, high-tech images
  that were instrumental in selling the company product (152 Co-op hours).   May 24–June 17, 19—
  Rated outstanding in 3D Modelling, gained summer work   Summer, 19—

Infinity Systems Design Group Incorporated   Victoria, BC
  Programmied in C language on the Amiga, creating programs
  that were successfully used to increase efficiency company-wide (150 Co-op hours).
  Successfully designed completion of the Pin Project.   March 14–April 15, 19—

Education

University of Victoria   Graduating 20—
Enrolled in second year.   Bachelor of Computer Science

Personal Attributes

| creative | ambitious | conscientious |
| personable | responsible | problem-solver |

References attached.

This résumé was prepared on a Macintosh Computer/LaserWriter using Microsoft Works

References

Ms. Jaqueline Gangaram, Executive Producer
Sanctuary Woods Multimedia Corporation
2739 Fairfield Street
Victoria, BC
V9W T2V
604/555-6789

Mr. Dan Redbird, President
Infinity Systems Design Group Incorporated
1598 Shelbourne Avenue
Victoria, BC
V8B 2T3
604/555-1212

Mrs. Rosemary Kelso
Co-operative Education Specialist
Lambrick Park Secondary School
4139 Torquay Drive
Victoria, BC
V8N 3L1
604/555-3636

Michael Haisell

8 Royal Avenue
Toronto, ON
M6M 4F4
Residence (416) 325-1234

E-mail: haisell@camosun.on.ca   Facsimile (416) 325-2344

Career Profile

A desktop operator experienced in *Graphic Design* working on a *Macintosh* computer, in *Quark XPress*, *Illustrator*, *Photoshop* and *FrameMaker*, and possessing creative problem-solving and organizational ability.

Career Summary

▶ **Desktop Publishing Professional** *(Copp Clark, 1989-1996)*

Desktop achievements:

- produced book layouts in *Quark XPress*; required special attention to editorial copy mark-up and art department spec sheets
- input and formatted projects ranging from 20-page medical flyers, French program manuals, and college readers, to a 2-colour, 600-page accounting text
- completed an average of 15-20 titles per year

Technical abilities:

- monitored quality control; advised the editorial and art department of discrepancies in copy mark-up, design, or writing style
- revised certain existing design elements to accommodate editorial requirements
- revised and imported *Illustrator* files into *Quark*
- input manuscripts into *Microsoft Word*; inputting speed about 100-120 wpm

Management skills:

- designed archive record sheet for more organized storage of files for reprint
- designed a time sheet to facilitate budget calculations

▶ **Data Entry Clerk** *(Dupont Canada; Human Resources Temp Services, 1988-1989)*

- recorded data from company invoices, purchase orders, and medical equipment
- service calls onto microfilm disks
- provided filing, photocopying, telephone support

▶ **Graphic Designer/Paste-up Assistant** *(Unitrade Press, 1987-1988)*

- provided book layouts and paste-ups
- created book cover designs
- designed promotional flyers in *Ventura* on an *IBM* computer
- handled copy mark-up in preparation for typesetting

Working Style

Task Oriented Consistent completion of objectives. Organized and industrious. High concentration and extensive general knowledge contribute to quality performance. Interested in challenges.

High Learning Curve Able to assimilate facts and adapt to rapid change. Able to correlate complex information streams.

Articulate Good verbal and writing skills. Very careful listener.

Congenial Manner Courteous and friendly. Enthusiastic. Team skills.

Selected References

Mr. Clayton Wingert
Assistant Manager
McDonald's Restaurants of Canada
4000 Yonge Street
Toronto, ON
M6M 8P9
416/555-1234

Mrs. L. Holland
Piano Teacher
Royal Conservatory of Music
20 Yarrow Road
Toronto, ON
M9X 6B7
416/325-5432

Mr. M. Kwok
Co-ordinator
Ministry of Transportation and Highways
252 Bloor Street West
Toronto, ON
M7C N8M
416/555-5678

Dr. Sally Morrison
Research Analyst
Institute for Meteorological
  Observation
116 Dupont Street
Toronto, ON
MIA T2M
416/555-0987

Additional personal, professional, and academic references provided upon request.

Chapter Summary Exercises

1. Prepare a one-page and/or a two-page perfect power résumé. Be sure to follow the Champion's Checklist when writing and printing your power résumé. After it has been evaluated and corrected to a perfect, power résumé, include it as a sample of your work in your portfolio.

Reflective Journal

After you have prepared your résumé, try to evaluate it from an employer's point of view. List the positive aspects that would make you a valuable employee. List any negative aspects. Now, are there any changes you want to make to your résumé?

Internet Activity

Browse through and experiment with the Internet to find the best possible place to post your résumé. While posting a résumé is only about three percent effective in obtaining work, it *is* another "contact."

If you are an advanced Internet user, construct your own www page where you can display your business card and résumé. You can also place it to the various search engines around the world.

Chapter 8

Cover Letters

objectives

After completing this chapter you should be able to:

▶ Explain the purpose of a cover letter.
▶ List what should be included in the cover letter.
▶ Define the major parts of a cover letter.
▶ Write an impressive cover letter.

introduction

A cover letter is a letter that goes along with, and covers, a résumé sent in response to an advertisement or a work referral, or sent to indicate interest in a company. The cover letter introduces you, points to your résumé and, ultimately, gets *you* the interview. The manner in which you make yourself stand out from the crowd in a cover letter shows that you are trying hard to get the work. A good cover letter is concise and to the point. It tells how you found out about the position and how your skills match it.

The information you present, the order in which you present it, and the way you present it are all very important. Done properly, a good cover letter can pique an employer's interest so that the résumé gets closer scrutiny—and eventually, so do you! Remember, that's what it's all about—*getting the interview!*

producing the cover letter

Make an elegant statement with your cover letter by doing the following:

▶ Word process letterhead on your cover letter stationery. The letterhead should copy exactly your name and address as it appears on the résumé. Use the same typeface, the same quality paper and the same colour of paper as the power résumé.
▶ Address your letter to a specific person. If you do not know the contact person's name, phone the company and get the full name and title. Be sure to get the correct spelling and ask if the individual prefers Ms., Mrs., Miss or Mr. (Names are not always clear indicators of gender.).

Remember, although people like to hear and see their own name in print, they are turned off by incorrect spelling or being addressed by the wrong gender.

▶ Keep the letter brief (no more than one page), personal, and tailored to the job.
▶ Show a keen interest in the company, letting the reader know how you can help the organization. Use businesslike language,

not flowery and overblown, with short words and sentences. Paragraphs can often be one sentence and should never be more than three sentences.

▶ Word process or type the letter but make sure that all spelling, grammar, and punctuation are correct. To get the employer's interest *and the interview*, this must be the perfect cover letter accompanying the perfect power résumé.

▶ Always laser print each cover letter—never photocopy. The first thing the employer sees is the cover letter so make a good, first impression.

Parts of a Cover Letter

1. **Personal letterhead:**
   - Word processed, centred, begin on first line.

2. **The date:**
   - Acceptable styles are 1998 05 30; month/day/year, e.g., May 30, 1998

3. **Inside Address:**
   - Name and title of contact person.
   - Company name and full address.

4. **Salutation:**
   - Addressed specifically to the contact person.

5. **Body:**
   ▶ First paragraph
   - Clearly state the job for which you are applying.
   - State how you learned of the position.
   - Dazzle with what you know about the company.

   ▶ Second paragraph
   - Tell how and why you are best suited for the position.
   - Highlight your major skills that relate to the position.
   - Highlight how these will benefit the employer.

   ▶ Third paragraph
   - Express your *enthusiasm* to work in this company.
   - Express your *appreciation* for the person's attention.
   - Request a personal interview.
   - Include hours and telephone number to reach you.
   - Indicate a follow-up call by you in about a week.

6. **Closing:**
   - Current style is "Sincerely."

7. **Signature:**
   - Sign your legal signature in ink.
   - Key your name in full after the signature.

8. **Notation:**
   - "Enclosure."

HEADING

Jamilah Fazal
2389 Castle Drive
Victoria, BC
V8N 5G7

E-mail: fazal@uvictoria.bc.ca   Telephone/Fax: (604) 555-1234

4 RETURNS

DATE

19-- 05 30

4 RETURNS

INSIDE ADDRESS

Ms. Mandy Morrison, Controller
Wildwood Software Inc.
989 Government Street
Victoria, BC
V3T 2P9

2 RETURNS

SALUTATION

Dear Ms. Morrison

2 RETURNS

BODY

Being aware of the excellent reputation held by *Wildwood Software Inc.*, I was excited to learn that you are currently expanding your operation. My background would ideally suit one of the system programmer openings that you advertised in the *Times-Colonist*, May 29. I have enclosed my résumé in application for such a position with *Wildwood Software Inc.*

2 RETURNS

I am currently a second-year student in a Computer Science Program at the University of Victoria. With my keen interest in the computer field and with the valuable experience I gained working this summer at *Sanctuary Woods*, I feel that I could immediately apply my skills to the exciting projects you have online. I bring energy, enthusiasm, high productivity and excellent problem-solving skills to the challenges that the software programmer position will provide.

2 RETURNS

I am available for an interview at your convenience and can be reached at (604) 555-1234 after 3:00 p.m. Monday through Friday (answering machine at other times). If you have not been able to contact me by next Monday, I will call to arrange for me to meet with you and to discuss how I can contribute to *Wildwood Software Inc.*'s success.

2 RETURNS

CLOSING

Sincerely

SIGNATURE

4 RETURNS

NAME

Jamilah Fazal

2 RETURNS

NOTATIONS

Enclosure

Jamilah Fazal
2389 Castle Drive
Victoria, BC
V8N 5G7

E-mail: fazal@uvictoria.bc.ca   Telephone/Fax: (604) 555-1234

19-- 05 30

Ms. Mandy Morrison, Controller
Wildwood Software Inc.
989 Government Street
Victoria, BC
V3T 2P9

Dear Ms. Morrison

Being aware of the excellent reputation held by *Wildwood Software Inc.*, I was excited to learn that you are currently expanding your operation. My background would ideally suit one of the system programmer openings that you advertised in the *Times-Colonist*, May 29. I have enclosed my résumé in application for such a position with *Wildwood Software Inc.*

I am currently a second-year student in a Computer Science Program at the University of Victoria. With my keen interest in the computer field and with the valuable experience I gained working this summer at *Sanctuary Woods*, I feel that I could immediately apply my skills to the exciting projects you have online. I bring energy, enthusiasm, high productivity and excellent problem-solving skills to the challenges that the software programmer position will provide.

I am available for an interview at your convenience and can be reached at (604) 555-1234 after 3:00 p.m. Monday through Friday (answering machine at other times). If you have not been able to contact me by next Monday, I will call to arrange for me to meet with you and to discuss how I can contribute to *Wildwood Software Inc.*'s success.

Sincerely

Jamilah Fazal

Enclosure

letter format

Two styles of letters are in common use in business today. With the **full block** style, all lines begin at the left margin including the date and closing. Use **open punctuation** with full block style letters. This means no punctuation is used at the end of the date line, at the end of lines in the inside address or letterhead, or after the salutation, closing or notation line.

Another letter style is the **block** style used with **mixed punctuation**. With block style, all lines begin at the left margin except the date, the complimentary closing, and the writer's name. These start at the centre of the page. Mixed punctuation means that a colon follows the salutation and a comma follows the complimentary closing. Always type a notation, such as "Enclosure," with a capital letter.

August 24, 19--

Mr. Stefan Usselman
Box 24
Allan, SK S0K 0C0

Dear Mr. Usselman

Sincerely

L. Bitz

Full block style, open punctuation

August 24, 19--

Mr. Stefan Usselman
Box 24
Allan, SK S0K 0C0

Dear Mr. Usselman:

Sincerely,

L. Bitz

Block style, mixed punctuation

Figure 8.1 Full block and block style letters

the business card

Business cards are an essential selling tool, well worth their cost. Printers and stationery businesses that sell business cards have many formats to choose from, or you can customize and produce your own design using your word processor with business card template software, laser printer, and the special business card paper found in "Do-it-yourself" business card kits. The business card is one of the most powerful networking tools available, and employers will be impressed that you have one. Attach your business card with a paper clip to the upper left hand corner of the cover letter/power résumé package. The employer must remove the paperclip to get to your package. The business card, therefore, is noted and filed. You need an edge over the competition—a business card provides one.

Be sure to have extra business cards in your pocket to give to the receptionist and others you meet at the business. Who knows? Even if a position is not available at this time, your business card may be passed on to another department, or to a similar type of business that is hiring, and you might just get a call.

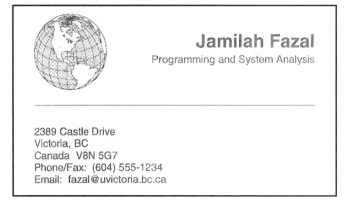

Figure 8.2 A business card

the envelope

Mail, courier, or hand deliver the power résumé and cover letter, with business card attached, in a white 9 x 12 envelope. (Do not fold, staple or mutilate!) The employer will find your power résumé package easier to read and file and it will stand out from other résumés and cover letters, especially if others have been folded.

If you are mailing the envelope, make sure you attach the correct postage. Otherwise, your package will be returned to you.

ANDREW PRINCE
5500 BEARD ROAD
NORTH BATTLEFORD SK S9A 0B8

MS. MARTA PIMI
DIRECTOR OF HUMAN RESOURCES
EVERLY COMPUTER COMPANY
23 TRENT STREET
SASKATOON SK S7N 2T9

Figure 8.3 Correctly prepared 9 x 12 envelope

ACTIVITY 1

Cover Letter Facts

Answer the following questions in your notebook, explaining each answer in detail.

1. What is the purpose of a cover letter?
2. The body of a cover letter usually has three main paragraphs. Describe in detail what should be included in each paragraph.
3. What are the recommended letter formats and what is the correct type of punctuation for each?
4. What type and size of stationery should be used for a cover letter?
5. List the parts of a letter and explain the function of each part.
6. If you don't know the name of the person who should receive your letter, what should you do?
7. What size of envelope should you use for your cover letter and power résumé?

Chapter Summary Exercises

1. Make a copy of the letter on page 97. Keep it as a model for any personal business letters you write (cover letters, request letters, compaint letters, etc.).
2. Imagine that you are applying for a job at Jetco Enterprises Inc., 2450 Delisle Road, (your community and your postal code). Prepare a cover letter to accompany the power résumé you prepared in the last chapter. Address the letter to Mr. Alfred Gallo, Human Resources Director. Include it as a sample of your work in your portfolio.
3. Investigate different styles of business cards. Prepare your own business card. If you have the technological capability, design and print your own business card. Otherwise, take a template of your business card to a printer and have it professionally done. This is a priority — don't go searching for work without it!

Reflective Journal

1. Three generic employability skills you possess that you could emphasize in your cover letter are...

Internet Activity

Search for a work opportunities bulletin board and download at least three interesting-sounding vacancies posted online by employers. If you are interested in working abroad, download three international vacancies that you fin in the Internet International Directory. Choose one national and one international opportunity and e-mail each, requesting more information. Print out your messages and the replies.

Chapter 9

Power Application Forms

objectives

After completing this chapter you should be able to:

▶ Explain the purpose of application forms.
▶ Understand the instructions on an application form.
▶ Actively participate in eliminating harassment in the workplace.
▶ Identify the types of employment discrimination that are illegal in your province or territory.

introduction

When you are seeking employment with a company, you are usually given an application form to complete. Anywhere from one to four pages long, the application form consists of questions that include everything from personal facts to your last place of employment. It is a compact way for the employer to keep your name and qualifications on file.

An application form is really a résumé in disguise so take a copy of your résumé and references with you when applying for work. Like the résumé, the application form screens out unqualified workers and sometimes well qualified workers, too! For example, your application will be eliminated if it is messy, contains spelling or grammar errors or shows evidence that directions have not been correctly followed. Sound familiar? Only if the application makes a good first impression on the employer will it lead to an interview. Power up your application form in the same way you powered up your résumé.

powering up your application

1. Read the *entire* form carefully before you start to complete it; follow directions carefully so that you don't risk disqualifying yourself.
2. Print or write *very* neatly. Use an erasable black ink pen to fill out the form or, if you take the form home, type it. A messy application will be rejected instantaneously.
3. Double-check your spelling and grammar. Make sure you know the spelling of technical terms related to the work you are seeking.
4. Request two copies of the form or photocopy it so that you can use one as a rough copy.
5. Answer every question. Write "N/A" (Not Applicable) or insert a dash (—) if a question does not apply to you.
6. Take the opportunity to provide additional positive information in the "Additional Information" line. For example, in the work experience section, list any unpaid (volunteer) experience or

special training in high school that relates to the work for which you applied.

7. Always ask for clarification if you don't understand a question.

8. Provide only positive information. Negative information will screen you out. Leave the item blank if an honest answer is negative or easily misunderstood. Be ready to explain the blank, because you will probably be asked during the interview. For example, if you were fired by your previous employer, you might be reluctant to answer the question: "Why did you leave your most recent position?" The circumstances might be more readily explained in person than by the very negative written statement: "I was fired." If the question doesn't come up during the interview and you get the work, be sure to explain the blank item. If it is discovered that you withheld pertinent information, you could be dismissed.

9. Be honest. Remember you have to sign your name to the information supplied in the application form.

10. If possible, personally give your completed application form, power résumé, and cover letter into the hands of the employer. It's an excellent way of making contact and that all-important first impression.

Study carefully the two sample application forms on pages 108 to 111, so that you will know what to expect when you apply for work. Using an erasable pen, complete the sample application form provided by your teacher. Make sure all dates, addresses, work experience, and other information are correct. When you have completed your perfect, practice application form, use it as your model when filling out other application forms.

discrimination in employment*

Notice that neither of the application forms at the end of this chapter asks for information about date of birth, sex, race, religion, or marital status. (There is a voluntary section at the end of the Government of Canada Application for Employment pertaining to employment equity). This is in line with human rights legislation that is in effect in every Canadian province and territory. Such legislation prohibits discrimination in employment, and employers usually are careful to abide by it.

There are some situations in which an employer might be justified in asking certain questions or refusing to hire a person on certain grounds, such as situations in which a person's age or a physical handicap might affect the legal or physical performance of a job.

The following table summarizes the types of employment discrimination that are illegal federally and in various provinces and territories. The items under the *Federal* heading apply to all companies and departments controlled by the federal government across Canada. As you can see, employment discrimination is illegal federally and in all of the provinces and territories on the basis of:

Employment: Prohibited grounds of discrimination*

Canadian Human Rights Commission
Tel: (613) 995-1151
TTY: (613) 996-5211

Prohibited Grounds	Federal	British Columbia	Alberta	Saskatchewan	Manitoba	Ontario	Quebec	New Brunswick	Prince Edward Island	Nova Scotia	Newfoundland	Northwest Territories	Yukon
Race or colour	•	•	•	•	•	•	•	•	•	•	•	•	•
Religion or creed	•	•	•	•	•	•	•	•	•	•	•	•	•
Age	•	• (19-65)	• (18+)	• (18-64)	•	• (18-65)	•	•	•	•	• (19-65)	•	•
Sex (incl. pregnancy or childbirth)	•	•[1]	•	•	•[2]	•	•	•	•[1]	•	•[1]	•[1]	•
Marital status	•	•	•	•	•	•	•[3]	•	•	•	•	•	•
Physical/Mental handicap or disability	•	•	•	•	•	•	•	•	•	•	•	•	•
Sexual orientation	•[4]	•		•	•	•	•	•	•[1]	•	•[1]		•
National or ethnic origin (incl. linguistic background)	•			•[5]	•	•[6]	•	•		•		•[5]	•
Family status	•	•		•	•	•	•[3]			•		•	•
Dependence on alcohol or drug	•	•[1]	•[1]	•[1]	•[1]	•[1]		•[1,7]	•[1]	•[7]			
Ancestry or place of origin		•	•	•	•	•		•				•[5]	•
Political belief		•			•		•	•	•		•		•
Based on association					•	•		•	•				•
Pardoned conviction	•	•				•	•				•		
Record of criminal conviction			•				•						•
Source of income				•[8]	•					•			
Place of residence												•	
Assignment, attachment or seizure of pay											•		
Social condition/origin							•				•		
Language							•						

Harassment on any of the prohibited grounds is considered
a form of discrimination.

* Any limitation, exclusion, denial or preference may be permitted
   if a bona fide occupational requirement can be demonstrated.
1) complaints accepted based on policy
2) includes gender-determined characteristics
3) Quebec uses the term "civil status"
4) pursuant to a 1992 Ontario Court of Appeal decision, the Canadian Human
   Rights Commission now accepts complaints on the ground of sexual orientation
5) defined as nationality
6) Ontario's Code includes only "citizenship"
7) previous dependence only
8) defined as "receipt of public assistance"

This document is also available on computer diskette and as a sound recording
to ensure it is accessible to people who are blind or vision impaired.

Threatening, intimidating or discriminating
against someone who has filed a complaint,
or hampering a complaint investigation,
is a violation of provincial human rights codes,
and at the federal level is a criminal offence.

This chart is for quick reference only.
For interpretation or further details,
call the appropriate commission.

August 1993

Source: "Prohibited Grounds of Discrimination in Employment" (ISBN 0-662-59835-0)

- ▶ Race
- ▶ Colour
- ▶ Religion
- ▶ Sex

- ▶ Age (with limitations in some provinces)
- ▶ Marital status
- ▶ Physical handicap or disability

In some cases, the type of protection varies in the different jurisdictions. For example, some jurisdictions that protect individuals on the basis of age set the upper limit at age 65, meaning that if you're younger than 65 you can't be refused employment on the basis of age. In some jurisdictions, age 18 is the lower limit of this protection, while in others the age is 19.

If you're not sure whether you're protected under federal or provincial legislation, contact your local human rights commission. Representatives can provide you with the information you need, advise you about your rights, and help you make a formal complaint if it appears that you have been treated unjustly.

*Based on information supplied by the Canadian Human Rights Commission.© Minister of Supply and Services Canada, August 1993. Cat. No. HR 21-44/1993.

harassment

What is harassment? It is any unwarranted or offensive comment or gesture. For example, someone tells a joke that is sexist or racist and is surprised when someone else is offended by it. Policies against harassment attempt to heighten the sensitivity of workers so that people can work together co-operatively and effectively, avoiding embarrassing and humiliating incidents.
Examples of other unwelcome behaviour include:

- ▶ verbal abuse or threats
- ▶ leering or other gestures
- ▶ unnecessary physical contact
- ▶ practical jokes which make people feel embarrassed or awkward
- ▶ displaying of pornographic, racist, or other offensive pictures
- ▶ unwelcome remarks, jokes or innuendo about a person's body, race, attire, marital status, sexual orientation, ethnic, or religious origins
- ▶ continued behaviour, such as condescension, that undermines an individual's self respect

How can a person play a role in fighting and eliminating harassment? First, do not take part in these demeaning behaviours. Be sensitive to your audience. If you suspect that your comments or actions may be interpreted negatively, think again before you speak or act.

If you are a victim of harassment, do not be afraid to speak up. Let others know you value yourself and that certain comments and actions are unacceptable. By taking a stand, you may prevent the same thing from happening again or to someone else. If providing feedback does not remedy the situation or if the harassment is severe, find a person you can trust who can help stop the harassing behaviour. Be prepared to provide specifics. Although this may be very embarrassing for you, do not ignore the problem. Besides eating away at your self-esteem, it can also be detrimental to your work performance.

Employment Discrimination

Study the "Prohibited Grounds of Discrimination in Employment" table on page 104, and list the grounds for discrimination that apply in your province or territory. Then look in the telephone book under the provincial government listings and write down the telephone number you would call to contact your local human rights commission. If you do not understand any of the categories listed in the table, call your local commission and ask for an explanation. Check first with your classmates to ensure that several of you do not call about the same category.

Chapter Summary Exercises

1. Answer the following questions in your notebook.

   a) What does a prospective employer hope to learn from a completed application form?
   b) What might cause an employer to discard an application form?
   c) What might a messy or incomplete form indicate about the applicant?

2. List the guidelines for successfully completing a power application form.
3. Complete a sample power application form to be included in your portfolio for easy reference in filling out work application forms.

Reflective Journal

1. What contacts or significant experiences have you had with minority groups?
2. Have you ever been discriminated against for any of the reasons listed on page 104 or for any other reason? How did this discrimination make you feel?
3. Is there evidence of racism or discrimination where you work or have worked?
4. How do you know the difference between sexual harassment and just trying to make social contact with someone you are interested in at your place of employment?
5. Are women and men treated equally with respect to pay, promotions, and access to the same types of work?

Internet Activity

1. Do research on the Internet about court cases in your province that have involved charges of discrimination in employment practices. The cases could involve discrimination in hiring,

treatment on the job, or wrongful dismissal (firing someone without a reason that is recognized by law). For example, a person can be fired for stealing from his or her employer, for being consistently late for work, or for frequently taking time off without permission. If necessary, ask the librarian for help in locating this type of material.

Then, choose one of the cases and prepare an essay that contains as many details of the case as possible, including:

a) The name of the plaintiff (the person who laid the charge) and his or her age and occupation.
b) The details of the charge that was laid by the plaintiff.
c) The name of the defendant (the person or company sued).
d) The date(s) that the case was heard in court.
e) The judge's decision of the case (whether the plaintiff won or lost, and the judge's explanation of why).
f) If the plaintiff won, provide details of what the judge directed the defendant to do and/or how much the person or company was ordered to pay the plaintiff.

Government *Application For Employment* reproduced by permission of the Public Service Commission of Canada.

Application for Employment

Demande d'emploi

PROTECTED / PROTÉGÉ

| | Mcp
Pcg | | Update
Mise à jour |

I wish to be considered for the following types of employment :
Je désire que ma candidature soit etudiée pour les genres d'emploi suivants :

Position title and reference number from advertisement.
Titre du poste et numéro de l'annonce.

OR
OU ▶

- **PLEASE TYPE OR PRINT**
- **DO NOT WRITE IN THE SHADED AREAS**
- **VEUILLEZ ÉCRIRE À LA MACHINE OU EN LETTRES MOULÉES**
- **NE PAS ÉCRIRE DANS LES CASES OMBRÉES**

Family name :
Nom :

Given name :
Prénom :

Initials :
Initiales :

Social ins. no. / N° d'ass. sociale

Mailing address (include your postal code) : Adresse postale (indiquez votre code)

Date of birth (excluding year)
Date de naissance (jour et mois seulement)

A of R / Z de R

Month   Mois   Day   Jour

Telephone number
Numéro de téléphone ▶

Home
Domicile

Area code
Indicatif régional

Other
Autre

Area code
Indicatif régional

NAIS no. / N° du SNRAC

RSO number
N° de l'ADR

Language of application
Langue de la demande
☐ English   ☐ French
Anglais   Français

Status
Statut

Reason
Raison

Letter / Lettre

Pop.

Date

Would you accept temporary employment?
Accepteriez-vous un emploi temporaire?

| 3 | Yes
Oui | 1 | No
Non |

It yes, indicate minimum acceptable period of employment. / Dans l'affirmative, indiquez la durée minimale acceptable de l'emploi.

| 4 | Less than 3 months
Moins de 3 mois | 5 | 3 to 6 months
De 3 à 6 mois | 2 | More than 6 months
Plus de 6 mois |

Would you accept part-time employment?
Accepteriez-vous un emploi à temps partiel?

| 3 | Yes
Oui | 1 | No
Non |

You are entitled to work in Canada by reason of : / Vous avez le droit de travailler au Canada du fait que vous possédez :

| 1 | Canadian citizenship
la citoyenneté canadienne | 2 | Permanent resident status
le statut de resident(e) permanent(e) | 3 | Work permit
un permis de travail |

List geographic locations where you would accept employment (cities, regions, provinces) : Indiquez les endroits où vous accepteriez un emploi (villes, régions, provinces).

Mobility/Mobilité

Text/Remarques

Which official language do you know best or speak most frequently?
Quelle langue officielle connaissez-vous le mieux ou utilisez-vous le plus souvent?

☐ English   ☐ French
Anglais   Français

In which official language(s) do you consider you have a **working ability?**
Dans quelle(s) langue(s) officielle(s) estimez-vous **pouvoir travailler?**

☐ English   ☐ French   ☐ Both
Anglais   Français   Les deux

EDUCATION
You will be required to present proof of your credentials

ÉTUDES
Vous devrez produire une preuve de vos titres et qualités

SECONDARY
SECONDAIRES

| 1 | Completed
Achevées | OR
OU | 2 | Incomplete
Inachevées |

▶ If incomplete, number of years completed
Si inachevées, nombre d'années terminées

Province or country   Province ou pays

ACADEMIC QUALIFICATIONS OBTAINED   TITRES SCOLAIRES

Level : Niveau	Year obtained Année d'obtention	Field of study Domaine d'études	Name of educational institution Nom de l'établissement

Professional or other qualifications / education / languages / skills / Titres professionnels ou autres qualités / études / langues / compétences

WORK EXPERIENCE

You need not complete this section if you are attaching a résumé that contains the information requested

EXPÉRIENCE DE TRAVAIL

Vous n'avez pas à remplir cette partie si vous annexez à votre demande un curriculum vitae contenant les renseignements suivants

Name of present or most recent employer / Nom de l'employeur actuel (ou du plus récent)	Period Période	From Du	M	Y/A	To Au	M	Y/A
	City / Ville			Prov. or country / Prov. ou pays			

Job title and description of duties / Titre du poste et description des fonctions

Name of previous employer / Nom de l'employeur précédent	Period Période	From Du	M	Y/A	To Au	M	Y/A
	City / Ville			Prov. or country / Prov. ou pays			

Job title and description of duties / Titre du poste et description des fonctions

EMPLOYMENT EQUITY (UNDERREPRESENTED GROUPS)

ÉQUITÉ EN MATIÈRE D'EMPLOI (GROUPES SOUS-REPRÉSENTÉS)

Your voluntary response to the four questions below will assist us in ensuring that the Public Service is fully representative of the public it serves and may also identify you as eligible for programs and services designed to improve representation of groups targeted by Employment Equity Programs in the Public Service of Canada.

To assist you in completing the questions below, please refer to the Employment Equity information on the next page.

Les réponses que vous fournirez volontairement aux quatre questions suivantes nous aideront à nous assurer que la fonction publique du Canada est entièrement représentative du public qu'elle sert. De plus, vous serez peut-être désigné(e) comme personne admissible aux programmes et aux services destinés à améliorer la représentation des groupes visés par les programmes d'équité en matière d'emploi dans la fonction publique du Canada.

Avant de remplir cette section, veuillez consulter les renseignements concernant les programmes d'équité en matière d'emploi sur la page suivante.

1. Are you / Êtes-vous

☐ a man? un homme? ☐ a woman? une femme?

2. If you are an aboriginal person of Canada, please specify the group to which you belong
Si vous êtes un(e) autochtone du Canada, veuillez préciser à quel groupe vous appartenez
▶

3. If by colour or race you are a visible minority, please specify the group that best describes your origin.
Si vous êtes membre d'une minorité visible en raison de votre couleur ou de votre race, veuillez préciser le groupe décrivant le mieux votre origine.
▶

4. If you are disabled, please describe your disability(ies) below.
Si vous êtes une personne handicapée, veuillez préciser ci-dessous votre ou vos handicap(s)
▶

DECLARATION / ATTESTATION

All the information I have given in this application is true and complete.

Tous les renseignements fournis dans la présente demande sont exacts et complets.

Signature   Date

Thank you for your interest in the Public Service of Canada and the time you have taken to complete this application

Nous apprécions l'intérêt que vous manifestez à l'égard de la fonction publique du Canada et vous remercions d'avoir pris le temps de remplir cette demande

Profiles / Profils

Skills / Compétences

Status Statut	Reason Raison	RSO / ADR	Purge flag Ind. d'épuration	LETTER / LETTRE Code	Signature RSO Sign. de l'ADR	Destination base office Bureau d'attache destinataire	Purge date Date d'épuration	Y/A	M	D/J	Base office Bureau d'attache
			☐1 Yes Oui								

Population Ind. / Ind. de population

			ELOST / ESANE		
☐1 NAIS SNRAC	☐U Univ. recruit. - Outside Recrut. univ. - Hors campagne	☐D College recruit. - Outside Recrut. collégial - Hors campagne	☐ Other Autre	Y/A M D/J	–

RSO initials/Initiales de l'ADR	Date	Entered by/Introduction par	Date

ADDISON-WESLEY PUBLISHERS LIMITED
26 PRINCE ANDREW PLACE, DON MILLS, ONTARIO M3C 2T8
PHONE: (416) 447-5101   FAX.: (416) 443-0948

POSITION APPLIED FOR	SALARY EXPECTED
	DATE AVAILABLE

APPLICATION FOR EMPLOYMENT

SURNAME	FIRST	MIDDLE	PHONE	POSTAL CODE
ADDRESS	STREET		TOWN	PROVINCE

ARE YOU LEGALLY ELIGIBLE TO WORK IN CANADA?   YES ☐   NO ☐

EDUCATION RECORD	MAJOR	DATES ATTENDED	CERTIFICATE / DEGREE LEVEL COMPLETED
SECONDARY			YES ☐ NO ☐ LEVEL COMPLETED:
BUSINESS, TRADE OR TECHNICAL SCHOOL			YES ☐ NO ☐ LEVEL COMPLETED:
COMMUNITY COLLEGE			YES ☐ NO ☐ LEVEL COMPLETED:
UNIVERSITY			YES ☐ NO ☐ LEVEL COMPLETED:
OTHER			YES ☐ NO ☐ LEVEL COMPLETED:

ADDITIONAL COURSES, WORKSHOPS, TRAINING: (Please note date of training)

DESCRIBE ANY OF YOUR SKILLS, EXPERIENCE, OR TRAINING THAT IS RELATED TO THE POSITION BEING APPLIED FOR.

LANGUAGE

	SPOKEN	WRITTEN
ENGLISH	☐	☐
FRENCH	☐	☐
OTHER	☐	☐

EMPLOYMENT RECORD   (OR SEE ATTACHED RESUME ☐)

COMPANY NAME (MOST RECENT)	TYPE OF BUSINESS	FROM:	TO:
ADDRESS		REASON FOR LEAVING	
POSITION AND RESPONSIBILITIES			

COMPANY NAME	TYPE OF BUSINESS	FROM:	TO:
ADDRESS		REASON FOR LEAVING	
POSITION AND RESPONSIBILITIES			

COMPANY NAME	TYPE OF BUSINESS	FROM:	TO:
ADDRESS		REASON FOR LEAVING	
POSITION AND RESPONSIBILITIES			

HAVE YOU EVER BEEN EMPLOYED BY ADDISON-WESLEY BEFORE?   YES ☐   NO ☐

HOW DID YOU LEARN ABOUT THIS POSITION?

OUTSIDE HOBBIES AND INTERESTS, SERVICE CLUBS OR PROFESSIONAL ASSOCIATIONS:
DO NOT LIST CLUBS OR ORGANIZATIONS OF A RELIGIOUS, RACIAL, POLITICAL OR NATIONAL CHARACTER.

REFERENCES: LIST TWO PERSONS TO WHOM WE MAY REFER WHO ARE NOT RELATIVES — PREVIOUS MANAGERS OR CO-WORKERS ARE PREFERRED

NAME	OCCUPATION	WK PHONE
ADDRESS		

NAME	OCCUPATION	WK PHONE
ADDRESS		

MAY WE CONTACT YOUR REFERENCES?   YES ☐   NO ☐

I HEREBY DECLARE THAT THE FOREGOING INFORMATION AND ANY ATTACHED INFORMATION IS TRUE AND COMPLETE TO MY KNOWLEDGE.
I UNDERSTAND THAT A FALSE WRITTEN OR VERBAL STATEMENT MAY DISQUALIFY ME FROM EMPLOYMENT, OR CAUSE MY DISMISSAL,
I FURTHER UNDERSTAND THAT IF THIS POSITION REQUIRES A VALID DRIVER'S LICENSE, PROOF WILL BE REQUIRED AFTER HIRE.

SIGNATURE: _____   DATE: _____

INTERVIEWER'S NOTES

INTERVIEWER'S COMMENTS

THIS SECTION TO BE COMPLETED ONLY IF APPLICANT HAS BEEN HIRED

IN CASE OF EMERGENCY NOTIFY: NAME	RELATIONSHIP TO YOU:
ADDRESS	WK PHONE RES PHONE
FAMILY DOCTOR	PHONE

Chapter 10

Work Interviews

objectives

After completing this chapter you should be able to:

▶ Prepare for a successful interview.
▶ Identify the types of questions an interviewer might ask.
▶ Understand what it means to "impress for success."
▶ List what to do and what not to do in an interview.
▶ Answer an interviewer's questions effectively.

introduction

So you've got the interview! Congratulations! Now you have just three seconds or less to pass the "first impression" test with the interviewer. Facts don't count, perceptions do—what does the person think of you? How you look? How you act? What you say and how you say it? If you blow the interview you won't get the work.

What is the main function of the interview? Your power résumé and impressive cover letter passed the five-second test and then convinced the employer that you had the skills and experience for the work or you would not have been called in for the interview. What does the employer hope to learn on seeing you? Mainly, to find out if you are *personable*—will your personality fit into that particular office, and will those who work there find you easy to get along with? Two powerful facial expressions, the smile and the eyebrow lift, can be used to show that you are pleasant and responsive. The smile is important in all cultures; use it throughout the interview. Use an eyebrow lift when you say hello and smile or to show interest in what was said. However, do not grin continuously or lift your eyebrows so often you appear to have a nervous twitch. Remember, the interview *eliminates* people—it does not *choose* people.

before the interview

The "Hustle" Component

▶ When setting up your interview, try to be the first or last person interviewed on any given day. Interviewers tend to remember the first and the last interviewee best.

▶ Go to the place of business a few days ahead of time, and talk to the receptionist. Find out about the work, the company and even the person who is interviewing you if you can. Tell the receptionist that you are scheduled for an interview in a few days and would like some information on the company and the work. Your keen interest in the company might be mentioned to the "right" person.

- ▶ Find out the receptionist's name. Addressing him or her by name as you leave and when you return for your interview will make a positive impression.

Better Never Than Late

- ▶ *Never* be late for the interview. If you are going to be late, phone and reschedule an appointment for another day, never for the same day. No matter how good your reason, being late is unforgiveable in the world of business.

Your pre-interview visit to the company's location will have shown you how long the journey is. On the day of the interview, allow plenty of extra time for the journey. If there is a delay, you will still be on time. If you are early, don't go directly to the company. Find a nearby coffee shop where you can sit and collect your thoughts, preparing to arrive at the company within ten minutes of your interview time.

What to take

- ▶ Take with you another copy of your résumé and a list of references in an envelope or portfolio (not a briefcase). After you are seated, if the interviewer has not already asked, offer your credentials to the interviewer.

You have a portfolio of employability skills (Chapter 4) that you have acquired through school activities, paid work, volunteer work, and family and social life. A portfolio also is a collection that showcases your natural abilities and contains samples demonstrating your acquired skills. Each unit in this book provides portfolio suggestions. Again, a portfolio might be the "edge" you need.

impress for success

First Impressions

As unfair as it may sound, all else being equal, 90 percent of men and women get work based on how they appear at the interview. Being successful means presenting yourself in dress and general demeanour as a resource that this company will want.

Remember the interviewer decides in three seconds or less upon seeing you as to whether you are a likely candidate for the work. The importance of how you are perceived by the interviewer in those first three seconds cannot be overstated. You need to capitalize on all your strengths.

How can you do it? First, when you do your pre-interview check of your prospective place of employment, take careful note of other employees. What does the way they dress suggest to you about the company? Does it seem formal or informal? Do the men wear suits, sports jackets (with or without a tie), sweaters and slacks or jeans? Do any wear their hair long? Do any wear earrings? Do the women wear suits, dresses, casual slacks and tops? Do any wear more than one earring or ear cuffs in one ear?

Second, think about the type of work for which you are applying. If you are looking for work as an auto mechanic or a plumber's assistant, you'll probably dress differently from the individual who hopes to be in sales or in a law office. No matter what kind of work you are applying for, your first concern is to be clean, neat, and very presentable. A few days prior to the interview, have your hair trimmed, if necessary, so that it looks neat.

The evening before your interview, select the outfit you will wear and make sure it is clean and pressed. This applies even if the work you will do is in a warehouse where appropriate dress is jeans and a T-shirt. If the work you want is in an office, again, take your cue from the employees you observed earlier and dress like them or a little more formally. Whatever you choose to wear, make sure you feel comfortable in it, both sitting and standing, and that you feel really good wearing it. As with your résumé, conservative styles and colours are the order of the day. Make sure your shoes are polished and not down-at-heel or scuffed. Have them repaired, if necessary. On the day of the interview, pay careful attention to personal hygiene. Be conservative in your use of make-up, perfume, or after-shave. When selecting your jewellery, choose subtle rather than showy items. Remember, *you're* the important commodity in this situation, so keep the attention on yourself and the skills you have to offer, not on your clothes or jewellery.

during the interview

▶ Wait for the offer of a handshake. Be sure your hand is dry by surreptitiously wiping your palm on your clothes as you lift if for the handshake. Shake firmly and briefly. Your handshake should be at least as firm as the other person's—but don't make it a wrestling match!

▶ Wait for the interviewer to offer you a seat and wait until the interviewer is seated before you sit. Do not fidget! You want to appear calm.

▶ Maintain eye contact. By so doing, you are signaling that you are listening—completely. The interviewer will be assessing you to see that you are listening hard to everything that is said.

▶ Use names. If you are given only the first and last name of the interviewer, use Ms. or Mr., unless a female interviewer expresses her preference for "Miss" or "Mrs."

▶ Speak clearly, neither too loudly nor too softly. Stay positive and show enthusiasm.

▶ Especially during the interview never criticize or complain about *anyone* or *anything*. You want to be seen as a person of high integrity with a positive attitude. Do not be afraid of silence. Use no offensive or vulgar language, and do not contradict the interviewer. You are there to provide and obtain information, and your task will be difficult if you alienate the interviewer by getting into an argument.

▶ Do not chew gum or smoke cigarettes, even if one is offered.

▶ Ask and answer all questions according to the other person's point of view.

Try to answer the questions accurately, taking care not to answer in monosyllables, but don't say any more than is necessary. It's easy, especially when you are nervous, to get off the track or even to completely lose track of the point you are making.

Figure 10. How to ace an interview.

	You and Your Skills	Interest in the Work	Commitment to the Work	Ability to Fulfil Work Requirements	Previous Employment
Employer will ask:	1. What do you consider your strengths? 2. Why should we hire you? 3. What are your most important abilities?	1. Why did you apply for this position? 2. What do you know about our company? 3. Why do you want to work for us?	1. Why have you had so many career changes? 2. Are you thinking about going back to school? 3. What are your future plans?	1. Are you willing to relocate? retrain? 2. Do you prefer to work by yourself? 3. Can you work under pressure?	1. Why did you leave your last place of employment? 2. How did you feel about your previous employer? 3. How much were you absent in your last position?
Employer's purpose in asking:	To find out how well your qualifications match the work and what makes you different from other applicants.	To find out if you understand his or her organization and to see how well you have prepared for the interview.	To find out if you're prepared to stay.	To find out how well you satisfy work requirements, he or she may describe a situation and ask how you would react.	To find out if you've had employment problems that would eliminate you for work in his or her company.
How you should prepare:	Analyze your qualifications and match them to the work.	Research before your interview, i.e., talk to people who work at the company, read about the industry.	Think through your career plans and write down answers that will show that this is not just a stopping point in your long-range goals.	Make sure you know what's important to you in terms of your lifestyle and working style.	Write down answers that emphasize the positive—for example, your desire to learn new skills or assume more responsibility.
Your answers:	Explain how your experience and accomplishments relate to the work. Describe situations in which you've demonstrated these skills. If you're over-qualified, stress your adaptability and flexibility.	State what you've found out about the company and its operations. Explain why you're interested in the position and how your skills would meet the company's needs.	Talk about the challenge of the work and its relation to your career. If you've held a number of positions, give a reasonable explanation and let the interviewer know how your experience will help you in this position.	If an interviewer wants your reaction to a situation, demonstrate your skills and knowledge to the best of your ability. If you can't fulfil the requirements, say so.	Explain that you're interested in having your career grow and develop and that you're seeking new opportunities. Avoid getting emotional, and don't make negative comments about your last position or employer.
Sample Q and A:	Q. What are your weaknesses? A. My public speaking skills need work, but I've volunteered to chair a fund-raising committee, and I'm building these skills.	Q. What is it about our products that interests you? A. Your company is in the forefront of development on (product). I'm interested in your cutting-edge technologies.	Q. What are your long-range goals? A. I'm interested in developing my communication skills to the point that I could deal directly with the public.	Q. What salary are you looking for? A. A salary that matches my experience and that of the nature and scope of the work.	Q. What did you dislike about your last position? A. I didn't get the chance to work in (product/service), which I hope to do at your company.

Adapted from *Prospects 1994*, Human Resources Development Canada, Y-101-10-94E

► People like to talk about themselves, so get the interviewer talking. When you are asked, "Do you have any questions?" one that might be useful to ask is "How did you get started in this business?" Other leading questions are "Do you like working here?" and "Are there some pointers you can give me?" As you can see, the answers to such questions will be informative and helpful to you in your own endeavours.

► Practise making a graceful exit from the interview, smiling and thanking the interviewer for his or her time. Say something positive that reflects your experience and interest in the work. Shake hands only if the interviewer offers his or her hand first. Do not stand and tell another story. Just smile, say goodbye, and go!

ACTIVITY 1

Role-Playing

Your teacher will assign partners to role-play an interviewer/interviewee situation. The interviewer will ask the interviewee four questions chosen from this chapter, making notes of the answers received. The partners will then switch roles and repeat the process. In each case, the person playing the interviewer will give her or his notes to the other person. Reviewing these notes should help you to see how good an impression you might have made in an actual interview. Videotape the interview with your partner and analyse it together, noting what went well and what needs improvement.

A Champion's Checklist:

► Rehearse! Work toward having the ready answers you will need and delivering them in a positive, self-assured manner.

► You are dressed for success and impeccably groomed.

► Use body language effectively—sit up and lean into the interview, look alert, and make eye contact.

► Be honest. Acknowledge it when you do not know something.

► Make a good impression on *everyone*. Say a friendly word to the receptionist as you leave. An interviewer often asks the receptionist for his or her impression after the applicant has left.

► Everyone likes to be around a winner, so act like one.

► Show enthusiasm—enthusiasm for the line of work, happiness to be there. Show some brightness and personality. Keep a positive attitude.

► Don't be afraid to ask for the job. "I really would like to work here. If you offer me the job, I know I will prove an asset to your company."

► Carry your day planner, extra copies of your résumé, your portfolio, and extra business cards with you to the interview.

► Keep a record of the interview. Make a few notes on how it went, what went well in your answers and what needs more

> work. Also note if a follow-up call by you or by the employer is
> to be made.
>
> And finally—did you remember to write a thank-you note?

Thank-You Letter

Immediately after the interview, write a thank-you letter. This is a courtesy that is always appreciated in the business world. It also reminds the interviewer of you and singles you out from the many others interviewed that day. In addition to thanking the person for the privilege of the interview, you could express your increased interest in the work, and mention again the skills and personal characteristics that you feel qualify you for the position. The sample thank-you letter below can be used as a guide. Use your own letterhead stationery as you did in the cover letter. The thank-you letter could just tip the scales in your favour, so do not procrastinate. (P.S. Don't forget to include your business card with the letter—another subtle reminder.)

Figure 10. Sample Thank-You Letter

(Current Date)

Ms. Mandy Morrison, Controller
Wildwood Software Inc.
989 Government Street
Victoria, BC V3T 2P9

Dear Ms. Morrison

Thank you for the time you spent with me today and the information on the exciting new expansion and direction of your company. As you noted, my previous experience, both in training and work experience, directly relates to the position advertised.

I am even more interested in working at *Wildwood Software Inc.* than ever and look forward to speaking to you again soon.

Sincerely

Jamilah Fazal

Follow-up in a Week

If you have not heard from the interviewer within the time period that was probably indicated at the end of your interview, a follow-up telephone call is in order. Remind the interviewer of who you are and what position you applied for, and ask whether a decision has been made yet. If the position has been filled, remain courteous and gracious and indicate your interest in working for the company should another position become available. Do not burn your bridges by becoming angry or hurt and lashing out at the person because you did not get the work. In fact, to better prepare for the next interview, ask in a non-confrontational way why you did not get the work. For example, you might ask: "Are there other skills you were looking for that I need to develop?" or "How might I have presented myself so that you would have chosen me?"

If you are declining a job offer or are no longer available, again thank the interviewer for considering your application and explain the circumstances. Such courtesy makes an excellent impression on prospective employers.

you didn't get the work?

If you didn't get the work you applied for, don't give up. Finding work takes time. Don't give in to feelings of depression or dejection. Go over your résumé, cover letter, skills portfolio, and interview techniques looking for ways to improve your presentation. Keep a positive outlook. Go back to your network for more work leads. There are always other options. A way to connect to the workplace and gain experience is volunteering or job shadowing. Consider creating your own work by becoming an entrepreneur (See pages 60-61, "Minding Your Own Business."). *Remember*, a person who knows how to conduct a work search will eventually be successful.

Chapter Summary Exercises

1. What is the main purpose of an interview?
2. List four strategies to follow before the interview.
3. You're being interviewed for work in your chosen field. The interviewer asks you what your weaknesses are. How would you reply?
4. Explain the strategy, "Better never than late."
5. If you are fully qualified for the work, why are first impressions so important?
6. You have three seconds to make a good impression in the interview. How do you do this successfully?
7. Eleven key points to remember during an interview were mentioned. What are they?
8. So you didn't get the work. What do you do now?
9. Describe behaviour that contributes to a successful interview.
10. Demonstrate appropriate interviewing techniques (portfolio presentation, questioning, dress, and etiquette).

Reflective Journal

1. Have you ever been to an interview? If so, how did you feel before and after the interview. Explain why you felt the way you did.
2. How can you best prepare for a work interview?
3. Can too much emphasis be placed on first impressions and appearance in the workplace? If so, what do you think can be done about it?

Internet Activity

Individually or in small groups access the Internet for more information on interviewing techniques. "Map" your journey on the Internet for others in your class to follow. What information on interviewing do's and don'ts seem to be stressed over and over again both in your text and on the information highway?

UNIT 3

Succeeding in the Workplace

introduction
The change from student to employee is a dramatic one; the rules are very different. For example, many of your new employer's expectations will not be stated and you will be expected to find out what these are. This unit will discuss how to handle your first day at work and employer expectations relating to attendance and efficiency at your workplace.

Chapter 11

Adjusting to the Workplace

objectives	After completing this chapter you should be able to:

> ▶ Accept that nervousness in a new work situation is normal.
> ▶ Define the term *probation period*.
> ▶ Plan ahead to lessen stress on your first day at work.
> ▶ List ten important "do's" and "don'ts" for a successful first day in a new workplace.
> ▶ Explain the importance of attendance and punctuality at work.
> ▶ Define *flextime* and *telecommuting*.
> ▶ List the guidelines for calling in to report that you will be absent from work.

introduction

The first day in a new workplace can be one of the most tension-filled days of a person's life. Many aspects of an employment situation are different from what you have experienced at school. The environment will be less casual, the "grading" will be different, and you will be completely responsible for the work you do.

The adjustment period can be difficult if you go about it the wrong way. Two important keys to success are: *getting along with your fellow workers* and *relating to your supervisor*. If you exercise tact, co-operation, and patience, you will enhance your chances of starting off on the right foot.

Starting new work requires you to become used to new situations, both physical and psychological. You will be meeting new people and might find yourself in situations where problems already exist. Be assured, though, that most people have at one time or another been just as nervous in a new work situation.

the probation period

Usually new employees are hired on a trial basis for a certain length of time, which is called a *probation period*. This period could last from a week to six months, as determined by the employer. It is a critical time for the new employee: your work habits are analysed, your conduct is graded, your ability to perform the work functions is rated, and your reaction under pressure is observed.

The probation period gives you the chance to show your employer the type of employee you can be. During this time, you must prove to your supervisor that you are capable of doing your job well and that you possess the other necessary characteristics of a good employee. This is also a time when you should carefully assess the company to ensure that it is what you anticipated and that any promises made to you on hiring are carried out.

appearance counts

You were hired and are scheduled to start Monday morning. What should you wear? Remember, you get only one chance to make a good first impression on your new supervisor and co-workers.

At some workplaces you will wear a uniform, so clothing will not be a problem. Other workplaces require protective clothing over street clothes, so the problem is lessened. For most work, however, you will have to make decisions every day about what to wear.

Basically, the type of clothing you wear will be determined by the type of work that you do. Dressing inappropriately not only could make you look ridiculous and feel uncomfortable, but also could be a safety hazard. It also might be an indication of a lack of understanding of your role or a lack of commitment to success in your work.

It might help to look at your co-workers' clothing. Sometimes a company has an image, either formal or informal, that it wants to project, which might be quite different from that of other similar companies. Usually your co-workers' clothing will reflect that desired image.

Good grooming is equally as important as appropriate clothing in making a good impression. Greasy hair, dirty fingernails, or bad breath can cancel out the good impression made by a smart suit, dress, or uniform.

ACTIVITY 1

Clothing and Grooming

1. In the occupation you would like to have, what clothing would be suitable? Name the occupation first, then describe the type of clothing required.
2. List ten examples of good grooming (e.g., clean, trimmed fingernails).

Planning Ahead

You know what date you are starting work and what clothes you will wear. What else should a new employee consider?

work schedule

What time are you supposed to report for work? When do you finish? When are the coffee and meal breaks? What is the company policy concerning overtime (hours worked in addition to the usual schedule)? Will you be doing shift work? The majority of these questions can be answered within the first few days by someone in the personnel or human resource department or by your supervisor.

trans- portation

Determine ahead of time how you will get to work. If you plan to take public transportation, call the transportation company to confirm the schedule and the pick-up and drop-off locations. If you are riding in someone else's car, consider the cost and inconvenience to that person. If you are driving your own car, make sure it is in good operating order and reliable. If you can walk to work, figure out ahead of time exactly how long the walk will take. Whatever mode of transportation you use, plan to arrive a little early on your first day, to allow for any possible problems.

food services

If your work hours include a meal break, you will need to find out what food service facilities are available. Some typical situations include:

- ▶ A cafeteria. Is it open during your shift?
- ▶ A food truck, which goes from company to company selling hot and cold snacks.
- ▶ Vending machines. Often a microwave oven is available for heating the food.
- ▶ A kitchen where you can store food in a refrigerator and perhaps heat it up on a stove or in a microwave.
- ▶ A kettle (useful for hot soup and coffee, etc.).
- ▶ A nearby restaurant.

personnel forms

When you first begin work you'll probably be required to complete a number of official forms. These are necessary to register you as an employee, to determine your tax situation, and to enrol you in company insurance and pension plans. To help you complete these forms, bring to work the personal information form you prepared in Chapter 6. Do not hesitate to ask the human resource officer for help in completing forms—they can be complicated.

first-day do's and don'ts

The boxed information below and on the next page offers a few do's and don'ts to help you have a successful first day at a new workplace. Actually, these are good suggestions for every day on the job.

DO:

1. Get a good night's rest.
2. Set your alarm. Allow yourself plenty of time to get ready.
3. Eat breakfast; it gives you much-needed energy.
4. Arrive a little ahead of time and be ready to work.
5. Follow the dress code of the workplace.
6. Follow the health and safety regulations of the workplace.
7. Be a team player—be cooperative, cheerful, and friendly with your co-workers.
8. Show your willingness to learn and apply new skills.
9. Accept criticism graciously.
10. Demonstrate resourcefulness, initiative, maturity and good judgment at all times.

DON'T:

1. Ask too many questions (but do ask the basic questions about location of supplies and whatever you need in order to do your work).
2. Bother people unnecessarily.
3. Be aggressive.
4. Be a show-off.
5. Speak critically about anyone or anything.
6. Try to become too familiar with co-workers or your supervisor.
7. Bring personal problems to work.
8. Use the telephone for personal calls.
9. Smoke, unless special areas are provided. If so, smoke only during your official breaks.
10. Show any strong emotions. Always remain calm and polite, no matter what the problem is.

punctuality

In the work world, *you* will have the main responsibility for being *where* you should be, and *when*. In school you had help: the bell rang to start classes, end classes, start lunch, end lunch, and so on. At work you're expected to keep track of time yourself. There are no bells to remind you.

You must be present for your complete work schedule. To an hourly paid worker, coming in three minutes late means the loss of a quarter-of-an-hour's wages! Being late could not only earn you your supervisor's disapproval, but also could be possible grounds for dismissal.

To be successful at work, you'll need to develop a mature and self-reliant attitude concerning punctuality. Regardless of the reason, you are responsible for the consequences of being late. Punctuality applies not only to starting and finishing times, but also to coffee and meal breaks.

If you don't have a watch, obtain one. You might not always be near a clock when it's important for you to know the time. Don't always be dependent on someone else to tell you the time, because you'll be bothering that person and interfering with her or his work.

If your work schedule is irregular, you'll have to be particularly careful. Write your schedule down and keep it where you'll see it often.

And remember, your work involves a commitment. If your schedule interferes with your social life, that's unfortunate but can't be helped. Your employer depends on you to be at work as scheduled. If you don't honour that schedule, you'll be out of work and will have difficulty obtaining it in future. Tardiness and excessive absenteeism are major offences in the work world.

flextime

Employees of many organizations today are able to take advantage of flextime. For management, flexible work arrangements have become a critical management tool for the '90s. Because the employee benefits, absenteeism is lowered and productivity improved, resulting in a measurable rise in morale within the company. Flextime is a work schedule that allows employees to choose their work-starting and work-ending times, although they are usually required to be at work during certain specified hours, called *core time*. For example, core time might be 10 a.m. to 3 p.m. Other than these hours, employees would be able to choose their own schedules, providing that the number of hours worked added up to the required total. So, if an eight-hour shift was required, some employees might choose to work from 7 a.m. to 3 p.m., while others might work from 9 a.m. to 5 p.m. Another type of flexible work arrangement may mean every second Monday is a day off, in lieu of starting work every day at 7 a.m. and working an hour or so longer than most.

Just remember: whether the company you work for uses flextime or regular-time schedules, you must be responsible for your timetable and ensure that you work the required minimum number of hours.

telecommuting (the home office)

Another flexible working arrangement that benefits both employer and employee is telecommuting. **Telecommuting** is an umbrella term covering a wide range of alternatives to the traditional office routine. In some cases, it refers to working from home when a special project demands uninterrupted time; in others, it is an arrangement whereby an employee works out of the office for two or three days a week. Some companies have eliminated office space completely and have their staff work entirely from remote locations. These remote locations might be the employees' homes or neighbourhood telework centres near the employees' homes. These fully equipped telework centres are a viable option for those who do not have sufficient office space or equipment in their homes or who do not like the isolation or distractions of working at home.

Telecommuting is not a passing fad. In 1994, 43.2 million North Americans were telecommuting, and projections are that the home-worker population will increase by approximately 15 percent a year. It is predicted that by the year 2000, 40 percent of Canadians will work out of their home.

Telecommuting has come into prominence because of the large number of personal computers in both workplaces and homes. The improvement in communications software, the development of inexpensive modems and fax machines and boards, and the increased sophistication of telecommunications services have provided the additional momentum.

Again, as with "traditional" commuting, employees who telecommute must adhere to the company's required number of working hours per week, and should be prepared to work during scheduled hours, making themselves available for business calls and other requirements of the business day.

ACTIVITY 2

Thoughts About Punctuality

1. List three thoughts that an employer might have about a worker who is always on time.
2. List three thoughts that an employer might have about a worker who is always late.
3. What are some tricks that you could use to help you to be punctual?
4. If you were telecommuting, would you have any difficulty in starting work "on time"? How could you help yourself to act professionally?

if you can't go to work

Always be at work unless you have a good reason not to be. If you're not there, no one else might be available, or able, to do your work, and the company's business activities might suffer. Then, too, when you do return to work, you'll have to work twice as hard to catch up. Also, if other employees have to do your work as well as their own too often, they'll probably become resentful. If you *must* miss work, be sure that you always follow the guidelines illustrated in the following scenarios.

1. You have terrible flu symptoms. You feel that you should stay home to avoid spreading germs and also because, in your present condition, you'd be inefficient. Yes, you have a good reason to stay home.
2. You have a good reason to stay home from work, so are you just going to turn over in bed, thinking, "I'll call the boss later"? No, it is your responsibility to let your employer know as soon as possible that you are unable to work. This gives your employer time to make arrangements to ensure that your absence won't interfere with business or put too much of a load on your co-workers.
3. It's 8:30 a.m. and your place of business is open. You call in and speak to the receptionist, asking that a message regarding your absence be passed on to your supervisor. *Now* you can go back to bed, right? Wrong! Never leave such a message with someone who might be too busy to pass the message on right away, or who might not appreciate what your absence will mean to your supervisor and co-workers. If you can't reach your supervisor when you call in, leave a message with the most responsible person you can, asking that your supervisor call you for a fuller explanation when convenient.
4. If you think that "I'm not coming in today" is all you need to say when you call in, you're wrong. You must explain clearly and fully why you're unable to go to work. If you can, identify when you will be able to return to work.
5. If your schedule for that day involves an urgent task, inform your supervisor and offer to provide over the telephone any help you can to the person who will have to do the task. Your supervisor will undoubtedly appreciate such a responsible attitude.

Being off work for special occasions (out-of-town weddings, family reunions, etc.) is something that should be arranged well in advance, as soon as you know about the event. Your employer will then be able to set up a work schedule that takes your absence into account. And, of course, you shouldn't expect time off very often for such events.

ACTIVITY 3

Calling In

The following are telephone conversations between employers' receptionists and employees who are going to be absent from work. In each case, write a possible continuation of the conversation in your notebook. Include what you think the person's supervisor's reaction will be and explain how the caller did or didn't follow the guidelines for calling in to report an absence. If you can think of a compromise that might help both the employer and the employee in any of the situations, include that too.

1. **Receptionist:** Good morning. Mackis and Company.
   Employee: Hi, Andrew. It's Ryan. I won't be in for my four o'clock shift today. I've got some type of stomach flu and I've been awake almost all night. I feel awful.
   Receptionist: Oh, that's too bad. I'm sorry to hear it.
   Employee: Well, I need to let my supervisor know. May I speak to Ms. Singh, please?
   Receptionist: Ms. Singh isn't here at the moment, but she should be back soon. Would you like me to pass on your message that you're sick and won't be in?

2. **Receptionist:** Season's greetings. Rinaldo Enterprises
   Employee: Hi, Lydia. It's Nikki.
   Receptionist: Oh, hi, Nikki. How are you?
   Employee: Not great! Just between you and me, I was out partying last night and I just can't handle coming in to work.
   Receptionist: Again!
   Employee: Oh, come on! I don't take that much time off! That's why I figured I was entitled to take today.
   Receptionist: You mean you're not coming in *at all*? I think your department is really counting on you today—Mr. Eastman's not going to be too happy. I'll transfer your call to his office.

3. **Receptionist:** Good morning. Bibeau Industries.
   Employee: Oh, Gord, it's Alina. I totally forgot until this morning that I have a dental appointment at eleven, so there's no point coming in to work until after.
   Receptionist: Uh-oh! Mrs. Gamit has already said that she needs you as soon as you come in. This'll be really inconvenient for her.
   Employee: Oh, that's too bad. Well, tell her I called.

4. Receptionist: Gillis and Company, your communications specialists.

   Employee: Hi, Ramesh. Guess what! I've just had a call from my favourite cousin. She's going to be in town for four hours and wants to spend the time with me. I'm heading out to meet her now, so I won't be in until later.

   Receptionist: That's great for you, but I think you'd better check with Mr. Demers first. He might really need you for something this morning.

5. Receptionist: Good morning. Fujimoto Enterprises.

   Employee: Delcy, it's Leo. I'm not coming in today. We've had this great three-day family reunion at the cottage planned for months, so I'm leaving for there now.

   Receptionist: Oh, then I guess your department's known for some time that you'll be away today.

   Employee: Well, no. I figured it would be less of a hassle to just call in and let them know on the day of the reunion. That way, I'm sure of getting the time off.

   Receptionist: You might find yourself with more time off than you'd like! I'd better transfer you to Miss Walters.

6. Receptionist: Good morning. Smith Storage.

   Employee: Hi, Mary. It's Malcolm. I can't come in today. Our babysitter is sick and I have to look after my little sister.

   Receptionist: Is no one else able to do it?

   Employee: Well, dad's away, and mom works.

   Receptionist: So do you.

   Employee: Oh, well, her work's a lot more important than mine.

   Receptionist: Not to our company! You'd better talk to Mr. Bradette.

Chapter Summary Exercises

1. What is meant by *probation period*? *Flextime*? *Telecommuting*?
2. In the work that you intend or want to do, what type of clothing will be appropriate? If you have work now, describe your usual work clothing. Give details, explaining why the clothing you wear (or will wear) is appropriate, takes safety precautions into account, etc.
3. a) List ten things you should do during your first day at work.
   b) List ten things you should *not* do.
4. Why is being punctual for work important?

5. When you are planning to be absent from work, what five guidelines should you follow?
6. In paragraph form, describe three situations that you think would be acceptable to an employer as reasons not to report for work.
7. Discuss the importance of punctuality, dependability, and interpersonal relations.

Reflective Journal

1. How can the physical and psychological situation in an office affect your adjustment to a new workplace?
2. Do you believe companies should have probation periods for their new employees? Explain your answer.
3. What aspects of personal dress and hygiene are important to you? Does your "code" meet your placement requirements?
4. Explain what the following statement means to you:
   "To be successful at work, you need to develop a mature and self-reliant attitude concerning punctuality."

Chapter 12

Efficiency in the Workplace

objectives

After completing this chapter you should be able to:

▶ Explain why employers value efficient employees.
▶ Use mentoring as a strategy for success.
▶ Realize the importance of using company equipment and supplies carefully and efficiently.
▶ Discuss why both quality and quantity of work are important.
▶ Assess the quality and quantity of your work.
▶ Show initiative and make decisions effectively.

introduction

One of the most desirable characteristics of an employee is efficiency. Efficiency at work is the ability to do your work without wasting time, energy, supplies, etc. You aren't born with efficient work habits; they are developed. Becoming efficient starts with learning the best way to do your work; discovering who is who at work; where to find what you need in order to do your work; how to take care of equipment and materials; being able to distinguish the difference between quality of work and quantity of work; and learning how to use your initiative and be an effective decision maker.

who's who at work

When you begin new work, you're introduced to many new people. This can be very confusing! However, these are the people you will need to communicate with to get your work done, so the sooner you can remember their names, the sooner you will be productive in your new employment. No one will expect you to remember everyone's name right away, so concentrate on the people in your immediate department with whom you are likely to work most closely. The following are a few tips that might help.

1. Ask for a list of employees' names, such as an internal telephone list. Refer to this to jog your memory and to make sure you spell names correctly.
2. When you are introduced, repeat the person's name and try to identify one outstanding feature of the person (e.g., unusual glasses, broad smile, outgoing personality, etc.).
3. Listen to how the other employees refer to each other. Do they use first names or family names? Is it Marie or Mrs. Bibeau? Roy or Mr. Sanna? In some companies, everyone is informal and only first names are used. In others, some people are addressed by their first names but others are addressed as "Mr.," "Mrs.,"

"Miss," or "Ms." Follow the lead of the majority of your co-workers. Addressing someone appropriately will make you both feel comfortable.

A Champion's Checklist

To help you *keep* the work once you get it:

1. Recognize that people like to feel important.
2. Smile and be pleasant, every day to everyone!
3. Names are the sweetest sound; remember and use them.
4. Be a good listener—encourage others to talk about themselves (but not when you are supposed to be working!)
5. Always talk in the other person's interest.
6. Never argue—never say or imply that another person is wrong.
7. If *you* are wrong be quick to admit it.
8. Let others talk their way into your ideas. It gives ownership, commitment and helps you to succeed.
9. Be noticed for being efficient, competent, and capable in handling human relations.

---

mentoring

Mentoring is a relationship usually between an older, more skilled individual and a novice. The purpose of mentoring is sharing or passing along wisdom or experience to the younger one—not for pay or for ulterior feedback. A mentor provides modelling, close supervision on special projects, and individualized help in many areas. A mentor telling you where to find resources or showing you how to do something gives you a step up from others. One of the greatest roles a mentor can play is to introduce you to the right people at the right time, that is, sharing his or her network of contacts to further your career.

The mentor who teaches, advises, and promotes your career may be your boss, a co-worker, someone higher up in the company, or an influential individual connected to the business.

To encourage mentoring listen carefully to feedback from senior employees and decide whether you can follow the advice. Always thank the person for the suggestions whether you use all of them or not. Show interest and enthusiasm by asking questions and making use of the answers, demonstrating that you want to learn and improve your performance. *Always be the best that you can be* at whatever task you are handed. Mentors who give up their time to help you want to see positive results from their mentoring. The more mentors you have, the more help you have to get ahead at work. Remember never, never, take your mentor for granted. Be modest and appreciative by sharing your successes with your mentor.

Getting Organized

No matter what your work, you will need some materials to produce results. An office worker needs stationery, scissors, a stapler, pens, and so on. An instrument technician needs a lab coat, tools, a magnifying glass, etc. An auto mechanic needs items such as protective clothing, tools, and access to auto parts.

The time you spend assembling your materials before you start to work is not productive. If you have to make several trips, production time is lost. If you have to ask someone the location of every item, even more time is wasted.

To avoid this situation, find out during the first day or two the location of all the basic supplies you will need and the procedures required to obtain them. Is someone's permission necessary or can you just help yourself? Sometimes you will need to fill in a requisition form and perhaps indicate a budget code. A budget code identifies the department to which the cost of the materials is to be charged. If a budget code is required, write it down and keep it in your work area for future reference.

Whenever you run out of a particular material and need to pick up more, take a moment to consider what other supplies also are low. Thinking ahead will reduce the number of interruptions and, therefore, the amount of time spent away from your work. Equipment and supplies are a major expense for most companies, so it is important for all employees to use and conserve these carefully. The following are some basic guidelines for doing this.

care and handling of equipment and supplies*

1. Before using a new piece of equipment, read the operating instructions and follow them carefully. If you are still unsure about the correct way to use the equipment, ask your supervisor or an experienced worker to show you how to do it.

2. Even if it takes longer, follow safety procedures when using equipment. Accidents happen to people who take chances. Remember, safety rules are based on previous accidents—if it happened to someone else, it could happen to you. Your basic rule should be: The safe way is the right way.

3. When you have finished with tools or equipment, put them away or turn them off. This will help to prevent them from getting lost, broken, or wearing out, and turning off the power conserves energy.

4. If the equipment you're using doesn't seem to be working properly, immediately report the problem to the person in charge. Often a minor flaw that is found early can save a major breakdown later. Also, it is difficult to produce high-quality work if the equipment you are using is defective.

*The rest of this chapter is adapted from: Guidance Centre, University of Toronto, in co-operation with Employment and Immigration Canada. PLACE. Guided Steps to Employment Readiness. "Part D: Doing Well on the Job." © Minister of Supply and Services Canada, 1984, pp. 27–30, 37–47. Reproduced with the permission of the Minister of Supply and Services Canada, 1990.

5. Don't waste company supplies. In the following case study, for example, Renée wasted fifty sheets of paper by running the photocopy machine carelessly. Then she added to her wastefulness by throwing the paper away. Paper, pens, erasers—all types of supplies—cost money.

6. Don't steal from the company. This costs everyone money—workers and consumers alike. Stealing includes stealing time from your work to run personal errands, stealing supplies or equipment, and "borrowing" things for your own use. Also, remember that theft is against the law. Not only can you be fired for it but also you can be prosecuted.

Case Study

Read the following case study and then answer the questions that appear at the end of it.

Renée was furious. "The equipment they give us around here is useless," she fumed to herself, giving her computer terminal an angry shove. "Especially this machine. Something's always going wrong with it. Yesterday the data set wasn't working. This morning the paper jammed. Half the time it doesn't accept the sign-on sequence. And now it won't even start! The thing is a pain in the neck."

She flicked the power switch a couple of times, then stood and glared at the machine.

Just then Nadia walked by. "What's the matter?" she asked with concern when she saw the expression on Renée's face.

"I don't know. The darn thing won't start."

"Here, let me look," Nadia said helpfully. She tried the power switch, made sure the data set was hooked up, then walked to the back of the machine. "Here's our problem," she said after a moment. "It's unplugged. There, it should work now." Sure enough, the terminal hummed happily.

"Thanks, Nadia. I wouldn't even have thought of anything so simple," Renée said, sitting down to start work.

Things didn't seem to get any better during the day. When she went to photocopy her printout, the photocopy machine was out of paper. She tried loading it, but it wouldn't work. She had to go and ask Mrs. Hansen to help. Renée knew it was part of her job to load the machine, but she just couldn't seem to get it right. The paper always jammed or she forgot to press the right switch. It was easier to get someone else to do it.

When the paper was loaded properly she started to make her copies, still feeling flustered. She needed fifty copies of each page. "At least this time I remembered to set it for the right number of copies," she thought.

While waiting for her copies, she rushed to her desk to make a personal telephone call. When she returned to the machine, she noted with a sinking sensation that the copies were blank. She'd put the original in wrong side up! Looking guiltily over her shoulder, she threw the fifty blank pages into the waste basket.

"I just won't record those copies in the record book," she decided. "After all, I didn't really make the copies and they don't ask us to list every page we have to throw away."

At 3:30 her supervisor went out, saying "I'll be back in an hour, Renée." Great! Now she could get the paper and supplies that her roommate had asked her to bring home. "After all," she argued, justifying her actions to herself, "the company is making lots of money. No one will even notice that the stuff is missing. Besides, my roommate really needs it. She's just a student and she can't afford to buy it herself." Gathering up several lined pads and some typing paper, pens, paper clips, and pencils, she made a neat pile on her desk. "I'll just wrap them up in some of this brown paper," she thought.

Halfway through her task, she got a creepy feeling and looked up. There stood her supervisor, looking very stern. "Oh, you're back already. Was the meeting shorter than you expected?" Renée asked breathlessly, trying to hide what she was doing.

"What are you doing, Renée?" he asked, ignoring her question.

"Oh, this...well...you see...my roommate is a student and she asked me to bring some...uh ...paper and stuff home...uh and...well...," her voice trailed off.

"Yes, I do see," Mr. Patel answered, rather grimly. "I think you and I had better have a talk. Come into my office, please."

Renée sat nervously in the chair while Mr. Patel looked out the window for a moment. Finally he turned and said, "I've been thinking for some time now that I should speak to you about your attitude toward company equipment and materials. You don't seem to understand that you have a responsibility to use them carefully and efficiently.

"For example, look at the way you use the photocopy machine. I've noticed that you waste a lot of paper. And even though it's part of your job, you haven't learned to load it properly. So you're costing the company money in two ways. First, you're increasing the cost of supplies, and second, you're keeping another employee from his or her work. If everyone was like you, the company would go bankrupt.

"Now I've caught you stealing. Stealing company supplies as well as company time. Everyone who works here, as well as everyone who buys our products, ends up having to pay for that kind of behaviour.

"When you decided to help yourself to company supplies, you probably figured that the company was rich and could afford the loss. Imagine what would happen if everyone behaved like you.

"Now, I'm going to give you one last chance. But I expect you to learn to operate the business machines properly and to stop wasting and stealing company supplies. Treat company materials as if they belonged to your best friend. You wouldn't steal from her or mistreat her property, would you?

"All right. You can go now. But be warned, next time you'll be dismissed."

Questions

1. In what ways did Renée misuse her company's supplies and equipment?
2. What would happen if every employee behaved like Renée?
3. Do you think it's a good idea to treat company materials as if they belonged to your best friend? Explain your answer.

In the case study, Renée showed her lack of concern about company equipment and materials by treating the equipment roughly, not learning to operate it properly, wasting supplies, and stealing company materials Like many people, she took the attitude that "the company can afford it." But employers can't afford to keep employees like Renée. It costs them money to repair or replace equipment that's damaged or broken by careless workers. And supplies cost money too. Careless, wasteful, and dishonest employees could, in the long run, cause the company to close its doors. Then Renée and her co-workers would be out of work. Also, the amount of money that a company has to spend on its office and plant is built into the prices that it charges for its products or services, so Renée, her co-workers, and the general public have to pay more for these.

Careless use of equipment and materials can have other serious effects also. For example, if you use large or dangerous machinery without proper care, you could injure yourself or others, and if your equipment is damaged, other employees might not be able get their work done either.

ACTIVITY 1

Assessing Your Use of Equipment and Supplies

1. Do you wait until something goes wrong before you bother to read the operating instructions?
2. When a machine isn't working, do you kick or shake it to try to get it going again?
3. When you've finished with a piece of equipment, do you leave it lying around?
4. Do you "borrow" company supplies or equipment for your personal use?

If you've answered "Yes" to any of these questions, you should examine your behaviour regarding your use of company equipment and supplies.

Quality of Work

At school and at work your teachers and your employer expect that the quality of work you produce will meet acceptable standards. Usually people produce poor-quality work not because they can't do better, but because they can't be bothered to do their best. Perhaps they don't like school or their work, maybe they think that a few mistakes don't matter, or maybe they're more concerned about getting their work done quickly than about doing it well.

The quantity of work produced is important, but the quality of that work is also extremely important. First of all, the mistakes you make can cause problems for other workers and increase company costs. This is particularly obvious on a production line. For example, Ali works in a bakery, taking buns out of the oven and placing them on a conveyor belt. If Ali jiggles the trays when he lays them on the belt, the buns end up out of position and don't get iced properly. The next workers in the sequence, who inspect and package the buns, have to remove all of the buns that aren't iced properly. This makes extra work for them and results in a lot of waste. By taking a little more time and being more careful, Ali can help to improve the overall productivity of his unit.

In some sense, in almost every type of work the individual worker is part of a production line. We are all dependent on the work of others in the organization. Take a few minutes to think about where your work fits in with the work of others and you'll realize that the quality of your work affects the overall production of the entire organization. This is why employers value employees who produce good-quality work.

Guidelines for Improving the Quality of Work Produced

1. Before starting a task, make sure you understand the instructions. Obviously, if you don't know what you're supposed to be doing, it'll be sheer luck if you do it correctly. Write down the instructions or repeat them to your teacher or supervisor to make sure you understand. Ask questions if you don't. If you are really unsure, do one example, then take it to your teacher or supervisor to check that you are on the right track before going further.
2. The first times you do a task, follow the instructions exactly. Only when you're completely familiar with the work should you start looking for shortcuts.
3. From time to time, check back over your instructions to make sure you haven't forgotten anything. It's easy to slip into bad habits or sloppy work procedures.
4. Concentrate on doing work properly. If your mind is on other things, you are more likely to make mistakes. You won't notice your mistakes unless you are concentrating on what you are doing.
5. Before you pass your work to the next person, double-check it. Everyone makes mistakes from time to time, so it's worth spending the few minutes it takes to check your completed tasks. It's particularly important to check your work the first few times you perform a new activity.
6. Be aware of and deal with problems you encounter in your work. Sometimes, for example, you might find yourself in situations for which you've received no instructions. If the problem is a minor one, try to solve it yourself. If it is something you don't feel

comfortable handling, however, report it to someone in authority right away. Don't ignore it in the hope that it will solve itself.

7. Accept the fact that you are responsible for the quality of your work. Don't look for excuses or blame others for your mistakes.

ACTIVITY 2

Assessing the Quality of Your Work

1. If you make a mistake do you let it go, thinking that someone else will find it?
2. Do you fail to double-check your work because you assume that you did it correctly the first time?
3. Do you tend to rush through your work as quickly as possible?
4. Does your teacher or supervisor criticize you for sloppy or inaccurate work?
5. When doing routine tasks, do you find that you let your thoughts wander?

If you have answered "Yes" to any of these questions, you should make an effort to improve the quality of your work.

Quantity of Work

In any organization, a slow worker can cause just as many problems as a careless worker, so the quantity of work produced is also important. For example, if the bakery worker, Ali, is slow getting the buns out of the oven and onto the conveyor belt, two holdups result: the baking of the next batch of buns will be delayed, and the people after Ali on the production line, the people who inspect and package the buns, will be left with nothing to do. So Ali's slowness affects everybody involved in the production of the buns.

In many types of work, employers set production quotas, which means that employees are expected to produce a certain number of products or perform a certain number of tasks in a set period of time. In other occupations, employees are paid for piecework, which means that their income depends on the number of items they produce. Even when formal production quotas aren't set, employers expect employees who are doing similar types of work to produce approximately the same quantity of work.

As an employee, therefore, you should aim to produce about the same quantity of work as the people you work with. If you're very slow, you'll interfere with the work of others, and they'll probably feel that you're not doing your share. At work, you're part of a team and you have a responsibility to the other team members. Your aim should be to do your fair share of work quickly and well.

Guidelines for Improving the Quantity of Work Produced

1. *Find out how much you are expected to produce.* When you start an assignment, your teacher or supervisor will usually tell you what tasks you are responsible for. Make a list of these tasks and use it to prepare a daily schedule. If you're not given specific instructions about the amount of work you should produce, find out what is expected by watching or asking other students or people with whom you work.

2. *Plan a daily routine.* Decide on the order in which you're going to do each of your assigned tasks and give yourself a time limit for each one. Having a routine helps you to save time because you don't have to stop after each activity and take time to decide what to do next.

3. *Before you begin a task, make sure you have all the necessary materials and equipment.* If you have to keep jumping up to get things you've forgotten or run out of, your productivity will decrease. By organizing yourself before you begin, you'll find that you get more done in the same amount of time.

4. *Work at a steady pace.* It's easy to waste a lot of time jumping up to get things, making personal phone calls, making unnecessary trips to the washroom, daydreaming, or chatting with other workers. You should try to avoid interruptions and keep your mind on the task at hand.

5. *When you've finished one task, don't sit and wait for someone to tell you what to do next.* Move on to the next activity you've planned as part of your daily routine. If you've finished your work for the day, you might either start on work that's due later or ask your teacher or supervisor for something else to do.

6. *Try to finish one task before beginning another.* Each time you switch to a new activity, it takes a few moments to get your thoughts organized. Obtain an in-basket and ask people to leave their work there. Then finish what you're doing before starting on the next thing in the basket.

7. *Try to avoid worrying about the work you still have to do.* This is easier said than done, but if you've planned a realistic daily routine, you should be able to get everything finished. Worrying about what's still to be done just slows you down.

ACTIVITY 3

Assessing the Quantity of your Work

1. Do you always seem to fall behind in your projects?
2. Do you often have to stay late to finish your tasks?
3. Does your teacher or supervisor usually ask for your work before you've finished it?
4. Do you usually meet your work deadlines?
5. Has your teacher or supervisor criticized you for slowness or poor productivity?
7. Do the people you work with regularly produce more work than you?
8. Do you spend a lot of time gazing around or talking to others?

If you've answered "Yes" to more than one of these questions, you're probably producing an inadequate quantity of work during your regular work hours. It's possible that your assigned workload is too heavy. To judge this, you should discuss the problem with your teacher or supervisor. However, if others doing similar tasks have the same amount of work and seem able to handle it, the problem must be poor productivity on your part and you should review the guidelines for improving the quantity of work produced.

Case Study

Read the following case study about two young employees who work for the same employer but have quite different working habits. Then answer the questions that appear at the end.

Sam and Marita are the two newest employees in a cafeteria located in a large, busy mall. They've been there only two weeks but already the difference in their work habits is clear to everyone.

As far as Sam was concerned, today had been the worst day yet. Here it was, only two o'clock, and it felt as though he'd been there forever. He was rushed off his feet and everything was going wrong.

"How can I be expected to serve properly if I can't even find the trays?" he asked himself crossly as he stuffed everything into one small bag. "Here you go," he smiled, handing the bag to his waiting customer, only to watch, horrified, as the bottom of the bag tore, spilling food and a soft drink all over the counter. Sighing, he cleaned up the mess and started over.

Out of the corner of his eye, he saw one of his regulars looking impatient. She must have been waiting ten minutes already, he groaned to himself, "Well, what'll it be today?" he asked, hurrying to her.

"I think I'll have a small cola, a cheeseburger, and do you have any chocolate ice cream?" she asked.

"Just a minute, I'll go check," he said, rushing off.

On his way, another customer interrupted. "Could you tell me where to find the straws?" he asked. "Right over there," Sam pointed.

"There aren't any there," the customer persisted. Sam turned back. Sure enough, they had run out of straws. "I'll get some more from the back," he promised, and started off.

When he came back with the straws, he noticed his first customer. What was it she'd wanted to know about? Oh yes, chocolate ice cream. He hurried back with the answer.

"Fine, I'll take two cones." she said.

As he reached for the cones, he realized with a sinking sensation that there wasn't enough ice cream. "I'll be right back with more," he called over his shoulder, diving into the back room.

"You'll have to wait a minute, there's none open," said Ferdie, the manager, when Sam explained what he wanted. So Sam waited.

Five minutes later, when Sam got back, he noticed that his customer had disappeared. Oh, there she was, at Marita's counter. He grabbed an ice cream cone and rushed over to her. "Here you go," he panted. "Is this what you wanted?"

The customer looked at him coldly. "Never mind," she said. "I got tired of waiting and decided to get something else instead."

Sam felt angry. Grumbling, he walked back to his counter and looked around. Well, at least there weren't any customers at the moment. He knew he should tidy up his area a bit, but first he'd have a drink and relax.

Sipping his drink, he looked over at Marita, who was working busily behind her counter. She seemed to have a really easy time of it. "Look at her now, cleaning up her counter when it doesn't even need it," he thought to himself. "I guess it's easier on her side of the restaurant. Besides, all my customers are in such a hurry." Still, he wondered.

At three o'clock, when he and Marita went for their coffee break together, the question was still on his mind. "You always look so cool." he said. "When I was going crazy trying to do three things at once and that customer was on my back, I looked over at your counter and there wasn't even anyone waiting. How do you do it?"

"Well, I don't know. It got pretty busy at my counter for a while there!" Marita answered, surprised. "I just don't let myself get upset. Instead, I concentrate on serving one customer at a time. I find that when I try to do more than that, I get mixed up and forget what everyone wants. It just slows me down.

"I try to be prepared, too. When it slows down a bit, I check to make sure there are enough trays and I tidy up under my counter, making sure that I have enough condiments, cups, plates—you know, the stuff that runs out. Then I don't have to keep running to the back when I need them.

"When I arrive in the morning, I like to follow a regular routine. For example, I always start by cleaning and tidying up my counter. That way I don't have to think about it later on. Then I read the price lists and try to memorize any changes. I find it saves time when customers come in, because I don't have to keep checking. And I'm trying to learn where everything is kept. That way I don't have to waste time searching for things. And once I've finished with something, I try to put it back in the same place each time. It makes it faster to find things."

Sam looked impressed. "So that's why you always manage to look cool. Maybe I should try it."

Questions

1. Who do you think did more work during an average day, Sam or Marita? Give reasons for your answer.
2. Why do you think it's important for your work to meet acceptable standards of quality? What happens when these standards are not met?
3. List ways of improving the quality of your work.
4. What can you do to improve the quantity of work you produce?
5. In what ways can being organized and tidy in your work habits lead to greater efficiency?

Initiative and Decision Making

As you become more experienced and knowledgeable in your work, you should be able to increase your value to your employer by developing your initiative and decision-making skills. Employers need employees with initiative, i.e., who take an interest in the work, who are versatile and adaptable, who anticipate and then do what needs to be done and come up with ways of completing work more efficiently.

Decision makers prove their worth to employees by being able to work independently without constantly interrupting others with questions about what to do and how to go about it.

Initiative and decision making should be exercised with some caution and discretion. Make sure you have all of the necessary information and that you make decisions that are appropriate for someone in your position.

The following activities will help you to assess your own initiative and decision-making skills and to be aware of how these skills are being exercised by others.

ACTIVITY 4

Assessing Your Initiative*

Answer "Yes" or "No to the following questions.

1. Do you wait until you are told before beginning a new task?
2. If you think something is being done wrong, do you think that it's someone else's problem?
3. Do you think that doing your work well is all that should matter to your supervisor?
4. Do you resent being asked to take over for another employee who is absent or overworked?
5. Do you avoid suggesting changes because you feel no one will listen or that it probably isn't a very good idea anyway?
6. Do you try to avoid talking to your supervisor?
7. Do you avoid working extra hours if you are asked?
8. Do you get to work barely on time and leave as soon as you can?

If you've answered "Yes" to more than one of these question, it's possible that you're unwilling or unable to show initiative. If you'd like to show more initiative but aren't sure how to go about it, the following guideline might help.

*This exercise and the next section are adapted from: Guidance Centre, University of Toronto, in co-operation with Employment and Immigration Canada. PLACE. *Guided Steps to Employment Readiness*. "Part D: Doing Well on the Job." © Minister of Supply and Services Canada, 1984, pp. 91-93.

ACTIVITY 5

Assessing Initiative

Interview three people who are employed. Find out how they or their co-workers show initiative at their place of work. Prepare a brief report that gives each person's title and then list the ways in which each person shows initiative.

You Decide

Showing initiative can lead to promotion and bonuses. pretend that you're the head supervisor of the physical Therapy Unit of the Clearbrook Hospital. The human resource manager has told you that you can promote two people in your department to supervisory positions. She has also given you $1000 in bonus money to distribute among the workers on the basis of how well they have shown initiative. An individual can receive any amount up to $1000. Read the employee descriptions below and decide whom you would promote and how much bonus money you would give to each. Explain the reasons for your decisions.

Marissa: Works overtime when asked. Often helps patients on her own time. Does not participate in hospital social activities.

Lazlo: Seldom has to be told what to do. Has missed work often, usually because of family problems. Absences irritate co-workers. Enrolled at a local community college in a two-year program that will qualify him for a higher position in physical therapy.

Simone: Works very well alone. Usually does not help other co-workers except when asked. Has thought of new ways to get the work done more efficiently.

Huan: Does not watch the clock; if extra hours are required, works them cheerfully. Is thinking of looking for higher-paying work at another hospital.

Selma: Gets along very well with co-workers but has quite a few disagreements with supervisors. Volunteers to come in on days off if the hospital is short-staffed.

Effective Decision Makers

Before making a decision, ask yourself:

1. Is this my decision to make or am I making a decision for someone else?
2. Should I be sharing the responsibility for this decision with other people?
3. Am I being rushed or pressured to make a decision?

Think about an important decision you need to make or have recently made. Now work through the following procedure to increase your effectiveness in reaching a decision. If the decision is already made, how might this strategy have helped you make a wiser decision?

When you have answered these question to your satisfaction, you are ready to begin in the decision-making process, which is as follows:

Step 1: Define the problem.

Carefully examine the problem to make sure you understand it. Write the problem down, stating all the facts. For example, if you are constantly short of money, you could define the problem as being the fact that you spend too much or that you need to earn more money. You might need the help of others in defining the problem.

Step 2: List all possible solutions to the problem.

After careful thought and necessary research (including talking to other people, if necessary), write down all of the possible solutions to the problem. Don't try to make a final decision at this point.

Step 3: Evaluate all of the possible alternatives and choose the best solution.

Don't jump to conclusions and choose the first solution that seems to make sense. Look at the problem from every possible angle and assess each alternative in every possible context. Avoid procrastinating but don't make hasty decisions. Use the information you gathered, your intuition, and your post experience to come to a workable decision that reflects your values and goals.

Step 4: Develop a plan of action.

Write a list of the steps you need to take to implement your plan.

ACTIVITY 8

Apply the decision-making process to the following situations. In each case:
Ask yourself:

1. Is this the employee's decision, or is it being made for someone else?
2. Should responsibility for the decision be shared with someone else?
3. Is there a rush or pressure on the person to make a decision?

Then,

▶ Define the employee's problem.
▶ List all possible solutions.
▶ Evaluate the alternatives and choose the best one.
▶ Detail a plan of action.

You could set this up in your notebook as follows.

Step 1: The problem:
Step 2: Possible solutions:
Step 3: Best solution:
Step 4: Plan of action:

1. Lately Tak has been under a lot of financial pressure. It seems he never has enough money for things he needs. Tak goes to university full time, and on weekends and some week nights he works for the minimum wage at a local restaurant. In the summers he works as a lifeguard and swimming instructor also. He lives in a very inexpensive apartment on a quiet street near

the hospital where he takes some courses. After two more years of university he will graduate as an physical therapist. He is looking forward to having a secure income.

2. David works in a large office building in the suburbs. He is a customer service representative. At work he often feels tired and has headaches. Some of the other workers complain of the same symptoms. During his two-week summer vacation he feels in the best of health. When David returns to work after the holidays, his symptoms return. He suspects that the building's inadequate air circulation system might be the cause of his problems.

3. Eva has had permanent part-time work as a circulation clerk in the college library for three years. She is well-liked by staff and students. Eva is pleasant with the library users and follows the library policies. Eva's supervisor, Linda, is not officially in charge of hiring circulation staff but often makes strong recommendations to her supervisor. Often Linda's friends and family are hired. A full-time position will soon be available. People are aware that Eva realizes that a more recent part-time worker, one of Linda's friends, has been given the vacation weeks that Eva requested. Eva is resentful of Linda but is aware that she must be careful if she wants full-time work.

4. Tibor works as a sales representative in a small office. All of the items he sells are packaged and shrink-wrapped in set amounts. On his sales calls, he often receives requests from customers who want different quantities than the packages offer or who want to mix and match packages of items. Tibor usually decides to repackage items in order to sell customers exactly what they want. This causes all kinds of problems back at this office where accounting, the order department, and the warehouse are wasting time figuring out and putting his orders together and then billing and collecting for them. Tibor's supervisor is also involved when staff from other departments complain about the extra work his orders entail and when customers complain because mistakes have been made. Should Tibor be exercising his decision-making skills with more discretion? How might such situations be handled?

5. You might know of a problem at your place of work. Write down the details of the problem and, using the decision-making process, explain how you think the problem could be solved.

Chapter Summary Exercises

1. What does the word *efficiency* mean?
2. What does being efficient on the job involve?
3. Describe some methods you can use to remember co-workers' names.
4. What is mentoring, and how can it benefit you?
5. What is the first step you should take before beginning a task?
6. Briefly describe six things that are important in relation to the care and handling of company equipment and supplies.
7. Is taking company supplies such as pens, paper, etc., for personal use acceptable? Explain why or why not.
8. a) Why is the *quality* of work produced important?
   b) Why is the *quality* of work produced important?
9. a) List four ways in which the *quality* of work can be improved.
   b) List four ways in which the *quality* of work can be improved.
10. Read again the case study on page 139 and make notes of each thing Sam did that you think was the result of inefficiency. Then, in paragraph form, describe each example of inefficiency and explain how he could have avoided the problem.
11. Discuss and role-play the positive and negative effects of a well-developed work ethic on workers and workplace productivity.
12. Identify steps in the decision-making process.
13. Discuss consequences of decisions.
14. Describe how career development is a continuous process with a series of choices.

Reflective Journal

1. If you had a chance to do one thing at work over again, what would it be?
2. Have you ever "borrowed" any equipment or supplies from your workplace and then wished you hadn't Why did you borrow the materials?
3. Name one adult at school or at work whom you admire. Tell why?
4. Have you ever had a mentor? How did the experience help you? If you could choose someone to be your mentor, whom would you choose? Why?

UNIT 4

Coping Skills for Today's Workplace

introduction

Success in the workplace depends on more than a person's knowledge, practical skills, attendance, and efficiency. Having a positive attitude, demonstrating professionalism, getting along well with supervisors and co-workers, and effectively handling stress are also very important.

This unit discusses these aspects of work life, including chapters on how to be assertive, not aggressive; how to handle anger; and how to really *listen*, not just hear, including a section on telephone skills.

Chapter 13

Importance of a Positive Attitude

objectives

After completing this chapter you should be able to:

► Explain the importance of a positive attitude in all situations.
► Assess your own attitude.
► Accept orders and follow instructions effectively.
► Define your own level of trustworthiness.
► Explain what the word *professionalism* means.
► List some of the ways in which professionalism can be demonstrated.

introduction

The word *attitude* means a way of thinking, acting, or feeling. Attitudes can be either positive or negative. Negative attitudes lead to negative results, so a positive attitude is necessary for you to make the most of your life, both personally and at work. A positive attitude is a greatly valued characteristic of an employee.

A positive attitude makes every situation more enjoyable for everyone. At work, the employer feels that any reasonable request will be willingly handled by an employee with a positive attitude. If you enjoy what you're doing, you'll probably have a positive attitude toward your work. Even if you *don't* enjoy what you're doing, however, a positive attitude helps.

Attitudes colour every aspect of our lives. A positive attitude brightens our lives with every colour of the rainbow, while a negative attitude darkens the world to grey and black. Which attitudes colour *your* world?

ACTIVITY 1

Is Your Attitude Showing?

The following survey will help you to assess your attitude toward others and toward situations in which you might find yourself. The results will indicate if your attitude needs improvement. In your notebook, write down the number of each question and then put beside it the number in the key below that best describes your first reaction to the question.

5 = Yes   2 = Usually No
4 = Usually Yes   1 = No
3 = Sometimes Yes/Sometimes No

1. Are you friendly and outgoing?
2. Do you avoid being a complainer?
3. Can you be optimistic when others are depressed?

4. Do you refrain from boasting or bragging?
5. Do you have a sense of duty and responsibility?
6. Do you control your temper?
7. Do you speak well of your employer?
8. Do you feel well most of the time?
9. Do you follow directions willingly, asking questions when necessary?
10. Do you keep promises?
11. Do you organize your work and stay on schedule?
12. Do you readily admit your mistakes?
13. Can you be a leader without being bossy?
14. Is it easy for you to like most people?
15. Can you stick to a tiresome task without being prodded?
16. Do you know your weaknesses and attempt to correct them?
17. Can you stand being teased?
18. Do you avoid feeling sorry for yourself?
19. Are you courteous to others?
20. Are you neat in your personal appearance and work habits?
21. Do you respect the opinions of others?
22. Are you a good loser?
23. Can you adapt to new and unexpected situations readily?
24. Are you tolerant of other people's beliefs?
25. Do you refrain from sulking when things don't go as you'd like?
26. Are you a good listener?
27. Are you the type of friend that you expect others to be?
28. Can you disagree without being disagreeable?
29. Are you punctual?
30. Are you a considerate and careful driver?
31. Do you generally speak well of others?
32. Can you take criticism without being resentful or feeling hurt?
33. Are you careful to pay back all loans, however small?
34. Do you generally look at the bright side of things?
35. Does your voice usually sound cheerful?
36. Can you work with people you dislike?
37. Are you pleasant to others even when something displeases you?
38. Do you show enthusiasm for the interests of others?
39. Do you tend to be enthusiastic about whatever you do?
40. Are you honest and sincere with others?

Attitude Scoring

There are 40 questions; a perfect score would be 200. Total your score and rate yourself according to the following scale.

175–200:   You're terrific.
150–174:   Your attitude toward others is admirable.
110–149:   Your attitude needs polishing in certain areas.
Below 110: Take a close look at your attitude. You might need to pay particular attention to those questions you answered with a 1 or 2. Can you see any room for improvement there?

Question

How can negative attitudes be changed to positive attitudes? Give some examples.

characteristics of a person with a good attitude

If you have a good attitude, you are:

Helpful
Willing
Orderly
Co-operative
Considerate
Cheerful
Prompt
Trustworthy

Polite
Persistent
Even-tempered
Responsible
Interested in work
Enthusiastic
Eager to improve
Accepting of criticism

ACTIVITY 2

Take a Look At Yourself

In your notebook, write down the numbers of the following questions. Then, beside each number, answer each question by writing "Yes," "No," or "Not sure."

1. Do you always wish it were the weekend?
2. Do you look forward to your future?
3. Do you enjoy tackling new challenges?
4. Can you keep a secret?
5. Do you feel that you don't get what you deserve?
6. Are you always late?
7. Do you often do things at the last minute?
8. Do you trust your own judgment?
9. Do you find it difficult to concentrate on finishing one task at a time?
10. Are you understanding about other people's problems?
11. Are you a good listener?
12. Are you able to work alone without supervision?
13. Do you always look for the easy way out?
14. Do you feel confident about your skills and abilities?
15. Do you find it difficult to meet new people?
16. Are you able to admire other people's accomplishments without feeling jealous?
17. Do you refrain from gossiping?
18. Are you tolerant of other people's opinions?
19. Do you know the difference between what you can change and what you can't?
20. Do you give and accept praise graciously?
21. Are you neat in your personal appearance?
22. Are you sympathetic? Do you try to put yourself in the other person's situation?
23. Do you frequently interrupt other people while they are speaking?
24. Do you enjoy meeting new people?
25. Are you patient with other people?

Questions

1. Which questions did you answer "Not sure"? Why?
2. Identify the questions that you answered "No" and explain why you answered this way. Could the attitude indicated by your answer to these questions determine the type of employee you are or might be?
3. Describe the characteristics of a person with a positive attitude toward her or his work.

ACTIVITY 3

An Interview

What does it mean to have a positive attitude in the workplace? What's it like to work with people who have a positive attitude—and with people who don't ? How does having a positive attitude affect the way the negative aspects of a work situation are handled? Ask someone who likes his or her work some questions like the following ones. Add some questions of your own.

1. Why do you like your work?
2. Are there people you work with who make your work easier? How?
3. Are there people you work with who make your work more difficult? How?
4. Do you think that one person's attitude can affect the company as a whole? How?
5. What do you dislike about your work?
6. How do you handle it when you really don't feel like going to work?
7. Do you know how your co-workers handle not wanting to go to work? What's your opinion of their methods?

Accepting Orders

Like it or not, most people have to take orders from others for at least part of their working lives. Remember that the person who is giving orders is in that position because he or she has demonstrated an ability to do that job well or to make sure that it is done properly.

By indicating your willingness to take and carry out orders, you show your willingness to co-operate in doing what your employer feels is best for the company. So, when you are given an order:
1. Look willing.
2. Make sure you understand what is required.
3. Respond positively and cheerfully.
4. Carry out the task to the best of your ability.

Read the following case studies to see how some employees accept and carry out orders. In your notebook, rewrite these case studies so that they follow the four guidelines for accepting orders. Finally, use your own work experience to write your own case study about a person who accepts orders well.

1. Shawna's supervisor asked Shawna to interrupt her work in the stockroom to help at the cash desk during a busy period. Shawna shrugged and said, "O.K., but don't blame me if the new stock doesn't get sorted today."

2. When Dimitri arrived at the restaurant for his shift, his supervisor was very glad to see him. "We're so short-handed today! Would you please help to clear the tables, instead of your usual task of helping to make desserts?" Dimitri's face fell. "I guess so," he said. He worked as slowly as he could, to show his supervisor how annoyed he was.

3. Maral worked part-time at the local library. She enjoyed working at the check-out desk and meeting the library patrons. One day, her supervisor said, "I'd like you to look after reshelving the books and making sure that the shelves are tidy." Maral thought that this would be boring, but she nodded, smiled, and began to carefully put books away in their proper places on the shelves.

ACTIVITY 4

Getting Things Straight

You're following directions properly when you do things in the right order. If you're not sure what the right order is, ask your teacher or supervisor. Read the following scenarios and, in your notebook, write down the letters that indicate the order in which you think the tasks should be done.

1. You work in a small coffee shop. Your supervisor has told you that attending to patrons and making sure that they're comfortable must always be your first priority. The various jobs you do in the coffee shop involve:

    a) Clearing and wiping tables.
    b) Sweeping the floor and mopping up spills.
    c) Serving glasses of water to customers when they first sit down.
    d) Replacing placemats and cutlery.
    e) Refilling napkin and condiment containers.
    f) Regrouping chairs and tables as necessary.

    You've just had an extremely busy lunch hour. All of your tables are now dirty, and you're busy cleaning up a sticky spill on the floor. Suddenly, a group of ten people comes in, wanting to sit together. In what order would you carry out your tasks? Explain why.

2. You work in a clothing store. The owner has told you that the customer always comes first. Your work involves:

    a) Helping customers to find the items they want.
    b) Working on the cash desk.
    c) Directing customers to the fitting rooms.
    d) Keeping shelves stocked with merchandise.
    e) Recording new stock as it arrives.
    f) Keeping the store neat and tidy.

    One day, while you're busy with a customer, new stock is delivered and left in the main store area instead of in the stockroom. Just as you're about to move it, start updating your records, and refilling some of the almost-empty shelves, a customer asks you where to find a certain size of a garment and if it's possible to try it on. At the same time, another customer rushes up, saying, ''I'm in a terrible hurry. Will you please take the money for this purchase right away?'' In what order would you carry out your tasks? Explain why.

3. You are the customer. You're ordering a meal in a fast-food restaurant. Your server has to:

    a) Take your order.
    b) Obtain your food and drink.
    c) Take your money for the meal.
    d) Provide ketchup and vinegar.
    e) Inform the customer of reasons for any delay.
    f) Check on the progress of food preparation.

    You order a hamburger, French fries, and a glass of milk. Your server notices that all of the pre-prepared hamburgers have been used during the lunchtime rush, but figures more are probably being prepared. Some fries are ready, so he puts them in a container and puts the container on your tray. He then pours milk from the milk dispenser and places it on your tray. He leans against the counter, waiting for the hamburger.

    After a while, you hear one of the cooks call, "Any more burgers needed? We can start on them now." Your server announces that you have ordered one. Several minutes later, the hamburger is ready. Your server now adds up your order and asks for the money. You pay, take several steps away from the counter, and are stopped by the server calling, "Oh, 'scuse me, but do you need ketchup and vinegar?"

    As the customer, in what order would you have preferred that your server carry out his tasks?

4. You have part-time work in an office. You assist your supervisor by:

    a) Keying letters and memos.
    b) Keeping files up to date.
    c) Delivering interoffice materials and packages.
    d) Sending out external mail.
    e) Operating the photocopier.
    f) Operating the fax machine.

Your supervisor will be in a meeting all day and has left you some notes about the work that must be done today. The instructions include:

▶ Key the handwritten letters in the attached folder. Sign them for me and make sure they get out in the last mail pick-up at 4 p.m.

▶ Key the memo to Ms. Lum. She'll need the information in this memo in order to write a letter that must go out today.

▶ Send the attached fax to our Vancouver branch. It must arrive there first thing this morning (don't forget the time difference—it's three hours earlier there).

▶ Do the big photocopying job that you'll find on my desk. It'll probably take a couple of hours. Good thing we have the automatic multi-page photocopier, right?

▶ There are two documents regarding the Baron Corporation somewhere in the pile of filing that I've left on your desk. They and the rest of the file will be needed for a meeting tomorrow morning. The rest of the pile can be filed any time.

In your notebook, write down the order in which you'd do these tasks. Explain why.

Figure 13.1 Calendar for Activity 5

OCTOBER						
SUNDAY	MONDAY	TUESDAY	WEDNESDAY	THURSDAY	FRIDAY	SATURDAY
	1 Coffee machine this week: Vida. Thanksgiving Charity Drive all week: 12-1p.m. daily-cafeteria. Come and donate your time.	2 New employees' orientation meeting 9-10am.	3	4 Accounting Dept. meeting 3-4pm.	5	6
7	8 Holiday THANKSGIVING DAY	9 Coffee machine this week: Les	10 Community Blood Donor Clinic: Please plan to attend. 12-2p.m.	11	12 All-employees meeting to demonstrate new telephone system: 10-11a.m.	13
14	15 Coffee machine: Baldeo	16 Farewell party for Ann Sava at 4:30 in the cafeteria. Wine + cheese	17	18 Employee Job Appraisal meetings to be held all day in the boardroom	19	20
21	22 Managers' meeting: 9-12 Coffee machine: Carla	23	24 New security system goes into effect. Before 7a.m. and after 6p.m. every day, use front doors only.	25	26 Warehouse closes at 2p.m. for inventory.	27
28	29 Coffee machine: Hank	30	31 Halloween Lunch presented by the Social Club, 12p.m. All invited. $3.50 each. HALLOWEEN			

ACTIVITY 5

Calendar Exercise

Figure 13.1 on the previous page shows a calendar in an office. It tells employees when various events are happening. Read the notes on the calendar and answer the questions below.

1. What is the date and time of the Accounting Department meeting?
2. Wing Yan arrived to work at the Thanksgiving Charity Drive at 2 p.m. on Monday. Did she come in at the right time?
3. What time should Joe go to the farewell party for Ann?
4. Who is in charge of the coffee machine during the second week?
5. At 6:10 p.m. on October 29, Kaaydah left the building. How should she have left?
6. What must Social Club members do before lunchtime on October 31 ?
7. By when should the employees be ready for their job appraisals?
8. If Ann's dad comes on October 26 at 3 p.m. to pick up an order from the warehouse, will he be able to get it?
9. What type of meeting should all new employees attend? When?
10. If Len wants to attend the Blood Donor Clinic, when should he go?
11. When do employees have a long weekend?
12. Should employees be at the information meeting regarding the new telephone system first thing in the morning?

Getting Along with Supervisors

It's important to have a good working relationship with your supervisor. Your work environment will be pleasanter and you'll have a greater sense of satisfaction in your work if you get along well with the people in authority.

ACTIVITY 6

Problems with Supervisors

Read the following scenarios and note the words in boldface that describe a supervisor's actions or attitude. Note also how the employee responded to the supervisor in each case. In your notebook, write your opinion of whether the supervisor's actions were acceptable or unacceptable, and whether the employee made an acceptable or an unacceptable response to the supervisor. In each case, explain your opinion. If you feel that the actions or attitudes of either person were unacceptable, state what you think the other person should have done.

1. Vida worked at a food concession at a busy convention centre. She enjoyed working with the public and took pride in being efficient and cheerful. Her supervisor **never complimented her, however, but always seemed to be pointing out what Vida should do next.** Vida would promptly start on the next task, but began

to wonder if she was doing her job as well as she should or could.

Once the convention season was in full swing, another person was hired to work in the booth. Vida noticed that **the supervisor gave the other person the task of serving most of the time, while Vida was told to keep the area clean and make sure that there were always plenty of supplies.** Vida felt that the supervisor was playing favourites and that her skills weren't being used properly. She wondered if she should discuss the situation with the supervisor, but never got around to doing so.

Eventually, Vida became resentful and put less and less effort into her work. **The supervisor told her that her work was unsatisfactory, but didn't explain in what way.** Vida became angry, and quit.

Months later, after being unable to find other employment, Vida wondered if there might have been some other way to resolve her difficulties with her supervisor.

2. Les had always had a good working relationship with the supervisor of the warehouse where he worked. **His supervisor gave him a variety of tasks to do, to find out what Les did best,** and Les did well at each task.

One day, the supervisor told Les that a new shipping procedure was going to be used in the warehouse. **She didn't have time to explain it very well, but said that she was sure that Les would "pick it up quickly."**

Les felt a little nervous about the new procedure. There were other people who knew how it worked, but Les didn't bother to ask them, figuring it would all work out all right.

A short time later, **Les's supervisor angrily called Les into her office.** An important order for which Les was responsible had gone astray. The mistake would probably cost the company a lot of money.

"You're the one who's stupid," Les told his supervisor. "How can you expect me to do the job when you don't explain it to me? The mistake is your fault!"

Being Trustworthy

Trustworthiness—being dependable, reliable, and honest—is another very important trait, whether at work, in school, at home, or with friends and acquaintances.

Rating Others' Trustworthiness

If you're trustworthy, your employer can depend on you to do your work, even when the supervisor isn't watching you. In your notebook, describe what you think would be the most trustworthy thing to do in each of the following situations.

1. Mario's employer always found it easier to pay Mario cash, since Mario didn't work many hours and his shifts varied. One day, Mario realized that he had been overpaid. He told a friend, and the friend's opinion was, "You might as well keep the extra money.

   "It's cash, so your boss won't have a record of it. Besides, he can afford it." What should Mario do?

2. Reba's supervisor often sends her out of the office on errands. Reba enjoys the chance to get out. Lately, she's started to go into stores and look around while out on errands. She hurries to do the errands to give herself extra time to shop. She feels that she isn't doing anything wrong, particularly since her supervisor has never said anything about how long the errands have taken.

3. Jack works in a small variety store. One day, a customer comes in and buys a number of items. When Jack has finished adding up the various prices, the customer asks, "Did you charge me the sale price for the facial tissues?" Jack hadn't realized that the tissues were on sale. If he changes the price now, he'll have to write out a "Void" slip for the store owner. This will take time, and several customers are waiting in line. It's possible that the customer won't check her sales slip—he could even "forget" to put it into her bag. What should Jack do?

ACTIVITY 8

Rating Your Own Trustworthiness

When someone trusts you, that person expects to be able to count on your behaving in a certain way. This puts a certain responsibility on you. If you behave in a trustworthy manner, employers will respect you and will probably give you greater responsibility.

In your notebook, make two columns, one headed "Yes" and the other "No." In whichever column best represents your reaction to each of the following statements, write the number of the statement.

1. At work, I try to give good value for my wages.
2. I always do what's expected of me at work.
3. I work hard and take longer breaks than I should only when I know it won't affect anyone.
4. I speak well of my employer when I'm away from work.
5. I believe in being truthful, so I let everyone know that my employer is a jerk.
6. I take good care of my employer's equipment and supplies.
7. If I break something, I admit that I did it.
8. If I break something that I know I couldn't afford to replace, I keep quiet about it.
9. When my supervisor gives me more money than is necessary to buy juice and muffins for a meeting, I always return the extra money.
10. If my supervisor asks me to do something that isn't part of my job, I cheerfully do it.
11. When quitting time comes, I quit, regardless of the work I've left unfinished.
12. I always tell new employees about everything I think is wrong with the company.

Questions

1. Take a look at your results. In which areas could you improve?
2. Have you ever been in a situation that you found hard to deal with honestly? Try to come up with suggestions on different ways in which this situation could have been dealt with honestly and comfortably.

Professionalism

Being professional at work means more than doing your work competently. Professionalism, which means demonstrating the habits and attitudes of a professional, involves having a personal code of ethics in relation to work attendance and punctuality, dependability, loyalty, self-control, gossip, personal appearance, and maintenance of work equipment and work area.

Being at Work—And On Time

As discussed in Chapter 11, punctuality and being at work when you're supposed to be are very important. Even if you don't have to sign in or punch a clock, being even a few minutes late is not professional and is actually cheating your employer. And staying away from work because you partied too well the night before is also a betrayal of your employer's trust.

Dependability

A true professional takes responsibility for properly completing all projects and tasks that have been assigned. Making up excuses for failure or blaming someone else for it are not acceptable behaviours. If you have a problem with some aspect of your work, speak to your supervisor and ask for help or guidance.

Loyalty

Don't tell outsiders any information that your company might consider to be confidential. Don't bad-mouth your company or your supervisor to outsiders or co-workers. If you have a lot of complaints, perhaps it's time you looked for other work.

Self-Control

Having self-control means more than just avoiding tears or outbursts of anger at work. It also means keeping your mind on your work and not letting your personal life infringe on your work life. Try to arrange to make and receive as few personal telephone calls as possible. Don't discuss your personal problems with anyone at work or spend valuable time broadcasting details about what a great or miserable weekend you had.

Gossip

Always remember that there's a big difference between facts and gossip. If someone is gossiping to you, ask yourself: "Why is this person telling me this?" "Should I trust a person who gossips?" "Would I like to be the subject of such gossip?" Gossiping takes time and thought away from work. Also, if you're the gossiper and the rumour proves to be untrue, your trustworthiness will always be in question. Look for ways to compliment other people and to speak well of them. Always heed the old saying: "If you can't say anything nice, don't say anything at all."

Personal Appearance

As discussed in Chapter 11, you should dress appropriately for work but always be as clean and tidy as possible. Your appearance affects the way in which your supervisor, co-workers, and clients or customers react to you. Many studies have shown that people tend to judge other people's personal qualities and characteristics based on their clothing and grooming. People are more likely to respect and trust a well-groomed, neatly dressed person.

Be aware that personal image is negatively affected by the use of bad grammar and too much slang or street language, as well as by mannerisms such as chewing gum, cracking knuckles, fussing too much with hair, and coughing or sneezing without covering the mouth.

Equipment and Work Area Maintenance

The importance of properly caring for company equipment and maintaining a tidy work area were discussed in Chapter 12. Besides the major items of concern, you should also think of the little things. For example, if you occasionally have to eat your lunch at your desk or workbench, dispose of the remains carefully. Your co-workers wouldn't appreciate smelling your tuna sandwich all afternoon! Also, avoid overpersonalizing your work area with photos, clippings, knick-knacks, etc.

Chapter Summary Exercises

1. What does the word *attitude* mean?
2. What are the benefits of having a positive attitude?
3. Should you work hard, even when you're not being supervised? Explain your answer.
4. How can you demonstrate a positive attitude when you're receiving an order?
5. Why is it important to receive criticism with a positive attitude?
6. What positive attitudes are required to co-operate with others?
7. Describe in detail a work situation in which trustworthiness is required.

8. Why is it important to demonstrate to your employer that you're a reliable worker?
9. a) Discuss how personal beliefs and attitudes affect decision making.
   b) Determine what attitudes are needed for career success.
   c) Explain how honesty and integrity of co-workers affect work performance.

Reflective Journal

1. Are you an optimist or a pessimist? What personality traits do you possess that make you one or the other?
2. Do you control your temper? Describe some techniques you use to keep your temper under control. What are your impressions of people who don't control their temper?
3. Why is it important to respect other people's opinions?

Chapter 14

Assertiveness Is Not a Bad Word

After completing this chapter you should be able to:

- ▶ Describe the characteristics of assertive, aggressive, and passive people.
- ▶ Act assertively, (without being overbearing).
- ▶ Accept and give criticism constructively.

introduction People want to feel as if they have some control over their lives, and to make their own choices. Some people, however, spend most of their time trying to be "nice," no matter how they *really* feel inside. Others react aggressively to almost every situation, demanding that things go their way. Happily, there's a middle road that doesn't involve being "good" or being "bad." People have the choice to be assertive.

Assertive, aggressive, or passive?

Assertive people:

- ▶ Are confident and certain of their likes and dislikes.
- ▶ Honestly express their feelings without being rude or unpleasant.
- ▶ Choose for themselves what they want to do or not do, based on their values.
- ▶ Allow and encourage others to achieve their goals.
- ▶ Respect themselves and others.
- ▶ Understand and like themselves.
- ▶ Avoid behaviour that makes them feel helpless, depressed, or dissatisfied, but don't do things that infringe on the rights of others.

So, assertive people are well-balanced and know how to achieve happiness and success without hurting anyone else in the process. Aggressive people, however:

- ▶ Achieve their own ends at the expense of others.
- ▶ Express their feelings without thought for the sensitivities of others.
- ▶ Impose their opinions and choices on others.
- ▶ Think only of themselves and their desires.

- Have no respect for other people.
- Always think that they're right and everyone else is wrong.

Just as unbalanced, but in the opposite direction, are passive people, who:

- Have a poor sense of their own self-worth; are always putting themselves down.
- Don't express their real feelings even though they often feel hurt and anxious; are afraid people won't like them if they do.
- Allow others to make choices for them, so they seldom get what they want; look to others to solve their problems or tell them what to do.
- Feel that they're always wrong and others are always right.
- Are often disappointed because other people don't live up to their expectations.
- Are often taken advantage of by aggressive people, who identify the weakness of passive people.

Case Study

Read the following case studies and then explain how each person could behave assertively in the situations described.

1. Diane works in a small department of about 12 people. A colleague decided that it would be a treat for someone who was having a birthday to be taken out for lunch by everyone else. The group has gone out a couple of times, and Diane is feeling quite uncomfortable about it. When they go, the entire department is left unstaffed, and, being "celebrations," the lunches are always extended well beyond the regular lunch hour. Diane has heard irritated comments from others in the company who have been unable to contact people at those times. As well, although Diane doesn't dislike any of her colleagues, she isn't close to all of them and wouldn't necessarily choose to go out to lunch with them, nor does she feel comfortable being "treated" by them on her birthday. Occasionally, there are two birthdays in a week, and neither Diane's budget nor her workload can cope with two long, pricey lunches.

2. Paul works in an office that enjoys considerable after-hours social contact. One of the supervisors is very outgoing and sociable and likes to organize get-togethers after work, either at his home or at a local restaurant. Paul sometimes doesn't feel like going but finds it difficult to say no, particularly since he knows that the rest of the group will take the opportunity to indulge in a little gossip about any non-attenders. Paul would prefer to spend his leisure time with his own friends and not participate in the office "intrigue."

3. After the high school prom there's going to be a party where Corey expects there will be drinking. He's anxious to go to the party because all of his friends will be there. After talking to his date, Dana, about the party, he doesn't know what to do. Dana

would like to please Corey but she doesn't want to go because she's afraid they might have to get a ride home with someone who has been drinking.

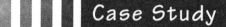

Case Study

Study the following list of common characteristics of aggressive people. Then read each case study and identify which person should learn to be more assertive. Aggressive people:

- ▶ Manipulate others to achieve their own ends.
- ▶ Want things done their way.
- ▶ Often speak without thinking.
- ▶ Know it all.
- ▶ Are very critical of other people.
- ▶ Demand a lot of attention from others.

1. Susan's company held an information meeting to inform staff about a reorganization of offices, staff, and work stations. Susan was surprised to learn that she is *not* being assigned a partially enclosed, private work station much coveted by everyone, and close to those for whom Susan works. Instead she will be in an open area that will be somewhat inconvenient for her work. Susan realizes that Michelle has for some time been planting ideas in the minds of the supervisors responsible for the reorganization. By exaggerating some facts and ignoring those that wouldn't work to her advantage, Michelle has persuaded the supervisors that she really ought to have the enclosed area.

2. Yasif and Steven have worked part-time as clerks in a sporting goods store for more than a year. Part of their wage is based on commissions. When a customer comes in who looks fairly well off, Yasif makes sure that he serves that person.

3. The staff in Olivia's department has a weekly meeting to keep everyone up to date and to make sure that work is divided equitably and efficiently. Danny has worked in that department a long time and the supervisor tends to listen to his ideas and suggestions, of which he has many. Olivia is new to the office, but she can see that things could be done more efficiently. She also sees that it's important to Danny that things be done his way.

4. Janet and Marna share an apartment. Janet is the better cook so she usually cooks supper on week nights. Marna does the cleaning up but resents it. Hoping that Janet will realize she hates cleaning up, Marna has started leaving a few dishes unwashed in the sink.

5. Asma has her own freelance business. A year ago, she did a small job for a company that she hoped would become a good client. Her contact at the company didn't pass along any complaints about the work she did, but she hasn't had any other work, and she feels that the contact person is trying to avoid her.

6. Midori has had a job at a popcorn store at the mall for three months. She usually enjoys her work, but lately she's started to

feel uncomfortable around the assistant manager, Mark. He often calls her into the back for no good reason and then asks her personal questions, which she tries to avoid answering. Mark has offered to drive her home a few times, but she always refuses. Midori doesn't want to have anything to do with him. She just wants to get through her shifts without incident when he is on duty.

Making Criticism Work for You

The word *criticize* can mean to judge, appraise, assess, evaluate, estimate, examine, analyse, survey, and comment on. It also can mean to attack, disapprove, find fault with, shoot down, condemn, denounce, blame, censure, reprove, reproach, take exception to, take offence.

As you can see from these possible synonyms, not all of the actions described would lead to good communication. Some of the inappropriate, negative actions are used by aggressive people in criticizing other people's ways of doing things. To be able to accept and give criticism in an assertive and constructive way, however, are important skills that can help to smooth the process of working and living with other people.

To have good relationships at work it's essential to have good communication. As an employee, you're part of an organization that has goals. A supervisor might criticize your actions when he or she thinks that a change in these would assist the organization to achieve its goals. The giving and taking of constructive criticism require care and much thought if the result is to be of benefit to the people involved and to the organization.

Who criticizes you now? Perhaps it feels as though many people do but that there are only certain people from whom you will accept criticism without feeling hurt. At work you'll have to learn to accept criticism from your supervisor and co-workers, and you must be aware that criticism doesn't need to bring anger or hurt. A suggestion for improvement should be welcomed.

Criticism and putdowns are not the same thing. If you're feeling unsure of yourself, however, you might interpret any critical comment as an attempt to belittle you. Constructive criticism, however, can help you to be better at the work you do, and is offered with caring, respect, and a genuine desire to help. Everyone has different strengths, weaknesses, and perceptions. You can profit from the experience and skills of others if you're willing to listen to different ideas and suggestions.

Nobody enjoys being criticized, but we can't expect to be able to please everyone all of the time, and we all have something to learn. If you interpret every comment as an unfair criticism or if you believe that any criticism you receive is proof of your worthlessness, you're setting yourself up to feel upset.

At work you'll be with people of different ages, backgrounds, and levels of experience. Sometimes people disagree and sometimes people make mistakes. No one is perfect all the time. Taking and giving constructive criticism well is a skill that can avoid unnecessary conflict in the workplace, at school, and at home. The following are some guidelines for accepting and giving criticism constructively.

Accepting Criticism Constructively

1. It helps to remember that neither you nor anyone else is perfect, so everyone deserves criticism at least some of the time.
2. It's often very difficult for the person who is criticizing you. He or she might feel uncomfortable and worried about hurting your feelings. If you keep in mind that constructive criticism will help you to grow and improve in your work, you could make it easier for the other person to help you. For example, you could demonstrate by means of your body language and facial expression that you are prepared to listen positively.
3. Looking as though you're listening is important, but you must also *hear* what is being said to you. Ask questions if you need to clarify certain aspects. Repeat the criticism in your own words so that both you and the other person know that you understand.
4. Try to put yourself in the other person's shoes. How would you feel about your performance if you were in her or his position? What does this person (or the organization) require from you that you are not providing?

Giving Criticism Constructively

Listening to criticism requires certain attitudes, but giving criticism requires skills as well. The following guidelines should help.

1. Give some forethought to the person and the task. Your goal is to contribute to the organization by helping the individual develop in his or her position. Ask yourself whether you're being too critical or not critical enough. When a person is in a new position, you might need to help him or her understand the "big picture"—how that work fits into the company program and how the details fit into the work. If the person understands the scope of the work, the details will have more meaning and are more likely to be attended to.
2. Try to understand from the other person's point of view why she or he is doing the work in a way you consider to be faulty. Has the person understood completely what is expected? Does she or he believe that the work is actually being done correctly and efficiently? Give the individual an opportunity to explain. For example, rather than saying, "This isn't the way you're supposed to do this," you might say, "I wondered why you chose to do it this way."
3. Explain why the work must be done in the manner you require, letting the person know that other ways might well be acceptable, but this is the most efficient way anyone has identified so far.

4. End the discussion on a positive note, taking into account the positive aspects of the person's work skills and accomplishments. Be sincere. Most people can tell when you're saying something positive just to be "nice." Make sure that, when you see improvement in the person's performance, you remark on it to the individual concerned.

Case Study

Read each of the following case studies and imagine that you are the person's supervisor. In your notebook, write a brief description of how you, as the supervisor, would handle each situation.

1. Naomi is a member of the support staff in a busy office. Several individuals count on her for her computer skills and her knowledge of where everything is. She also takes calls from other departments when staff in her area is away. Sometimes, her work takes her away from her desk. She might go to the warehouse, to the departmental supply room, to accounting, to marketing, and even out of the office on specific errands. Often, she forgets to let anyone know where she is or how long she expects to be away.

2. Dana, a publisher's representative, shares the services of a support staff member with several others. When Dana is going to be away from the office on a business trip, she often leaves notes for the support staff regarding work that is to be done or calls that might come in while she's away. She tends to write in short form and often the support staff member can't decipher her handwriting and ends up interrupting the work of others while they all try to figure out Dana's writing.

3. Everyone likes Nick. He has a great sense of humour. He's a great hit at company social events, and he can make the most boring meetings enjoyable. More importantly, he is able to defuse tense moments with his humour, helping life around the office to run more smoothly. His supervisor has noticed that lately he seems to spend more time kibbitzing than working.

4. Juri works irregular hours, sometimes leaving at the same time as everyone else but sometimes much later. He often forgets to punch out when he leaves, and his supervisor can't be sure how many hours he has worked.

Chapter Summary Exercises

Put yourself in the following situations and suggest assertive ways of dealing with them.

1. You'd like to buy two bananas, but all of them are priced and packaged in large quantities.

2. Two weeks ago someone borrowed some money from you. The person has not returned the money, and this week you are low on cash.

3. It's ten o'clock on a Saturday night. Your neighbour telephones you and says, "You're coming over. We're having a party." You're tired and you want to go to bed.

4. Someone pushes ahead of you in a movie line.

5. A car cuts in front of you on the highway.

6. A colleague at work keeps asking you to carry out tasks that you think would be more appropriate for her to do.

7. You and a supervisor sometimes work late. When everyone else has left, she often smokes, although your office is a smoke-free building.

8. Your best friend cancels a planned outing for a reason you don't think is very valid.

9. Your family is trying to deal with a crisis. Family members keep telephoning you at work to discuss the crisis.

10. The coffee area at work has been left in a mess again!

11. Your neighbours are playing music so loud that you're getting a headache.

12. You're presenting some information to a group of colleagues at a meeting. The person with whom you worked to gather the information keeps interrupting you.

13. Someone is giving you information that you think was given to that person in confidence.

14. A colleague often whistles popular tunes quietly while she works. It drives you crazy.

15. You work with two friends who both have higher paying jobs than yours. The three of you go out for lunch, sometimes two or three times a week. They like to go to an expensive restaurant.

16. You're invited to a reception. You go to the reception and you don't know anyone.

17. You receive your bill at a restaurant. You're disappointed with the quality of the food and displeased with the service.

18. A friend has planned a surprise party for a mutual friend. You know the friend will feel uncomfortable at being surprised.

19. At a social gathering you're cornered by someone who's boring you.

20. Provide an example of your own.

Reflective Journal

1. Have you been criticized at work? How did you react to the criticism? If the experience was negative, describe how you could have made it more positive by modifying your response.

Chapter 15

Handling Anger

objectives

After completing this chapter you should be able to:

- ▶ Accept that everyone becomes angry sometimes.
- ▶ Understand the negative consequences of insulting or belittling people.
- ▶ Handle anger in a positive manner.
- ▶ Recognize situations in which an apology is advisable.
- ▶ Take steps to diffuse anger.

introduction

Everyone becomes angry sometimes. It can happen anytime, anywhere. Your roommate left the apartment in a mess again and anger wells up inside you. Someone says something you think is unfair and you feel angry. A passing bus splashes you, or a co-worker is rude and unco-operative. Some days everything seems to go wrong and you feel anger and frustration building inside you.

Even if you're usually good-natured, you'll sometimes become angry when things don't go well at work or at home. It's normal to have both negative and positive feelings. Anger isn't something to fear or ignore: it's a signal that something is wrong. Analysis of the situation that's making you angry usually clarifies how a particular problem can be solved. It's necessary to handle anger constructively and to deal with others' anger toward us. In this way, we can control our feelings instead of having them control us.

While anger is a natural reaction to some situations, if it gets out of control or is kept inside, anger can be dangerous and destructive. Displays of uncontrolled anger toward other people can lead to hurt feelings and damaged relationships, or even to violence.

On the other hand, if we don't express our feelings when something upsets us, the anger simmers deep inside us. It doesn't just go away. This is called *repressed anger* and can actually lead to physical and mental illness, including high blood pressure, tension, and depression.

Prevention is always better than a cure for this very powerful emotion. The best prevention is open and direct communication with other people. This helps in avoiding the misunderstandings and hurt feelings that can cause anger.

Do you feel that you're being treated unfairly? Do you think you're getting less than you deserve? Are you being misunderstood? What's your style for resolving life's conflicts? Do you shout it out or do you grin and bear it?

positive ways to deal with anger

1. **Identify the real source of your anger.** Ask yourself the following questions.

   ▶ What is the real issue here?
   ▶ What is it about the situation that makes me angry?
   ▶ What do I want to change?
   ▶ What do I want to accomplish?
   ▶ What are the things I will or won't do?
   ▶ Am I trying to control or change a person who doesn't want to change?

2. **Control yourself.** Erupting in anger might clear the air in some relationships, but you wouldn't want to do this at work. Use some control techniques, such as silently counting to ten. Postpone getting angry. Take time to sort your thoughts out. If you do have an angry outburst, apologize and admit that you should have controlled yourself.

3. **Appreciate the fact that everyone is different.** No two people see a situation the same way and rarely is one person totally right or totally wrong. Different perspectives and ways of reacting are not necessarily wrong. Arguing about what's "right" won't resolve the conflict. It's pointless to tell someone what they should feel or think; they have a right to their own feelings and thoughts.

4. **Recognize that each person is responsible for his or her own behaviour and feelings.** No matter what the situation, it's not the other person's fault that you're angry. You *choose* to react with anger, so don't blame other people for how *you* feel.

5. **Show respect for yourself and for the other person.** Blaming, preaching, lecturing, and ridiculing won't resolve anything. Make it clear that you value the other person and simply want to clear up a specific problem.

6. **Listen to what the other person is saying.** Are you really trying to understand that person's point of view? Or are you just hearing what you want to hear?

7. **State your feelings calmly and clearly.** Use the word "I" often as you explain your feelings: "I think...," "I'm afraid...," "I want..." Saying "You did..." or "You are..." makes your statements accusatory, and could make the situation worse. Remember, we are responsible for our feelings; the other person is not making us be angry. Also, saying something like "Everyone thinks you're..." doesn't help either. Speak for yourself.

8. **Avoid gossip.** If you're angry with someone, tell that person, not everyone else. Avoid getting other people involved with your problems. Talking over a problem with a responsible person might help you to feel better, but you still must resolve your problem with the person involved in it. If you're angry with someone, that's the person you should tell.

9. **Offer suggestions to resolve the conflict.** Let the person know specifically what you want. You can't expect other people to know what you want if you make vague requests.

avoiding negative reactions

Insulting or belittling the other person when we're angry might offer some satisfaction at the moment but always creates new problems. We might feel guilty or embarrassed later, the other person probably feels resentful, onlookers might be negatively impressed, and nothing has been accomplished in solving the problem. The consequences of such a reaction can be short-term or long-term and can be direct or indirect.

If a person reacts to an insult with another insult, the typical result is an argument that no one can win. Nothing is resolved and things are said that might be regretted later.

In a work situation, the after-effects of an unresolved argument can be very disruptive. The "wronged" individual might be unwilling to work and co-operate with the other party, affecting the quality and quantity of work produced. Gossip and attempted sabotage of the other person's work are also possibilities.

ACTIVITY 1

Handling Anger Negatively

The following are negative ways of handling anger. In your notebook list two ways in which each response could make life more difficult for you or for other people.

1. Insult the other person.
2. Control your anger with the person involved but take it out on your family.
3. Control your anger, walk away, and try to forget the problem.
4. Say nothing but use as many indirect ways as you can think of to let others know you are displeased.

ACTIVITY 2

How Do You Handle Your Anger?

Write the following statements in your notebook, completing each with the word or phrase that best describes how you usually react. If none of the items describes your reaction, add your own description.

1. When I'm angry I usually:
   a) Yell.
   b) Sulk.
   c) Explain what's wrong.

   Immediately I feel:
   (emotion)
   a) Guilty.
   b) Relieved.
   c) Powerful.

   Later I feel:
   a) Foolish.
   b) Content.
   c) Guilty.

2. Last time I was angry I:
   (behaviour)
   a) Yelled.
   b) Sulked.
   c) Explained what was wrong.

   Immediately I felt:
   (emotion)
   a) Guilty.
   b) Relieved.
   c) Powerful.

Later I felt: a) Foolish.
(emotion) b) Content.
  c) Guilty.

3. How does your teacher or supervisor react when he or she becomes angry?
4. How does your parent or guardian handle her or his anger?
5. How does your best friend handle his or her anger?

apologizing

An apology is defined as "an acknowledgment of some fault, injury, or insult, with an expression of regret and a plea for pardon." So an apology has two elements:

1. Admitting that we are at fault.
2. Asking for forgiveness.

An apology can be an excellent way to reduce stress and to deal with a situation that makes us angry. Everyone makes mistakes from time to time and a simple apology can heal hurt feelings.

Whatever the situation, we have to face the consequences of our actions. We add to the stress if we try to defend inappropriate behaviour. Such defence can result in even more stressful emotional levels, exaggeration, and even lying, perhaps making the situation worse and definitely making it more difficult to apologize. It is far easier to admit our weaknesses or errors, apologize, and correct the situation immediately.

On the other hand, if you find yourself always apologizing, that too can signal a problem. Take a look at the situations and why you're apologizing so often. Perhaps you have trouble areas that you could work to improve. On the other hand, you might be apologizing too often for situations that aren't your fault. Talking to a parent, teacher, co-worker, or supervisor might help you to figure out what is wrong and to find a solution.

ACTIVITY 3

Analysing Apologies

1. Think of some apologies that you have heard in the last few days. Write down an example. Did the person sound sincere? Did the apology seem to clear the air?
2. Do you have different ways of apologizing to different people?
3. How do you feel when someone says "I'm sorry" to you?
4. How do you react to an apology?
5. What do you say to the person who is apologizing?
6. In each of the following situations, an apology is in order. With a classmate, role-play each situation twice, so that each of you has the opportunity to play the apologizer. Write down ahead of time what you will say.
   a) You promised to telephone a friend and you didn't.
   b) You use the last bit of milk in the carton at work for your coffee and then realize that it belonged to someone who had brought it from home.
   c) You promised to have your part of a project ready by the deadline, but you haven't completed it.

responses to anger

Sometimes when we're angry we respond in an apologetic manner and don't express our real feelings. We hide our hurt and disappointment and do nothing to solve the basic problem. Then again, sometimes we erupt in anger at another person and don't give that person a chance to respond. We condemn or insult the person, perhaps unfairly, or blow the whole incident out of proportion.

The sensible, positive way to handle anger is to express calmly and clearly how we feel and what is making us feel that way. Then we should specify what we would like changed and motivate the person to make that change. The motivation could be either positive (an explanation of how the change would improve the situation) or negative (a warning of the possible consequences if the change is not effected).

Case Study

Read the following case studies and choose what you think would be the best response in each case. Give reasons for your choice.

1. Carmela and Ramesh are members of the office social committee. They are planning to go shopping for the upcoming children's Christmas party and will be allowed an extended lunch hour to buy gifts and edible treats for the party. Erin, also a member of the social committee, has given a lot of thought to the kinds of gifts they might buy and is looking forward to sharing her ideas and buying the gifts. They make tentative plans to go out the following Wednesday at 11:45. Erin's department has a weekly meeting on Wednesdays which usually ends at 11:30. When Erin isn't out at 12:15, Carmela and Ramesh leave, feeling that time is getting too short for them to try to organize the expedition for another day that will suit all three of them. On their return, Erin is waiting for them and is angry because they went without her. Which of the following reactions would indicate that Erin handled her anger in a positive manner? Explain your answer.

    a) You could have waited for me. You two always leave me out of things. I don't feel as though I'm really a part of this committee. We didn't set a definite time to leave, and you must have known I really wanted to go. I can never depend on you to keep your word.

    b) I'm sorry you ended up waiting for me for so long. I was disappointed that I didn't get to go with you, but I can understand that you couldn't afford to wait any longer and that it might have been difficult to set up another day for us to go.

    c) I'm really disappointed. I wanted to go shopping with you, and I thought we'd agreed that we'd go after my meeting. My part in the meeting was over, anyway, and I could have left if I'd known you were leaving then. Next time, maybe you could let me know before you leave or maybe we should make more definite plans in future.

2. Luisa fell and broke her left wrist. It wasn't a bad break, and she was back at work two days later, struggling with an unwieldy cast and feeling somewhat sheepish. A few months later, Lidy fell and broke her right wrist. It was a bad break and she had to stay home for three weeks until the wrist has healed to the point where she could drive again. Luisa saw a card from Lidy on the company bulletin board, thanking everyone for the flowers she had received from the social club. Luisa was angry because she hadn't received any flowers when she broke her wrist. What would be the probable results if Luisa handled her anger in each of the following ways?

   a) She says nothing about that particular incident but she tells the company administrative assistant that she no longer wishes to be part of the social club and does not want the $2/month deducted from her pay. From now on, she will not participate in any of the social committee-sponsored barbecues, pizza lunches, Christmas parties, or other endeavours to brighten life in the office.

   b) She marches down to the administrative assistant and, in front of several other people, yells at her that she plays favourites and that she shouldn't have responsibility for any decisions regarding money collected from social club members.

   c) During discussion about other matters with the administrative assistant, she quietly mentions that, although she realizes it's a small matter, she was a little upset that she didn't receive flowers under what appeared to be the same circumstances as Lidey's, and wondered why she hadn't been treated the same.

3. Ruta's company is moving to a new building. New furniture is being ordered and all staff have had an opportunity to look at catalogues and make suggestions about desks and chairs that will be purchased for their use. Ruta has been busy getting ready for an important out-of-town presentation and, while she knows the types of chairs she does and doesn't like, she hasn't given any specific information to anyone. When she returns from her presentation, she finds that the order for new furniture has been placed. Angus, the person responsible for placing the order in Ruta's department, has ordered the type of chair that most other people have requested. It is exactly what Ruta would *not* want. How should she handle the situation? Explain your answer.

   a) How could you be so stupid! Didn't you look at the chair I have now? I need extra support for my back and this is the only type of chair that provides it. I'm going to go out and buy a special back support cushion, and *you* can explain the expense to the company accountant.

   b) Ruta says nothing, but, after the move to the new building, she takes every opportunity to complain to all and sundry of her terrible back pain and how inconsiderate it was of the company to purchase these particular chairs.

   c) I'm upset that you went ahead and ordered that chair for me. I tend to have back problems and I really need one similar to the one I've been using. I know I didn't get back to you after I looked at the catalogues, but I was just so busy. I could have used a reminder.

guidelines for diffusing anger

1. Postpone showing your anger. Remember to count to ten before saying anything. Once you're able to put it off, you'll have learned control.
2. Keep an "anger journal," recording the time, place, and frequency of the occasions when you get angry. This might help you determine the real cause of your anger. The next step is to discuss ways of eliminating the cause.
3. Don't *expect* other people to behave in certain ways. Remind yourself that other people have a right to behave in whatever way they choose.
4. Be aware of how you sound to others.
5. After an angry outburst, apologize for your lack of control and try to discuss the matter calmly and constructively.
6. Learn to tolerate things you might dislike.
7. Be kind to yourself. Don't burden yourself with self-destructive anger.
8. Keep in mind that expressing anger in a positive way is better than storing it up.

Chapter Summary Exercises

1. List five ways of diffusing anger.
2. Why is it a good idea to make apologies?
3. What are the dangers of insulting or belittling people?
4. When you are angry with someone and you want to correct the situation, what are four good rules to follow?
5. Describe the importance of personal qualities as they relate to employability (e.g., handling anger, promptness, getting along with others, dependability).

Reflective Journal

1. Describe a situation from your experience in which you became very angry. What caused your anger? Did it have negative effects on anyone else? Did you lose control? Do you regret having done so?
2. If you could replay the situation you described above, how would you handle it differently?

Chapter 16

Learning to Listen/Listening to Learn

<table>
<tr><td>objectives</td><td>After completing this chapter you should be able to:

▶ Explain why listening involves more than hearing.
▶ Describe the listening process.
▶ List ways in which you can be a better listener.
▶ Define non-verbal cues (including body language) and recognize your own and those of others.
▶ Use your improved listening skills on the telephone.
▶ Handle business telephone calls efficiently.</td></tr>
</table>

introduction

Listening is a skill that involves more than just *hearing* what others are saying. The three basic components of the listening process are:

▶ Understanding the message that is sent to the brain.
▶ Evaluating the information the brain has received.
▶ Reacting or responding to what has been heard.

Interestingly enough:

▶ We absorb only 25 percent of what we hear.
▶ About 45 percent of our waking time is spent listening.
▶ People speak at the rate of approximately 100 words per minute, while the brain is capable of absorbing some 600 words per minute.

In a classroom, a teacher once asked a daydreaming student if he had trouble hearing. He replied, "No ma'am, I have trouble listening." Hearing is simply the receiving of sounds, a physical perception, while listening is a mental activity. Listening requires concentration, co-operation, and an open mind.

You might be listening in order to learn how to do a task, to help you make a decision, or to achieve friendly relations with other people. But in every case, it's important to get beneath the surface of what the speaker is saying.

To do that you must listen with more than your ears. You need to be alert to tone of voice, facial expressions, gestures, and body posture. These verbal and non-verbal messages supply added information that will help you to grasp the speaker's full meaning.

Good listening habits are an important ingredient for success. If you practise careful listening, you'll become more efficient in your work, more knowledgeable, and more able to get along with people. You'll understand and remember the information and points of view that you hear. Responsible, patient listening is a rare skill, but it can be developed.

what is listening?

1. The ear is focussed by the mind on sounds.
2. According to some psychologists, minds are always listening, detecting, and selecting sounds on which to focus.
3. The purpose of listening is to recreate in the mind of the listener the information that is presented by the speaker.

For our purpose, the listening process can be described in four steps:

▶ Attention
▶ Reception
▶ Perception
▶ Examination

Paying full *attention* to a person who is speaking is probably the most important part of the listening process. If you don't do this, the other parts of the process are ineffective. Attention is an all-or-nothing proposition—there is no such thing as "divided attention." You're either paying attention or you're not.

Attention is conditioned by many factors, some of which are motivation, mood, and situation. The importance to you of what is being said is the motivation. If you really care, you'll listen carefully. If not, your attention will probably wander.

Mood, of course, means how you feel at the time. If you're upset about something, you won't be able to concentrate as much as you should on what's being said.

The situation also affects your ability to concentrate. If you're in a distracting situation, your attention is bound to wander from the speaker.

Reception, or hearing, is the receiving stage of listening. Visual cues (facial expressions, gestures, nodding) are very important to the listening process.

Perception means seeing in the mind. Perception also involves word recognition and association with past experience.

Examination involves the interpretation of the sounds being received. Who is speaking? How is that person feeling? What is the person saying?

Many people don't realize that they have listening problems. When they do stop to think about what happens when they don't listen, they manage to identify quite a few habits (mostly variations on "I was thinking of something else") that interfere with their listening. The following are some that have been mentioned.

▶ I have a tendency to be too concerned with how people see me.
▶ I don't listen things out; I jump in before the other person has finished speaking.
▶ My mind wanders to things I think are more relevant.
▶ When I'm bored as I listen, I fantasize, do my own thing, or am critical of what's going on.
▶ Sometimes I stop listening when I become more interested in the speaker's physical features than in what the person is saying.

▶ When the subject is of personal interest, I anticipate and wait for the other person to stop so I can defend my idea. If I become impatient, I interrupt.
▶ I'm thinking ahead to what I'll say next.

ACTIVITY 1

How Well Do *You* Listen?

Review the explanations given above about why people don't listen. To increase your awareness of the ways in which *you* listen, answer the following questions.

1. When you're bored with what's going on in a discussion or meeting, how do you usually listen?
2. When you want to start a good working relationship with a person of whom you are in awe, how do you listen?
3. Your supervisor asks you to do something that you're uncertain about being able to do well. You also want to hide the fact that you feel inadequate. How effectively do you think you would listen in this situation? Explain your answer.

effective listening

Employees have to do a lot of listening at work. Being able to listen to directions from your customers, employer, and other employees is very important, so companies want employees who are good listeners. Good listeners get the job done correctly the first time. The efficiency of many businesses could be doubled if only their employees knew how to listen well.

By listening in a courteous and attentive manner, you create a positive image of yourself and of your company. This calls for active listening: you must not only concentrate on what is being said but also watch for the visual cues that tell you how the speaker feels about what he or she is saying. Active listening will show your supervisor, co-workers, and customers that you care.

Listening is one of the most necessary but least understood communication skills. Since you've been listening all your life, you might be unaware that some improvement is necessary. The following are some techniques that will help you to become a better listener.

1. Look at the person who is talking. This will help you to concentrate on what is being said, and you'll be able to watch for visual cues.
2. Demonstrate that you're listening. The speaker can't be sure of this unless you respond in some way, such as appropriate facial expressions (a smile) or gestures (such as nodding your head).
3. Remain aware of your and the speaker's body language, the visual cues that often say more than words. If you're nodding your head in agreement but thinking, "What an idiot!" this *could* show on your face or in some involuntary movement. Watch the speaker for the same type of signal. A customer might swear that she or he had paid the bill, but not be able to look you in the eye while speaking. This should alert you to a possible problem, although you would investigate carefully before following through on your hunch!

4. Avoid interrupting the speaker. Hear him or her out to make sure that you understand exactly what is being said. This will lessen the chance of negative feelings due to misunderstanding. Save your questions until the speaker is finished.
5. When the speaker has finished, ask clear, concise questions about anything you didn't understand. Listen carefully, and take notes if necessary. Then repeat the instructions or information to ensure that you understood it.

ACTIVITY 2

Good and Bad Listening Habits

The following is a list of good and bad listening habits. Write the items in your notebook, then beside each write *G* if you think it's a good habit or *B* if you think it's a bad one.

1. Interrupts.
2. Changes the subject.
3. Repeats some of the things said.
4. Asks questions when the speaker is finished.
5. Rushes the other person.
6. Looks at the speaker.
7. Finishes the speaker's sentences.
8. Does not give responses.
9. Pays close attention.
10. Has a wandering gaze.
11. Does not interrupt.
12. Is impatient.
13. Jumps to conclusions.
14. Shows sympathy.
15. Reacts with a nod or smile.

Now think about *your* listening habits and list areas in which you feel you could improve.

ACTIVITY 3

Listening Interview

To learn what others think about listening habits, ask a person you know well to give you three or more characteristics of a good listener. Ask the same person for three characteristics of a poor listener. Prepare a brief report on the interview results.

ACTIVITY 4

Analysing Others' Listening Habits

Observe the listening habits of two of your classmates or co-workers, then write down your observations of whether they:

1. Look directly at people who are speaking to them.
2. Respond in some way to the speaker.
3. Use only positive body language.
4. Allow the speaker to finish, uninterrupted.
5. Ask questions or repeat the information to make sure they've understood.

Listening Reports

During the next full day of school or work, use some time during your breaks to keep a log of two conversations or listening experiences that you have. Complete a report for each listening experience, summarizing the conversation. You don't need to repeat the conversation word for word or detail who said what. Just briefly describe the conversation as it flowed from one topic to another. You might want to record it in the form of a list. Record the date of each conversation, the location where the conversation took place, who was speaking, and then your summary of what was said.

The Wordless Game

Write the topics listed below on twelve slips of paper, fold the slips so that the statements are not visible, and mix them together. The "speaker" should draw a slip and attempt to communicate the message on it without using words or sounds. The listener's job is to guess which statement the speaker is trying to convey. The listener does not have to give the statement word for word.

1. Come on. Let's get going, we're late.
2. Sh! We don't want anybody to hear us.
3. I don't know. I'm undecided.
4. I'm really hungry. Let's eat.
5. I'm fed up with this whole deal.
6. I'm so sleepy I can hardly keep my eyes open.
7. Look over there!
8. Stop what you're doing and follow me.
9. Did you say something? I can't hear you.
10. This whole thing bores me. I wish I could leave.
11. I'm broke. Can you lend me some money?
12. You and I should talk.

It's Not What You Say, It's How You Say It

The tone of voice that a person uses to express a thought can alter or even completely change the meaning of words. Read each of the following statements several times out loud, changing the tone of your voice each time. Discuss with your classmates the different meanings that are conveyed each time.

1. Yeah, sure, you can borrow my car. Do you know how to start it? It's kind of tricky. Just give it a little bit of gas, not too much, until the engine starts running smoothly. Don't try to drive away until the engine's warm. No, really, I trust you. Go ahead. Here are the keys.
2. I'm sorry I'm late, but I just can't seem to get everything done. I work all day, and then I have to rush home and do practically another whole day's work. I really envy those people who can go home and relax. I'm not complaining, but there's just nobody but me to keep things going.

3. Oh, you're sick, huh? Gee, that's too bad. Well, I guess we'll just have to go on without you. Maybe you can go another time. We'll miss you.
4. Yes, I feel sure we'll be able to meet the deadline. It doesn't give us much time, but I'm sure we can do it. I don't see any major problems that could cause delays. Yes, I think we're okay.

ACTIVITY 8

Non-Verbal Cues (Body Language)

Non-verbal cues are a very important part of the listening process. You must be aware of the type of cues that you use when listening to another person; otherwise, you'll be sending negative messages, no matter what you actually say. In this exercise, put yourself in the place of a person who is speaking and observing the non-verbal cues of a listener. Write each item in your notebook and then, beside each item, write the letter *P* if you think you would interpret this as a positive cue, and the letter *N* if the cue would strike you as being negative.

1. Raises an eyebrow.
2. Smiles.
3. Nods head.
4. Sits forward in chair.
5. Remains silent.
6. Frowns.
7. Looks away from the speaker.
8. Rolls eyes.
9. Relaxes body posture.
10. Touches you.
11. Stiffens body posture.
12. Moves away slightly.
13. Stays absolutely still.
14. Fidgets.
15. Looks at the floor.
16. Lets head almost touch shoulder.
17. Looks delighted.
18. Scowls.
19. Shakes head.
20. Slumps in chair.
21. Folds arms across chest.
22. Looks at the ceiling.
23. Narrows eyes.
24. Stretches.
25. Moves closer.
26. Looks disapproving.
27. Looks straight at you.
28. Drums fingers.
29. Shrugs shoulders.

Handling Telehphone Calls

You set the mood of an entire conversation the moment you speak into a telephone. Just as your smile brings a smile to the face of others—your voice can spark the interest and enthusiasm of your listener. Your voice can compel, persuade, convince, invite confidence—all vital advantages in the business world.

With good telephone manners you can expect good business relations. With proper use of your telephone, you can increase your efficiency and that of your firm. Modern business practices demand that firms create a favourable impression on the customer. The art of getting good results by telephone involves dealing with others as you would have them deal with you.

Telephone Skills

1. ### BEGINNING THE CALL

    ▶ Use the *four answering courtesies*:
    - Greet the caller.
    - State your company (or department).
    - Introduce yourself.
    - Offer your help.
    ▶ Be enthusiastic when you answer.
    - Make the caller feel very welcomed.
    ▶ Use friendly phrases as part of your greeting.
    ▶ Remember to *smile* as you pick up the receiver.

2. ### EFFECTIVE LISTENING

    ▶ Customers usually have three types of expression:
    - Make statements.
    - Offer objections.
    - Ask questions.
    ▶ If you do not listen closely, three things could happen:
    - You will hear what you *want* to hear.
    - You will hear what you *expect* to hear.
    - You will not know how to respond appropriately.

For example: "Your prices are a little higher than I thought they would be" is obviously not just a statement of fact; it's an expression of concern, bordering on complaint. Answering, "Yes, you're right. They *are* high" won't do you or your company any good. Appreciating what the customer is really saying will help you to make a more appropriate response such as, "For the quality and service we provide, I think you'll find that our prices are not out of line" or "You can purchase these items more cheaply elsewhere, but we guarantee our product, so it's worth paying a little extra."

3. ### HOW TO ASK QUESTIONS
At the beginning of most calls you need to know what your caller wants, so you should use *open questions*.

> Open questions begin with:
> *How? Why? When? Who? What? Where?*
> For example: How often does that happen?
> What did you do before the problem began?
> Who is responsible for your orders?
> When did the package arrive?
> Later, when all you need is a *yes* or *no*, use *closed questions*.
> Closed questions begin with:
> *Did? Can? Have? Do? Is? Will? Would?*
> For example: Did you call them?
> Do you have your copy of the bill?
> Have you received your refund?
> Will you attend our seminar?
> May I do that for you?

4. STATEMENTS TO AVOID

Always be careful about the type of information you give over the telephone. Keep in mind that the person at the other end of the telephone knows nothing about the inner workings of your company, and your snippets of information may give a very wrong impression. For example, suppose your supervisor is having a very hectic day. At 2:45, she tells you she is going out to pick up a sandwich to eat at her desk. At 2:58, you answer her phone and say, "Oh she isn't back from lunch yet." Instead of realizing, as you do, that your supervisor has been terribly busy all day, the caller thinks she is relaxing over an excessively long lunch. What kind of impression does this give?

ACTIVITY 9

Giving Appropriate Information

Restate the following statements to reflect correct telephone skills.

a) I'm sorry. Mrs. Ashfield is still at lunch.
b) I don't know where he is, may I take your number and have him call you?
c) I think she is still having coffee. I'll have her call you.
d) She is in the middle of a big customer problem. Would you like to leave a message.
e) He is at the doctor's office.
f) She went home early.
g) I'm sorry, Ms. Sato has not come in yet.
h) Our service department takes forever to answer the phone.

5. CLOSING THE CONVERSATION
You should:

- Thank the customer for calling.
- Let the customer know you appreciate his or her business.
- Provide assurance that any promises will be kept.
- Leave the customer with a positive feeling.
- Let the customer hang up first.

ACTIVITY 10

Customer Perception

Rate the following statements "Good" or "Poor" as if you were the customer.

a) Good morning, Widget Factory, Joan speaking, how may I help you?
b) Sorry that's not my job. You will have to call the order processing department.
c) Good morning, Widget Factory.
d) Mrs. Laver is out. Any message?
e) Thanks for your order.
f) I don't work in that department so I don't know anything about it.
g) Good morning, customer service.
h) I really don't know why our service person didn't return your call. Did you try calling again?

i) I'm sorry it took so long to get back to you. I'm sure we can solve your problem with this call. Now, how may I help you?

j) Ms. Little I'm sorry you received the wrong material but I wrote the order down just as you gave it to me.

voice communication

Your own communication system:

a) Speak distinctly and directly into the mouthpiece.
b) Answer promptly and identify yourself.
c) If you leave the phone, excuse yourself and hurry back.
d) Answer another person's telephone as politely as you answer your own.
e) Before putting a call on hold, ask if you can do so and, if there's time, explain why.
f) Leave a message when you leave your telephone.
g) Hang up gently.
h) Keep pad and pencil handy.

A Champion's Checklist:

When using the telephone, I know how to:

1. Handle the telephone and use all of its features.
2. Extend courtesy on every call.
3. Address the caller.
4. Transmit a positive attitude.
5. Answer calls using four courtesies.
6. Listen to distinguish what response is appropriate.
7. Ask questions. (Use open and closed questions appropriately.)
8. Avoid using statements that will create the wrong customer perception.
9. Speak clearly and distinctly.

---

effective use of the telephone to gain an interview

Consider the following:

1. The employer is not sitting at his or her desk waiting for applicants to call. You work through key people such as the receptionist, assistants, or secretaries when trying to reach the employer. (They are also the people you greet politely with a smile when you first step through the office door!)
   - They know the employer's schedule.
   - They know when the employer will be able to take a call or return messages.
   - They know if the employer is out of town for several days and whether someone else will be doing the interview.
   - Their job is to 'screen' calls and facilitate the employer's daily agenda.

2. If the company does not have voice mail, messages are usually recorded on message forms. When you phone an employer who is busy; and you are asked if there is a message, be sure to leave one. Say "Would you please give Ms. Gamit the message, Margaret Campbell, a co-op student at Oakland Secondary called." Even if you are not asked if there is a message you must ask to leave one. You want it on the record that you called so it is known you were not negligent or forgetful.

2. The onus is *not* on the employer to phone you; it is the other way around. Hence say, "Could you suggest the best time for me to reach Ms. Gamit?"

3. You need telephone practice in order to gain confidence:
   - SMILE even before dialling.
   - IDENTIFY yourself: "This is Margaret Campbell. I am a Co-op Ed student."
   - STATE PURPOSE of your call: "Ms. Gamit was expecting my call. I would like to arrange a convenient time to be interviewed by her."
   - Determine the BEST TIME to call back: "Could you advise me when it would be best for me to call back?"
   - CALL BACK PROMPTLY at the time suggested.
   - Start the above process over again on your call back.

ACTIVITY 11

Telephone Skills—Assignment

Calling for an Interview

As a practice for telephoning for an interview, write a list of things you want to ask and to say when you make your call. You will be practising these skills with a partner in class. Your list should include the following:

1. Asking for your contact by name (Dr., Ms., Mrs., Miss, Mr. Ng).
2. Introducing yourself and explaining who you are.
3. Confirming the days and hours during the week that you are available.
4. Establishing a date, time, and place for the interview.
5. Thanking the contact for taking the time to talk to you and developing a statement about "looking forward to meeting with you on _____ at _____" to confirm the interview.

Interview Information for the Workplace Employer (contact)

As a workplace employer in the practice session, you will need to establish what business you are representing, how you will respond, and the questions you want to ask before you start the practice telephone call. Please consider the following:

1. Your initial response to the student.
2. Information regarding the student's career interest that you wish to ask.
3. Information you need to know about available hours.
4. Confirming the interview date, time, place.
5. Closure.

ACTIVITY 12 → **Telephone Skills—Feedback**

Rate the following skills (your teacher will provide a form). Discuss the rating with your partner. Give the sheet to the person you rated. Use ratings *Good*, *Fair*, or *Need Improvement*.
Voice - Clear, Cheerful, Friendly, Confident.
Content - Opening, Questions Asked, Answers, Closure.

taking telephone messages

For a complete telephone message, the following information should be recorded:

1. Name of the person called (enunciate names clearly).
2. Name of the caller and his or her company (spell out names if in doubt).
3. Caller's telephone number and extension number, area code if necessary, e.g., Toronto (repeat numbers for accuracy).
4. The caller's city and province (if long distance).
5. The message.
6. The action requested and promised.
7. The date and hour of the call.
8. Name of the person who recorded the message.

Following is a typical message form:

MESSAGE FOR

M _____

WHILE YOU WERE OUT

M _____

OF _____

PHONE NO. _____

TELEPHONED		RETURNED YOUR CALL	
CALLED TO SEE YOU		PLEASE CALL	
WANTS TO SEE YOU		WILL CALL AGAIN	

MESSAGE: _____

_____

_____

_____

_____

DATE _____ TIME _____

RECEIVED BY _____

Figure 16.1
Telephone message form

messages on answering machines and voice mail

As our communication system becomes more automated, a new set of communication skills must evolve. Following are suggestions on both leaving messages and replying to messages on answering machines and voice mail.

1. At the start of every message and reply, identify yourself by name and telephone number, time and date of call, as well as subject of the call. For example: "Hello, Ms. Sairsingh. This is Jackie Krysa at 321-1212. It is 2:15 p.m. Friday, November 24th and I'm calling about an opening in your sales department."
2. Think ahead. Compose your message or reply before commencing your call. Be specific.
3. Be brief. Consider the listener's busy schedule.
4. After identifying yourself and stating the subject of the call, immediately state your request. Many callers skip through long messages and your request could be missed. For example: "I am very interested in working in your sales department and would like to set up a time for an interview. I am available both Monday and Tuesday. If these days are inconvenient for you please call me at 321-1212 so we can find an acceptable day for both of us. If I have not heard from you in two or three days, I will call again. Thank you."

telephone directory

Part of your telephone skills includes making full use of your telephone directory. Most directories have four main sections:

Introductory Pages:

1. Emergency Numbers Page
2. Customer Services
3. Free Calling Areas
4. Types of Long Distance Calls and Rates
5. Direct Distance Dialling
6. Area Codes and Time Zones

Alphabetical Listing:

1. Names are listed alphabetically.
2. Business firms containing the name of an individual are usually alphabetized by the surname. For example, Henderson James Sales Inc. (James Henderson Sales Inc.)

Government Listings:

These pages, usually blue, follow the white pages and provide listings for federal, provincial, and municipal government services.

Yellow Pages:

In larger cities, the Yellow Pages may be a separate publication from the White Pages. Whether it's a separate publication or part of a single volume, there is an index of headings at the beginning of the Yellow Pages. Names of business firms are listed alphabetically under the appropriate heading.

 **Using Your Directory**

Use your local telephone directories to solve the following problems:

1. Find the address of the nearest copy shop.
2. Locate the nearest doctor.
3. Obtain the name and telephone number of the nearest restaurant.
4. Given the name of the local business that sells office furniture, find its telephone number in the Yellow Pages.
5. Given the address, only, of a local printer, find the correct telephone number.
6. Given the address and only part of the name of the trucking firm, locate its telephone number and supply the entire business name.
7. Locate "Government" and "City" listings.

Chapter Summary Exercises

1. Demonstrate the importance of effective listening skills, study habits, test–taking skills and learning skills.
2. Why are excellent telephone techniques essential?
3. In your notebook, copy the following sentences, supplying the missing word or phrase.

   a. When others really listen to me I feel _____.
   b. When I want to show that I'm really listening to others I _____.
   c. One of my family members provides the non-verbal cue of _____ to show that he or she is really listening.
   d. I think good listeners make friends easily because _____.
   e. The most difficult time I have in listening to others is _____.
   f. The communication in my family could be improved if I would _____.
   g. What I definitely will do this week to improve my communication skills is _____.
   h. When I answer the telephone at work, I am _____ my employer.
   i. I will always take time to be _____ when handling telephone calls.
   j. Five important things to remember when taking telephone calls are _____.
   k. Five suggestions to remember when leaving or replying to a message on an answering machine or voice mail are _____.

Reflective Journal

1. What non-verbal cues do you use? You may not be aware of them all. Ask someone who knows you well to look over the list on page 179 and point out the cues he or she has observed you using. Are there any surprises for you? Are all of your cues positive? Make lists of the positive and negative non-verbal cues you use.

2. Has a misunderstanding ever sparked an argument between you and someone else?
   Describe the incident. What mixed messages did you or the other person receive?

Chapter 17

Handling Stress in the Workplace

objectives	After completing this chapter you should be able to:

- ▶ Define the word *stress*.
- ▶ Explain how stress can be good as well as bad.
- ▶ Analyse your own level of stress.
- ▶ Use stress management techniques.
- ▶ Recognize situations in which stress can work for *you*.

introduction

Some stress in our lives is essential and desirable. It helps to keep us alert, stimulated, and interested in what we are doing. Without some stress, life would be boring. Coping with life's stressful demands positively is a challenge and can result in personal growth and increased competence.

Too much stress, however—too many demands, for too long a time—can cause problems. The businessperson who worries continually about work problems while at home or about home problems while at work, the employee who dislikes his or her work but makes no effort to find a better situation, and the student who studies all day and works after school and on weekends, are all subjecting themselves to continuous stress. Unless such stress is handled properly, physical or even mental illness could result.

One of the main challenges today is learning how to deal with stress. Stress has been defined as the response of the body to any demand put or made on it. Anything and everything is a possible source of stress: waking up, deciding what you're going to wear, catching a bus, playing hockey, writing an exam, starting in a new work situation, getting married, moving to a new home, meeting a deadline, driving a car.

It's our response to events and not the events themselves that determines whether the stress will have a positive or negative effect on us. Our goal shouldn't be to eliminate stress from our lives, but to make it work for us. Stress is a natural result of almost all activity. We must accept this fact and learn to recognize the danger signals that we are under more stress than we can tolerate. We must then try to identify the factor that is causing the unhealthy level of stress, in order to eliminate it, or find some way to make the situation less stressful. In some cases, assertiveness and handling anger positively can reduce stress, as discussed in earlier chapters. Other effective stress management techniques include relaxation, physical exercise, and good sleeping and eating habits.

reaction to stress

In the 1930s, the late Dr. Hans Selye of Montreal, president of the International Institute of Stress, defined stress as the "non-specific response of the body to any demand made upon it." In other words, it is the body's initial reaction to any change it has to deal with.

Dr. Walter B. Canon, a noted Harvard professor of physiology, called the body's response to a stressful stimulus the "flight or fight response." This response prepares us for action in the same way it did our predecessors in the Stone Age. When confronted with danger, people in early civilizations would either stand and fight or flee a life-threatening enemy. Either way, the stressful situation was soon resolved and the people could go back to their everyday ways of functioning.

Today, we're confronted with quite a different set of circumstances. Many situations can't be dealt with head-on and then forgotten. Where do we run or with whom do we fight when dealing with increasing crime or inflation rates? And if we're not able to fight them and there's no place to flee, how do we get rid of the pressures caused by such situations?

The answer to this question is stress management. If we're unsuccessful in our efforts to cope with stress, we burn ourselves out—our "energy battery" runs low. The overload on our body systems exhausts us and makes us vulnerable to such physical ailments as hypertension, heart disease, ulcers, gastrointestinal problems, asthma, arthritis, cancer, and migraine headaches. These are enemies that are every bit as ferocious as any wild animal faced by Stone Age people.

Stress is a great equalizer. It does not discriminate against age, gender, race, colour, creed, or socio-economic standing. All of us experience at least occasional overdoses of tension and stress in our lives.

ACTIVITY 1

Do You Have a Stress-Prone Personality?

Rate yourself based on how you typically react in each of the situations listed below. There are no right or wrong answers. Write down the situation numbers in your notebook and then, beside each number, write the number from the following key that best represents your reaction. Then total your score and consult the scale at the end of the exercise.

3 = Frequently   2 = Sometimes   1 = Never

1. Do you try to do as much as possible in the least amount of time?
2. Do you become impatient with delays or interruptions?
3. Do you always have to win at games to enjoy yourself?
4. Do you find yourself speeding up to beat a red light?
5. Do you hesitate to ask for help with problems?
6. Do you constantly seek the respect and admiration of others?
7. Are you overly critical of the way others do their work?
8. Do you have the habit of looking at your watch or clock often?
9. Do you constantly strive to better your position and achievements?
10. Do you spread yourself "too thin" in terms of your time?

11. Do you have the habit of doing more than one thing at a time?
12. Do you frequently get angry or irritable?
13. Do you have little time for hobbies or time by yourself?
14. Do you have a tendency to talk quickly or hurry conversations?
15. Do you consider yourself hard-driving?
16. Do your friends or relatives consider you hard-driving?
17. Do you have a tendency to get involved in many projects at the same time?
18. Do you have a lot of deadlines at school or in your work?
19. Do you feel vaguely guilty if you relax and do nothing during your leisure time?
20. Do you take on too many responsibilities?

Stress-Prone Personality Scale

Score:

20–30: Individual tends to be non-productive. Life lacks stimulation.

31–50: A good balance exists between the ability to handle and control stress.

51–60: Individual is bordering on becoming excessively tense.

If you're in the higher score categories, it's recommended that you reduce the stress level in your life by taking some of the steps described earlier in this chapter.

what causes stress?

Some events known to be stressful include:

▶ Death in the family.
▶ Divorce or marital separation.
▶ Personal injury or illness.
▶ Changes in work responsibilities.
▶ Trouble with members of the family.
▶ Change in working hours.
▶ Change in working place.
▶ Change in school.
▶ Change in personal habits.
▶ Work you dislike.
▶ Spending time with people who make you feel uncomfortable.
▶ A problem child or a troubled relationship.
▶ Feeling torn between what you want to do and what others expect you to do.
▶ A schedule that doesn't leave any time for you to relax and act naturally.

Stress has been blamed for a lot of things: headaches, heart disease, obesity, drug addiction, high blood pressure, strokes, ulcers, and many other ailments. Stress is not caused by stressful events, however, but by a person's response to these events.

You can't always control what happens to you, but you *can* control your response to what happens. A stressful event for one person is not necessarily stressful for another. If you respond with fear or anger to an event, stress will take its toll. If you can use constructively the energy that you would have used being angry or fearful, maybe you can turn the situation around.

People experience stress when they feel powerless, alienated, or threatened. To combat a feeling of powerlessness, a person needs to take control by:

- ▶ Analysing the situation. Don't take things at face value.
- ▶ Believing and acting as if you can influence the situation.
- ▶ Thinking about how to turn the situation to your advantage.
- ▶ Learning the difference between situations and people that you can change and those that cannot be changed.
- ▶ Developing options and showing initiative.
- ▶ Learning to say "No."

A feeling of alienation, of feeling alone or cut off from other people, can be overcome by making a commitment to use and develop your skills, to reach goals that you set for yourself. Sitting around feeling sorry for yourself achieves nothing.

If situations appear to be threatening, as in the case of changes in your personal, school, or work life, treat the situations as challenges, not threats. After all, change is normal; lack of change means that no growth is occurring. If you treat change as a challenge, it becomes a stimulant to performance, not an upset in your life. And, of course, not all changes are for the worse. Think it through.

Life is demanding, but it's also interesting and challenging. Gain comfort and confidence from your ability to cope.

ACTIVITY 2

Stress In My Life

List six factors that have caused stress in your life. For each, explain how you reacted.

coping with stress

Exercise is an excellent way of coping with stress. When you're feeling stressed, take several slow, deep breaths; go for a walk; ride a bicycle; take part in a sport; or try yoga. When the muscles in your neck and arms begin to relax, you'll start to feel better.

You can also work off tension by taking up a hobby. Don't just watch television—do something you enjoy that takes your mind off stressful situations.

A technique called imagery can also be effective. Think about how you want a situation to turn out and then concentrate on the positive aspects. For instance, you could rehearse in your mind a work interview and concentrate on how well you'll behave, how calm you'll be, and what a good impression you'll make. Positive imagery is like a positive attitude. It pays off in increased confidence.

The level of stress that can be tolerated differs from person to person. For some people, high levels of stress are the spice of life. Through personal experience, they've developed successful ways of coping with stress and using it to their benefit. Usually these people view unexpected events as challenges rather than threats; they're in control of their lives.

The following are some stress management techniques to help cope with stress at school or at work.

1. When you have a break, get some exercise (take a walk, climb some stairs, etc.).
2. If possible, switch your tasks around, rotating stressful ones with ones that are easier to do.
3. When possible, share your workload if you're handling too much. Asking for assistance doesn't mean you're incompetent but rather that you're a concerned employee who wants to meet company requirements and deadlines.
4. Discuss your workload with your teacher or supervisor. Outline what you feel you can reasonably handle and suggest alternatives for getting the rest of the work done. Agree on a workable arrangement.
5. Concentrate on the positive aspects of school or work: the hours, the people, the physical environment, the atmosphere, the actual work you're doing, the type of company, the opportunities for promotion, or the chances for self-improvement.
6. Give yourself pep talks. Counter each negative thought with a positive response: "I'm not a failure; I've succeeded at many things"; "I'll be as prepared as I can be under the circumstances."
7. Avoid comparing yourself to others; recognize your capabilities and limitations. Believe in yourself—you can do it!
8. Get moral support by talking in confidence about your concerns with supportive family members and friends.
9. Recognize your limits in relation to energy and time, and set priorities.
10. Stay healthy. Build resistance through regular sleep, physical exercise, relaxation, and good eating habits.
11. Have a sense of humour. Laughter is therapeutic; it's a release from tension.
12. Live a balanced life by allotting time for work, family, and leisure.

work-related stress

If you find that you're unable to cope with certain stressful work situations after trying the various stress management techniques, you might have to take more drastic action. This could involve changing your attitude, methods, habits—or even your work! Consider some of the following alternatives:

1. *Change your expectations of work and/or of yourself.* Maybe you've had unrealistic goals and expectations. Revise or change them so you're not trying to achieve the impossible. Some of your personal needs might never be met through this work. Question yourself about your true values and needs. You might discover a gap between them and what your present work offers.
2. *Make a substantial change.* You might have to work for change within the organization, transfer to a different workplace or course, look at retraining possibilities, or look for other work.
3. *Map out possible courses of action,* taking into account the possible consequences in each case.

4. *Seek professional help.* Attend workshops or seminars that deal with work dissatisfaction or stress management. Discuss your situation with a counsellor.

5. *Take control*; make yourself happy—you're the best friend you'll ever have. If you don't like what you're doing or what's happening around you, make some changes. You're the *only* person totally responsible for your life.

ACTIVITY 3

How to Handle Stress

In each of the following cases, state what the person should do to reduce stress.

1. A co-worker criticizes Pamela for not completing an assignment on time. She thinks she *did* complete it on time.
2. Derek has been doing the same work for three years. His supervisor has often told him that he's doing a good job. Yet other workers hired after him have been promoted. He doesn't understand why he's been passed over.
3. Inga feels she's always overloaded with work. She asks herself, "Am I being given too much work, or am I too slow to handle it?"
4. Damir often argues with his co-workers. He doesn't think it's his fault. However, a friend has told Damir that his supervisor has noticed the arguing and is annoyed.
5. Tanny's supervisor in a retail clothing store criticizes her in public for not keeping her merchandise neat and orderly. Tanny is very hurt and embarrassed.
6. Kenji has been with the same company for five years. He has noticed that many workers who have been with the company three or four years are being laid off. Since his company doesn't seem to be doing much business, Kenji is worried about being out of work.

Chapter Summary Exercises

1. Should stress be eliminated from our lives? Why or why not?
2. Why can some people handle high levels of stress?
3. List some techniques that can help you to cope with stress.
4. a) Demonstrate the steps involved in resolving a conflict/stress situation.
   b) Discuss strategies for responding to and working with individuals who are under stress.

Reflective Journal

1. Give three examples of stressful situations you have experienced and how you dealt with them. Look over the stress management techniques listed on page 192. Are there any techniques that you could have used to make the stress work more positively?

UNIT 5

Safety Issues, Benefits, and Unions

introduction

Workplace safety is the responsibility of both employees and employers. In this unit you will learn what such responsibility involves. This unit also discusses the types of benefits that employees usually receive and various employer policies, in addition to the history and functions of labour unions.

Chapter 18

Work Safety Concerns

objectives	After completing this chapter you should be able to:

> ▶ Explain employers' and employees' responsibilities in relation to safety in the workplace.
> ▶ List possible safety hazards and the steps that can be taken to avoid work-related injury or illness.
> ▶ Define the term *workplace accident.*
> ▶ Explain the role of workers' compensation.
> ▶ Describe the steps required if you are to receive compensation because of a workplace accident.

introduction

Safety is defined as freedom from danger, injury, or damage, or the state of being protected against harm. Employers must provide reasonably safe working conditions, and employees must develop an awareness of safe procedures and follow the rules that promote safety. Despite good safety habits, however, accidents occasionally do happen and, when they do, it's important to know the correct procedures to follow. This chapter provides information on safety in the workplace, as well as what to do in case of workplace accidents.

occupational health and safety

Most workers across Canada are to some degree protected by laws or codes from workplace health and safety hazards. These laws and codes are administered and enacted by the federal and provincial governments and set minimum standards for health and safety in a variety of sectors, including the industrial, construction, mining, forestry, and petroleum industries. In addition to workplace health and safety laws, employees who work with materials, conditions, or equipment considered to be hazardous are covered by legislation and codes relating to these, such as pesticides, chemicals, X-rays, communicable diseases, explosives, environmental contaminants, fire hazards, and the transportation of dangerous goods.

Employers have a legal duty to conduct their operations in a manner that prevents or reduces their employees' risk of injury or loss of health. The basic elements of employee safety programs are specific health and safety policies, defined responsibilities for safety, and measures to maintain safe working conditions, such as inspections, safety training, and first aid training.

Employees themselves have a personal responsibility for carrying out safety procedures to protect themselves and their fellow workers and to wear protective clothing and equipment where this is designated. Employees must police themselves to a certain extent.

Employees are entitled to information about the health and safety hazards of their workplace and about safe performance procedures. For example, the *Workplace Hazardous Materials Information System* guarantees employees the right to know about controlled or hazardous products (usually chemicals) found in the workplace. This federal and provincial legislation, passed in 1988, requires that suppliers of hazardous materials clearly label all containers that enter the workplace, specifying any dangers or risks, precautions to be taken in handling, and first aid procedures, similar to warning labels found on some consumer products. In some cases, Material Safety Data Sheets must be provided to expand on the information on the labels. Some companies have health and safety committees that act as liaison agents between the organization and employees to gather and provide information.

As a general rule, most employees have a right by law to refuse to perform work that would endanger their or a co-worker's health and safety. These laws protect the worker from being disciplined for refusing to do such work. Some workers in some provinces, however, don't have this right, if refusal to work would endanger another person.

ACTIVITY 1

Work Safety Quiz

Write the numbers of the following statements in your notebook. Then, beside each, write the letter of the answer that you think is correct. If you don't know the answer immediately, think about each alternative and choose the one that seems to be the safest. If more than one answer seems to be correct, indicate this also.

1. Everyone should know the following about fire extinguishers:
   a) How to operate them.
   b) Which types to use on different fires.
   c) Where they're located.
   d) All of these.

2. Injuries often happen to people who:
   a) Always take chances.
   b) Commit unsafe acts.
   c) Ignore safety procedures.
   d) None of these.

3. It pays to develop:
   a) Safety consciousness.
   b) Safe habits.
   c) Safe attitudes.
   d) All of these.

4. Chemicals should be handled only:
   a) If they are labelled.
   b) If safe handling precautions are explained.
   c) If safety and health precautions are followed.
   d) All of these.

5. Safety and health information on chemicals should be available:
   a) On labels.
   b) In Material Safety Data Sheets.
   c) From your supervisor.
   d) All of these.

6. Machines should be cleaned after use:
   a) With a brush or rag.
   b) With your hand.
   c) According to instructions.
   d) None of these.

7. Your work area should always be:
   a) Cluttered.
   b) Clean and tidy.
   c) Dirty.
   d) None of these.

8. Scrap materials should be placed:
   a) On the corner of workbenches.
   b) In provided containers.
   c) On the floor near your work area.
   d) None of these.

9. Tools should always be:
   a) Left on workbenches.
   b) Left on machines.
   c) Put away when not in use.
   d) None of these.

10. Spilled chemicals should be:
    a) Left alone.
    b) Handled according to instructions on labels and/or Material Safety Data Sheets.
    c) Barricaded off.
    d) All of these.

11. Materials and parts should be:
    a) Properly stored.
    b) Stored in designated areas.
    c) Arranged so no one will trip over or brush against them.
    d) All of these.

12. On any job, always use:
    a) The tool that is handiest.
    b) The tool for the job.
    c) A knife instead of a screwdriver.
    d) None of these.

13. Tools should be kept:
    a) Where they belong.
    b) Clean.
    c) In safe working condition.
    d) All of these.

14. Dull, broken, or worn-out tools should be:
    a) Reported to your supervisor.
    b) Used.
    c) Thrown away.
    d) None of these.

15. Cutting tools should never be:
    a) Dull.
    b) Carried in your pocket.
    c) Left lying around the work area.
    d) All of these.

16. Operate a machine only when:
    a) Your supervisor is out of the room.
    b) Told to do so by your supervisor.
    c) You see others operating the same type of machine.
    d) None of these.

17. If you don't thoroughly understand some part of your job:
    a) Ask questions.
    b) Go ahead anyway.
    c) Do nothing.
    d) None of these.

18. Before starting a machine, make sure that:
    a) Long hair and loose clothing are safely tied back.
    b) All machine safety guards are operative and in place.
    c) You're wearing safety goggles or other necessary protective equipment and clothes.
    d) All of these.

19. When working with power tools:
    a) Keep your mind on your job.
    b) Turn the tools off when you've finished using them.
    c) Use them only according to instructions.
    d) All of these.

20. Never leave a machine until:
    a) The power switch is turned off.
    b) It has completely stopped running.
    c) You have cleaned up the work area around it.
    d) All of these.

21. When cleaning, oiling, adjusting, or repairing a machine, make sure:
    a) You've been fully instructed in such procedures.
    b) The power switch is turned off and the machine has completely stopped running.
    c) All safety guards and mechanisms are re-installed.
    d) All of these.

22. Wear proper safety goggles and shoes, face shields, aprons, and other personal protective equipment:
    a) When your supervisor is in the room.
    b) On all jobs that require them.
    c) Only when made to do so.
    d) All of these.

23. Before operating a machine:
    a) Remove or tuck in loose clothing. Tie back long hair.
    b) Roll up your sleeves and secure them.
    c) Remove rings, watches, and other jewellery.
    d) All of these.

24. When using a machine for a small or fast job:
    a) It's not necessary to wear protective equipment.
    b) You can rely on machine safety guards for adequate protection.
    c) You don't have to worry about loose clothing or long hair.
    d) None of these.

25. When handling rough, heavy materials:
    a) Wear gloves.
    b) Wear safety shoes.
    c) Wear a heavy apron.
    d) All of these.

26. When welding:
    a) Protection of eyes is not important.
    b) Wear goggles with the proper type, colour, or shade of lenses.
    c) Sunglasses afford adequate protection.
    d) All of these.

27. Horseplay and practical jokes:
    a) Are permissible at all times.
    b) Should be carried on when the supervisor is out of the room.
    c) Are not safety hazards.
    d) None of these.

28. Distracting your co-worker's attention for a moment:
    a) Can cause an accident.
    b) Is permissible when the supervisor is out of the room.
    c) Keeps the co-worker alert.
    d) All of these.

29. All cuts, scratches, burns, or punctures:
    a) Can become infected.
    b) Should be reported to your supervisor.
    c) Should be treated immediately.
    d) All of these.

30. If something gets in your eye:
    a) Ask a co-worker to remove it.
    b) Report it to your supervisor immediately and obtain professional first aid.
    c) Flush the eye with water.
    d) All of these.

31. Acids or caustics can be poured from their containers:
    a) Straight into another receptacle.
    b) According to instructions for safe handling.
    c) When not wearing safety goggles, gloves, or any other required protective clothing.
    d) None of these.

32. Glass tubing should be inserted into rubber stoppers using:
    a) A facial tissue.
    b) A pencil.
    c) A heavy cloth in case the tubing breaks. Safety goggles also should be worn.
    d) None of these.

33. Water should never be poured into a container of:
    a) Sulphuric or nitric acid.
    b) Any clear, colourless liquid.
    c) Dyes.
    d) All of these.

34. If an object is heavy or awkward:
    a) Ask for help.
    b) Show your strength by lifting it yourself.
    c) Complain about having to handle such objects.
    d) None of these.

35. In preparing to lift an object:
    a) Place your feet close to the load to be lifted, properly spaced for balance.
    b) Make sure your back is straight and as nearly vertical as possible.
    c) Bend your knees, squat, and grasp the object firmly.
    d) All of these.

36. To raise a load, lift by:
    a) Straightening your legs.
    b) Straightening your back.
    c) Straightening your arms.
    d) All of these.

37. To change directions while carrying an object, do it by:
    a) Twisting the trunk of your body.
    b) Changing the position of your feet.
    c) Swinging your arms.
    d) None of these.

38. In piling materials:
    a) When a pile of boxes or bags is more than one metre high, taper the pile in toward the centre.
    b) Tie boxes or bags together securely.
    c) Block in objects that might roll off the pile or make the pile collapse.
    d) All of these.

39. When handling materials, be sure to:
    a) Use available mechanical equipment.
    b) Wear gloves and safety shoes.
    c) Handle them in such a way that they will not strike someone.
    d) All of these.

40. Before attempting to lift a load with a rope sling, be sure:
    a) To examine the sling.

b) That all hooks, rings, and other fittings are properly secured in place.
c) The rope is adequate for the job.
d) All of these.

41. Before climbing a ladder, make sure that it:
    a) Provides secure footing.
    b) Is extended to its full length.
    c) Is as nearly straight up or vertical as possible.
    d) All of these.

42. In climbing a ladder:
    a) It's not necessary to use your hands.
    b) Use both hands.
    c) Use only one hand to hold on.
    d) None of these.

43. When using a ladder:
    a) Reach out from it only within safe limits.
    b) Stand on the top rung of the ladder.
    c) Reach out as far as you can to avoid having to move the ladder.
    d) None of these.

44. Ladders with damaged rails, steps, or rungs should be:
    a) Used.
    b) Used only in an emergency.
    c) Repaired or discarded.
    d) All of these.

45. When using a stepladder, first open it fully, then:
    a) It is safe to climb.
    b) Set both spreaders before climbing.
    c) Set one of the spreaders before climbing.
    d) None of these.

46. All fire hazards should be:
    a) Reported to your supervisor.
    b) Ignored.
    c) Reported to your co-workers.
    d) All of these.

47. Oil waste and rags should be:
    a) Placed in a cardboard box.
    b) Placed in a metal container.
    c) Left where they are.
    d) All of these.

48. Fire doors, aisles, fire escapes, and stairways should be:
    a) Used as storage areas.
    b) Blocked off.
    c) Kept clear.
    d) None of these.

49. Injuries happen to people who:
    a) Sometimes are innocent bystanders.
    b) Don't know safety rules.

c) Wear loose clothing around machinery.
d) All of these.

50. Your safety on the job and elsewhere can best be guaranteed by:
a) Using common sense.
b) Following all instructions carefully.
c) Reading labels on containers and Material Safety Data Sheets.
d) All of these.

Based on information from the Industrial Accident Prevention Association. Toronto, ON.

workplace accidents

Victims of workplace accidents are by law entitled to compensation and certain services. A workplace accident is one that arises from or occurs during work, resulting in injury or illness. Such accidents include injury or illness that results from sustained and unusual effort and from strenuous activities that are a regular part of the work. In addition, a workplace accident might occur during the performance of a related task that is not part of the regular work but necessary to complete a job.

The law states that if a worker suffers an accident while under the employer's control, direction, or supervision, and if the activities are part of the working conditions, the accident is a workplace accident. In line with this, the law assumes that injuries that occur in the workplace while an employee is working are occupational injuries, and the employee does not have to prove this. An employer might contest an employee's claim, but it is up to the employer to prove that the accident was not work-related. The following are some examples of possible workplace accidents.

▶ Working in the woods, a worker is cut while operating a chain-saw.
▶ A restaurant worker spills hot grease on herself and is burned.
▶ A nurse who frequently lifts and moves patients develops severe back pain; the condition is caused directly by the nurse's work.
▶ A bank teller is traumatized by a bank robbery.
▶ A warehouse worker drops a heavy object on her foot.

ten safety questions to ask your employer*

1. What are the dangers of my job?
2. Are there any other hazards (noise, chemicals, radiation) that I should know about?
3. Will I receive job safety training? When?
4. Is there any safety gear I'll be expected to wear? Will I receive training in how to use it? When?
5. Will I be trained in emergency procedures (fire, chemical spill)? When?
6. Where are fire extinguishers, first aid kits and other emergency equipment located?
7. What are my health and safety responsibilities?
8. Whom do I ask if I have a health or safety question?
9. Do you have safety meetings?
10. What do I do if I get hurt? Who is the first-aid person?

*From Workers' Compensation Board of British Columbia, Prevention Division

workers' compensation

Workers' compensation provides compensation for employees who can't work because of workplace accidents or occupational diseases. When employees are injured in the course of their work they are not penalized, but rather are compensated for their loss of income due to their inability to work.

In theory, workers' compensation covers everyone in the paid labour force; however, in each province and territory certain groups are excluded from coverage, such as, in some cases, workers in charitable organizations, real estate operations, beauty salons, and employment agencies. In many provinces, workers' compensation boards allow employers to apply for coverage of employees who would otherwise be excluded. When starting work, it would be wise to check regarding your coverage by workers' compensation.

The first workers' compensation Act was passed in Ontario in 1914 as a result of the drastic increase in the number of injured workers due to rapid economic growth and mechanization. Other provinces soon followed suit. All Canadian jurisdictions now have workers' compensation Acts that provide medical rehabilitation services as well as financial benefits.

Prior to the passing of these Acts, injured employees sometimes sued their employers for negligence. When an employee was successful in a bid for compensation, the employer was forced to pay out sometimes large sums of money in damages. On the other hand, thousands of injured employees did not go to court—they and their families were deprived of necessary income and often faced great hardship.

The impetus to start a government compensation scheme came from employees' demands for improved protection and the concern of employers about increasingly costly court settlements.

Basic Principles of Workers' Compensation

Workers' compensation legislation sets out the following provisions.

- ▶ Compensation for workplace injuries and illnesses is a guaranteed right, regardless of fault.
- ▶ Benefits are based on lost earnings and are paid for as long as the worker is disabled.
- ▶ Compensation is administered by a board that is independent of both the government and management.
- ▶ Employers pay for the entire scheme through a collective insurance system.
- ▶ Injured workers are no longer able to sue their employers for negligence.

Compensation includes:

- ▶ Medical treatment and rehabilitation.
- ▶ Vocational rehabilitation.
- ▶ Temporary and permanent disability payments.
- ▶ Survivors' benefits to spouses and dependants in the case of death due to injury. In case you're the victim of a work-related

accident or occupational disease, it's important that you be familiar with the following details.

▶ Your employer or employer's representative must be notified as soon as possible. If you are unable to do so, a co-worker, union representative, family member, or friend can do this for you.

▶ You must receive first aid quickly. If necessary, you should be taken to a physician or health care centre, and then taken home if hospitalization is not necessary. The employer is responsible for transportation expenses on the day of the accident.

▶ The compensation board must be notified of all accidents requiring health care or involving lost wages or disability beyond the day of the accident. In general, all serious accidents must be reported to the body responsible for the administration of the general occupational health and safety legislation in the particular province.

▶ The employer must record all minor accidents in a register kept for this purpose.

▶ You must provide your employer with a medical certificate if an absence from work of longer than one day is required.

▶ Your employer is not allowed to penalize you in any way because you've suffered a workplace accident or exercised a legal right.

Chapter Summary Exercises

1. List three advantages of having and following safety procedures for
   a) the employee and   b) the employer.

2. Name three safety precautions in effect at school or at work.

3. Have you noticed any unsafe conditions at school or at work? If so, list the conditions and outline steps that should be taken to remedy them.

4. List ways in which you think the following body parts can be protected at work.

   a) Arms   c) Eyes   e) Hands   g) Legs
   b) Ears   d) Feet   f) Head   h) Lungs

5. If, at your workplace, you didn't wear safety gear to protect the parts of the body listed above, what types of illness or injuries could result? Name at least two injuries for each body part.

6. In paragraph form, explain in what ways you think stress could affect workplace safety.

7. Describe how you think unsafe working conditions could increase stress.

8. List four possible safety hazards related to your work (or to the type of work you'd like to have) that could result in accidents. After each item, indicate what steps could be taken to eliminate the hazard.

9. Explain why having a clean, tidy working area is a safety precaution.
10. On arriving at work or school, you smell smoke and discover a fire that has already had a good start. List at least three things you should do immediately.
11. Explain why tools, other equipment, and materials should always be put away when not in use.
12. What safety hazards might there be in a modern office?
13. What is the correct way to lift heavy objects?
14. Describe how the work safety factor in the workplace might influence one's behaviour.

Reflective Journal

1. Describe how you feel when you have to work with someone who is careless and does not follow proper safety procedures. Use an example if you can from your work placement.
2. Have you ever taken any risks at work? Explain.
3. Have you ever known someone who has been injured on the job? Explain how this can affect not only the injured person but others as well. How did you feel when you heard about the accident? What are your feelings now?

Internet Activity

The Canadian Centre for Occupational Health and Safety (CCOHS) is the authoritative information source for management, workers, government, community, and education groups, emergency organizations, medical professionals, legal experts, OSH specialists, and individuals from all across Canada. Contact CCOHS by e-mail: custserv@ccohs.ca and ask for the organization's brochure on *A Quick Guide to Health and Safety on the Internet*. CCOHS's Home Page at http://www.ccohs.ca has direct links to over a hundred key safety resources, as well as a list of newsgroups and mailing lists with instructions on how to subscribe.

Complete a search on the Internet for information on safety concerns involving your occupation of choice, and write a short report on what you found.

Note: Internet address can change rapidly; use search tools for new locations.

Chapter 19

Employee Benefits/Employer Policies

<table>
<tr>
<td>objectives</td>
<td>

After completing this chapter you should be able to:
- ▶ Explain what employee benefits are.
- ▶ Define compulsory payroll deductions and explain what these deductions cover.
- ▶ Discuss some of the employee benefits provided by employers.
- ▶ Describe some flexible work scheduling methods.
- ▶ Explain the process of employee bonding.
- ▶ List the important company policies, rules, and procedures with which you should be familiar.
- ▶ Handle employment termination professionally if you resign and be aware of your rights if you are dismissed.

</td>
</tr>
</table>

introduction

The primary payment that employees receive for their work is the amount that appears on their paycheques, but many employers offer other benefits and services to the people they employ. These are sometimes referred to as *fringe benefits* and might include a dental plan, extended health insurance plan, allowance of sick days, pension plan, daycare plan, or paid vacation. Two work opportunities that offer equal salaries could provide you with different levels of actual return because of the benefits and services that one of the employers provides for its employees.

Employers and employees share in the cost of some of these benefits. Money is deducted from employees' paycheques to pay the cost of their contributions. The cost of similar services bought by the employee on an individual basis without the contribution of the employer naturally would be much higher. In addition, the employee would pay income tax on the full amount of income it cost to pay for the service. Usually when the employer contributes toward benefits, employees are taxed only on their own contributions toward the benefits; however, some benefits provided are taxable. This is something you should check with your employer.

Employers are obliged to make deductions not only for taxes but also for employment insurance and a government pension plan. What you receive on your paycheque is your *net* pay; the full total of what you earned is your *gross* pay.

Time-off benefits also are important to employees. Statutory holidays, vacations, sick days, and personal leave days, all with full pay, are offered by many employers.

The scheduling of work is also important to employees. The length of work time, time of day, and days of the week worked all have an effect on employees' morale and quality of life. Some employers offer their workers the opportunity to work a compressed work week, so employees might work the equivalent of five days over a period of four days, working longer hours each day and taking the fifth day off. Other employers offer flexible starting and quitting times. Some employees are obligated to work rotating shifts.

Compulsory Deductions for Benefits

Compulsory deductions from all Canadian employees' paycheques are for income tax, the Canada Pension Plan or the Quebec Pension Plan, and employment insurance, all of which are forwarded to the government by the employer. In some provinces, compulsory deductions are also made for provincial health care insurance plans.

Income Tax

The largest single deduction from employees' paycheques is for payment of income tax. Canadians have been paying income tax since 1917, when it was brought into effect as a "temporary wartime measure" by Canada's eighth prime minister, Sir Robert Borden. Today, income taxes collected by the government are used to provide many social and business support services.

Employees pay both provincial and federal income taxes. In all of the territories and provinces except Québec, which collects its own provincial taxes, both income taxes are paid to the federal government (Revenue Canada Taxation), which then passes the money on to the provinces. Self-employed people are obligated to pay income tax on a quarterly basis.

When you start a new job, your employer will have you complete a TD1 form. This form lists your expected income for the year and the names and particulars of any dependants (such as a spouse and/or children), and is used to determine the amount of income tax deduction to which you're entitled. The balance after allowable deductions is your estimated taxable income, which indicates to the employer how much tax to deduct from each pay, according to a tax table provided by Revenue Canada.

By the end of February each year, you'll receive a T4 slip from each employer for whom you worked during the previous year. The T4 slips show how much salary you were paid and how much income tax was deducted from it.

Based on the information on the T4 slips, you must complete an income tax return annually and submit it to Revenue Canada by April 30. The calculations you do on this return will tell you whether you must pay additional taxes or whether you're entitled to a refund for having overpaid your taxes.

Canada Pension Plan and Québec Pension Plan

Both the Canada Pension Plan (CPP) and the Québec Pension Plan (QPP) came into effect in 1966, and are designed to provide pensions for the retired from the earnings of people who are employed. All income-earning people, including those who are self-employed, are required to contribute to either the CPP or QPP.

Both pension plans also provide survivors' benefits (spouses' pensions, orphans' benefits, and lump-sum death benefits) and disability benefits, and payments made by both plans are adjusted on the basis of the Consumer Price Index. The Consumer Price Index (CPI) is a report prepared monthly by the government to keep track of the retail prices of goods and services in Canada, as an indication of how much it costs the average Canadian to live.

Employers and employees contribute equally to the CPP and the QPP. Changes in jobs or residences do not affect the plans in any way.

Currently, pension payments begin at age 65 and are based on a contributor's earnings, calculated in terms of the wage standards existing at the time of retirement.

Employment Insurance (EI)

The first compulsory national program to provide income during periods of unemployment came into effect in Canada in 1941 to protect workers against loss of income due to unemployment.

In 1996, the program was reorganized and renamed the Employment Insurance program in order to place emphasis on employment rather than on unemployment. Employment insurance premiums are payable by both employers and employees and these contributions are based on a certain percentage of the employee's salary, with a maximum contribution allowed per year. These contributions, subsidized by the federal government, are used to pay unemployed workers on a regular basis for a certain period of time.

To qualify for employment insurance benefits, applicants must prove that they were previously employed for a certain number of weeks. This proof is a Record of Employment form issued by their former employers.

To receive benefits, applicants must file a claim stating that they are out of work, are willing to work, and are registered at a Canada Employment Centre. Following a waiting period, individuals are eligible to receive a percentage of their previous weekly insured earnings up to a maximum amount. The length of time for which benefits will be paid varies, depending on how long a person was employed and on the national and regional unemployment rate.

Voluntary Deductions and Employer-paid Benefits

Group Life Insurance Plans

Life insurance, which provides financial protection for your survivors in case of your death, is a common employee benefit in Canada. The employer signs up for a group life insurance plan (which is cheaper than if an individual buys a plan) and pays either all or part of the premium for the employees. If the employees contribute part of the premium, a set amount is deducted from their pay. Such deductions are voluntary, since an employee can choose not to take advantage of the plan.

In many companies, employees are insured according to a formula based on the income of the insured. For example, if the formula was two times the salary, a person earning $20 000 would have a policy that would pay $40 000 to survivors on his or her death; another employee earning $30 000 would have a policy that would pay $60 000.

Group Health Insurance Plans

Provincial health care programs provide for most health care expenses but extended group health insurance programs cover those that are not. Membership in a company's group plan might be optional or compulsory, depending on the terms and conditions of the plan. Premiums are usually paid in the form of payroll deductions.

Extended health insurance plans usually reimburse part or all of the cost of prescribed medication and specific services such as ambulances, private nursing care, physiotherapy, psychotherapy, and dental care.

Short- and Long-Term Disability Plans

As discussed in the previous chapter, workers' compensation coverage that employers must carry provides for employees in cases of work-related injury or illness. In addition, most employers grant paid sick leave for employees who must miss work due to non-occupational illnesses or injuries. This sick leave is for a limited time only, however, so most employers have short- and long-term disability plans to ensure that employees are covered in case of extended health-related absences from work.

Most disability insurance plans are administered and financed by the employer. A cumulative plan allows the employee to accumulate sick leave days from year to year. A non-cumulative plan is one in which credits are not transferable from year to year.

Another arrangement is a sickness indemnity insurance plan. Premiums are paid (usually all or in part by the employer) to an outside agency or insurance company. The benefits of these plans are usually limited to a certain length of time and are preceded by a waiting period during which no payments are received by the employee, a condition that is often waived in cases of accident. The waiting period is specified because these plans are designed to pay out for longer-term disabilities and illnesses, not for short-term ones such as the flu or a cold. Usually the benefits paid are a percentage of weekly earnings. Some employees receive the benefits of a combination of sick-leave days and a sickness indemnity insurance plan.

Long-term disability plans are designed for employees who are disabled for a prolonged length of time. The payments from these plans, usually a percentage of income, are often preceded by a long waiting period. These payments are usually made only until normal retirement age is reached.

Employment Income Security

Some employees have the protection of supplemental benefits when a layoff occurs, which means that employment insurance benefits are added to by the employer from money previously paid to a special fund. As long as the fund remains solvent, participating employees are assured of an income almost equal to their working wages.

Private Pension Plans

Some employers contribute money to private pension plans for their employees, to supplement the pensions provided by the CPP or QPP. In non-contributory plans only the employer contributes to the pension. In contributory plans both the employer and the employee are required to contribute.

Private pension plans are not as flexible as the CPP or QPP, which remain in effect even if an employee changes work. Some private pension plans are terminated if an employee leaves the organization (although the money the employee invested is returned), unless the employee has what are called *vested pension rights*. Vested pension rights means that the former employee retains the benefit of any contributions that she or he made. Such rights usually come into effect after several years of service. A portability clause allows the employee's pension rights to be transferred to another employer.

Where will the money come from when your retirement arrives? Some pensions are paid out of the current income of the company. This is called an *unfunded plan*. Funded plans are funds accumulated in advance from the employer and employee. This money, plus interest, covers the cost of the pensions that the fund will be required to pay out. Private pension funds are by law administered by a trust company or by an insurance company, to ensure that employees' funds are protected if a company goes out of business and to prevent misuse of pension funds by companies.

Some private pension funds offer employees the opportunity to retire before the age of 65. Usually, however, there is a penalty in the form of reduced pension benefits, since statistically the employee will be drawing benefits for a longer period of time.

Paid Time-Off Benefits

Wages paid for time periods when an employee is not actually working are referred to as *time-off benefits*. These can include rest and meal breaks, wash-up time, sick days, personal leave days, and time off for family emergencies. Vacation length is usually based on length of service, although all employees are entitled to at least two-weeks' vacation after one year of full-time service.

The granting of leaves of absence for pregnancy, birth, adoption, extended illness, accidents, etc., is sometimes part of a company's personnel policy. Union contracts sometimes outline specific cases. These leaves are generally granted without pay.

Bonding

Bonding is a form of insurance that protects an employer against financial loss due to employee theft or misconduct. Whether the employer or the employee pays for the bond depends on the type of bond and the individual employer.

In the event of a loss due to a dishonest act by a bonded employee, the employer will be reimbursed by the insurance company that provides the bond. The bonded employee will then be required to repay the loss to the bonding company. Specific requirements and procedures for bonding will vary, depending on your circumstances, the work you'll be doing, and the policy of the company that provides the bond.

A variety of types of bonds is available, but the two types that can be obtained by individuals are *surety* and individual *fidelity* bonds. Surety bonds are most common and are often required by law for certain types of work, such as that done by tradespeople, salespeople, and truck drivers. Obtaining such a bond is often dependent on the applicant's financial position.

Individual fidelity bonds can be purchased to provide protection from loss due to dishonest acts on the part of specific employees, for example, people who have previously been convicted of such offences. As a condition of holding such a bond, annual assessments of the employee's performance might be required by the bonding agent. The amount of a fidelity bond and its cost depend primarily on the type of work, how much money is being handled, and the control the employer exerts through office and bookkeeping procedures.

Procedure for Obtaining Bonding

When you find out that a bond is required, ask the employer which company it uses to bond its employees. You can then approach the bonding company directly.

In some situations, you might need to go through an agent or broker who deals directly with the bonding or surety company. Agents themselves do not issue bonds but will support and process applications for bonding. The agent will give you an application form to complete. For your application you might need references from a clergyman or a previous employer, for example, stating that you're trustworthy and reliable. The application form also might ask for information about previous employers and about your financial status. The completed form, along with the required letters of reference, are then submitted to the bonding company.

If you need an agent, look in the Yellow Pages of the telephone directory under "Insurance Brokers" to see which companies handle bonding in your area.

The next step in the process involves investigation by the bonding agent of your background and status. The investigation can include contacts with friends, neighbours, and relatives, as well as an examination of your financial records. If strong recommendations are made in the letters of reference, this type of inquiry might not be required.

In summary, the decision whether to bond depends primarily on the description of the work, type and amount of bond applied for, and references. Usually, if your employer also is willing to support your application for bond, the company will look on that favourably.

Adapted from Employment and Immigration Canada. PLACE. Guided Steps to Employment Readiness. "Part E: Personal Needs." © Minister of Supply and Services Canada, 1984, Unit 20. Reproduced with the permission of the Minister of Supply and Services Canada, 1990.

Bonding Quiz

1. Define the term *bonding*.
2. Who pays for the bond?
3. Name the types of bonds available to individuals and explain each in your own words.
4. List the procedures for obtaining bonding.
5. Why might you need references when applying for bonding?
6. What happens in the event of a loss caused by a dishonest bonded employee?

Knowing and Observing Company Policies

Employees are sometimes not fully aware of their employer's policies, rules, and procedures. Sometimes this is the fault of the employer in not providing the information, but often it is due to the employee's failure to read information that the company has provided. Rules define the obligations of the employer and the employee to each other and should be carefully read and followed. The following guidelines will help you to be a better employee.

1. Find out the rules. Read all information provided about your job and company policies and benefits. Keep this written information so that you can refer to it when the need arises. Do not discard such information or ignore it. Before accepting work you should inquire about basic company policies and procedures and then reconfirm these once you start the work. Either obtain printed information from the personnel or human resource department or write down the details in a notebook about:

   a) Working hours:
      - Starting and leaving times.
      - Number of hours per day.
      - Overtime policies.
      - Breaks.

   b) Leave Policies:
      - Holidays.
      - Vacation length and timing.
      - Sick leave.
      - Accident leave.
      - Compassionate leave.

   c) Employee benefits.
   d) Health and safety regulations.
   e) Union organization and agreement details.
   f) Grievance (complaint) procedures.
   g) Rules about privacy and confidentiality of information you learn at work.

2. Organizations usually have unwritten rules that you'll learn about only by observing the behaviour of other employees and listening to them. This can range from how to address certain senior company officials to what to wear to work. Keep your eyes and ears open!

3. If you don't understand a rule or feel that it's being enforced unfairly, ask your supervisor or co-workers for an explanation informally before grumbling or filing a formal complaint. Often an informal chat can resolve the situation.

4. Even when you disagree with a rule or policy, it's your obligation to follow it until it's been changed officially. You can and should make your complaint known, but if you just ignore the rules, you can be fired.

employment termination

If You Resign

You're expected to give notice to your employer when you decide to resign. It's wise to give this notice in writing as well as verbally. One of your most valuable references in the future could be from your employer, and any employer would hesitate to recommend a former employee who left without allowing some time for the finding of a replacement.

In some provinces, the employer has a right to insist that you give notice. Employees working under federal labour legislation are not obliged to give any notice at all. Most union and individual contracts throughout Canada contain a clause stipulating a notice period before you can leave a position.

So, no matter what reason you might have for leaving the position, resign in a professional manner. If possible, give at least two-weeks' notice. Finish any projects you might have started, and leave your work area organized and tidy for the next person. Give the personnel/human resource department an address at which you can be reached. Remember, you might want to work for the same employer at some time in the future.

If You Are Discharged

Under the Canada Labour Code, employees who are discharged are entitled to severance pay equal to regular wages for a specific time period if the employee has not been given notice and if the dismissal was not for just cause. Just cause could include such behaviour on the part of an employee as willful misconduct (such as theft), disobedience, or neglect of duty. In such cases, the dismissed employee would not be entitled to either notice or severance pay.

Some union contracts contain clauses that require the employer to pay severance compensation to the discharged employee according to a formula that takes into consideration the amount of time that the employee has worked.

For higher-income executives, severance pay sometimes equals six-months' to a year's salary. Some employees have fought and won legal battles to receive larger compensation because they felt they were unjustly discharged.

When an employee is discharged or quits, the company is required to furnish the employee with a Record of Employment. This is an official document that is required if an employee wants to apply for employment insurance. This paper is important even if the employee has not worked the number of weeks that are required to receive benefits. The required number of insurable weeks of employment can be accumulated with weeks of work from several employers. This is an important record that should be kept in a safe place.

Claimants of employment insurance who are fired or who have quit their jobs are penalized by having their benefits withheld for a prescribed number of weeks. Claimants have the right to appeal decisions about their claims to a tribunal if they feel that they are being unduly penalized.

Chapter Summary Exercises

1. Name some employee benefits offered by employers.
2. What compulsory deductions are made from wages?
3. Why is it less expensive for an employee to belong to a group life insurance plan than to buy it as an individual?
4. Name four benefits that a group health insurance plan might cover that a provincial health plan might not.
5. How is the amount of a pension received by a retired employee from the Canada Pension Plan or the Québec Pension Plan determined?
6. Name some usual paid time-off benefits.
7. What protection does a supplemental unemployment plan offer employees?
8. What is severance pay?
9. List important company policies that you should know about.
10. Analyse sample employee performance evaluations to assess strengths, weaknesses, and areas for improvement.
11. Describe appropriate techniques for resigning from a position.
12. Identify strategies for coping with loss of employment.

Reflective Journal

1. What effect can the decision to *leave* a position have on you? Think in terms of your work, home, social life.
2. What effect can being *discharged* from work have on you? Think in terms of your work, home and social life. What are the differences and similarities between leaving work because you want to and being dismissed?

Internet Activity

Refer to the Internet databases on work postings, and write a report on the most common employee benefits.

Do you see any differences between union and non-union employees as far as benefits are concerned?

Chapter 20

Labour Unions

objectives

After completing this chapter you should be able to:

- ▶ Explain what a union is, how it functions, and the issues it handles.
- ▶ Describe how and why unions first came into existence.
- ▶ Define the terms *collective bargaining* and *collective agreement* and explain the purpose of each.
- ▶ Discuss what grievances are and how these are handled in unionized organizations.

introduction

Labour unions in Canada are recognized as institutions with important economic and social functions, concerned not only with wages and working hours but also with more far-reaching issues. Unions attempt to have a voice in all phases of employee-employer relations, including employee safety and benefits, unemployment, disability insurance, retirement pensions, workers' compensation and other forms of social welfare, and unfair employment practices.

Unions are also involved in the reformation of social and political policies, expanding their original focus to issues dealing with poverty, discrimination of any type, the environment, housing, and the need for improvement in the health care system. Unions also are active in the area of job training and retraining, trying to help solve the problems created by the advance of technology, which has resulted in the disappearance of some work and the creation of new work for which additional training is required.

What were working conditions like before unions? How is a labour union formed? How do unions operate? All of these questions will be answered in this chapter.

history of labour unions in canada

When our society was based on an economy that was primarily agricultural, many people worked for themselves as farmers or in small shops. However, as technology advanced, many smaller businesses were unable to compete in the marketplace against the cheaper-priced goods that were mass-produced by larger businesses.

People who had previously produced some of the goods that their families required went to work for these businesses, creating an even larger market for commercially manufactured goods. Wages were usually low and working hours long, often twelve hours a day, six days a week. Working conditions generally were poor and often jeopardized the health and safety of employees. The tasks employees performed were usually monotonous and physically demanding. Complaints were few, however, because the employees were afraid of losing their jobs.

In addition, until as recently as the beginning of this century, child labour was common. Today, child labour is defined as the regular employment of children under the age of fifteen or sixteen, but in the late eighteenth century it was generally assumed that children from about the age of seven should be employed full-time outside their homes. These children worked long hours—often thirteen to sixteen hours a day with little or no time off—in bad and often hazardous working conditions. Young children were particularly of value in the mines, where their small size enabled them to work in narrow, low passages that adults couldn't enter. And, of course, children could be paid far less than adults, so factories, mills, and farms welcomed the cheap labour provided by children. The children's parents were usually extremely poor and had no choice but to send their children out to work, warning the youngsters that they must do everything they were told, without question, because employment was so hard to find and the family's welfare depended on them.

The jobs these children did were, for the most part, dead-end, menial occupations, with no hope of advancement, so the children were doomed to lives as poor as those of their parents. Education for other than the children of wealthy families was considered to be of little importance in Canada until the late nineteenth century and the early part of this century.

Finally, workers decided that something must be done and began to band together to demand fair treatment from employers. In the United States, unions began developing in the 1830s, followed in the 1860s by the United Kingdom and Canada. The purpose of these unions was to identify unfair wage levels, overly long work hours, unsafe or inhumane working conditions, and, in general, unacceptable treatment by employers. Where at one time individual employees had been afraid to speak up, suddenly employers were faced by the protests of all of the members of a certain trade and often of related trades, accompanied by threats that production would be stopped if problems weren't solved to the employees' satisfaction.

labour unions today

Unions operate on the same basic principle today, bargaining for such items as:

- ▶ Fair wages that take into account the rising cost of living.
- ▶ Work security.
- ▶ Safe, clean working conditions.
- ▶ Recognition of seniority in relation to promotions, layoffs, rehiring, and choice of working hours and vacation times.
- ▶ Discontinuance of favouritism and similar injustices to employees.
- ▶ Proper grievance procedures to enable employees to present justified complaints to unbiased committees.
- ▶ Agreements that provide extended maternity and sick leaves, and regular yearly vacations.
- ▶ Satisfactory retirement programs.

Today's labour unions play an important role in the working world. Union members account for more than 37 percent of the non-agricultural, paid labour force. Even non-unionized employees can thank the unions for the general improvement in working conditions and employee benefits. For example, wages are higher because both unionized and non-unionized companies compete for the same skilled and qualified employees.

Many of the occupations you might consider for your future are unionized or involve working closely with members of a union. Some of the Canadian unions with the largest membership are the Canadian Union of Public Employees; the National Union of Public and General Employees; the Public Service Alliance of Canada; the National Automobile, Aerospace and Agricultural Implement Workers' Union of Canada; the United Food and Commercial Workers' International Union; and the United Steelworkers of America.

ACTIVITY 1

Investigating Others' Opinions of Unions

1. Interview someone who belongs to a union. Ask the following questions and add some of your own. Prepare a brief report of your findings.

   a) What is your occupation?
   b) What is the name of your union?
   c) What does your union do for you?
   d) What do you think would happen if there wasn't a union?
   e) How is your union organized?
   f) Who makes the decisions for your union?
   g) How does a strike affect you?

2. Interview someone who does *not* belong to a union, asking the following questions and adding some of your own. Prepare a brief report.

   a) What is your occupation?
   b) Would you like to belong to a union?
   c) How do you and your co-workers handle problems you encounter at your workplace?

how unions operate

Labour unions are made up of people who work in similar occupations or organizations. The main function of each unit is collective bargaining, which means that representatives of the employees and of the employer bargain for improved wages, benefits, and working conditions. The agreement reached between the two sets of representatives is called a *collective agreement*, a legal document that lists the items agreed to by both sides during negotiations.

Unions must meet a number of legal requirements before they can represent their members. The vast majority of workers in Canada come under provincial jurisdiction. While the provisions of the law vary somewhat from province to province, they are in most essential ways very similar. A limited number of workers, such as those engaged in interprovincial transportation, communications, and a few other industries, as well as federal employees, are under federal jurisdiction.

how a union is formed

The following steps are involved in the formation of a union.

1. Identification of the group of employees that the union is to represent, such as people who work in certain trades or people who work in the same industry or in related industries. An auto workers' union, for example, might represent not only the people involved in the actual manufacture of vehicles but also people in related industries, such as tire and battery company employees.

2. An invitation is extended to the identified group of employees by the union organizers. Employees who want to join sign an application form and make a small initial payment of dues or pay an initiation fee to indicate their commitment.

3. When the union has the support of the majority of qualified employees, an application for certification is made to the appropriate labour relations board. Certification means that the union is granted official recognition by the government and is entitled to enter into collective bargaining on behalf of its members.

4. Once certification has been granted, the members of the new union elect their own officers, such as president, vice-president, secretary, and treasurer. The elected officers are in charge of all of the activities of the local union and are governed by its constitution. The members pay dues, part of which are kept by the local union and part of which go to the national or international union to which most local unions belong.

Various types of services are provided by the national and international unions, such as assistance in negotiations with an employer. The local union also has the benefit of the expertise of staff such as lawyers, economists, and other research specialists. Education in the form of brochures, newsletters, and training programs for local union officers is undertaken by the larger union.

Aspects of the operation of national and international unions are addressed at conventions held periodically, to which each local union is entitled to send delegates. These delegates help to decide the terms of the union constitution, make budgetary and policy decisions, and elect officers.

ACTIVITY 2

Researching Union Relationships

Identify a local union and then do research to find out if this union belongs to a national or international union. Your teacher will help you to get started on this project. Record the correct names of both the local union and the larger one, making sure that you have the spellings correct, the number of members in both unions, and the types of industries represented by both.

collective bargaining

A union can begin collective bargaining when it has the support of the majority of the employees and has received official certification. The most common procedure is for the members of the local union to hold a meeting, or more often a series of meetings, to decide on the proposals that will be made to management, the representatives of the employer. Members are selected to act on the bargaining committee. A negotiator or a specialist might be provided by the national or international union to provide consultation on wage scales, employee benefits, and negotiation strategies.

The contract proposal advanced by the union might cover a wide variety of issues. Wages and job security are the most common, but by no means the only, concerns. Suggestions might be advanced relating to vacations, pension plans, extended maternity and sick-leave benefits, cost of living allowances (COLA), medical insurance, seniority provisions governing promotions, and grievance procedures. The members of the local union vote on exactly what proposals are to be made. The elected bargaining committee then arranges to meet the representatives of management.

The spokesperson for management might be the head of the company, the director of the personnel department, or other company officials, usually depending on the size of the company.

Bargaining is often a slow process. The proposals advanced by the union might be met by counter-proposals from management, followed by a period of discussion, and often by concessions being made by each side. Periodically the two groups engaged in bargaining report back to their superiors; in the case of the union, the bargaining committee reports to a membership meeting, where it might receive additional instructions.

Approximately 90 percent of the time, voluntary agreement is finally reached between management and the employees. The terms of the agreement are then written into a contract. This contract governs the wages, hours, and other conditions of employment in that particular company for a specified period, normally between one to three years.

Problems in the Bargaining Process

If the two parties find it impossible to reach an agreement, then government assistance is provided under the labour laws of the various provinces and by federal legislation. The assistance given varies somewhat from province to province but usually is as follows.

1. A conciliation officer, usually an official of the government's labour department, is appointed. This person meets with union and management representatives to determine the nature and extent of their differences. If possible, the conciliation officer helps the two sides to resolve their differences, and a contract is signed.
2. If the first step fails, a conciliation board is often established, usually made up of a representative of the union, a representative of management, and a chairperson selected by these two representatives. If the two sides can't agree on the selection of a chairperson, one can be appointed by the Minister of Labour. The conciliation board conducts hearings, listens to both sides' arguments, and then prepares a report. If agreement can be reached at this stage, a contract is signed. If not, employees are in a legal position to strike, after a time period specified by law.

strikes

The final decision as to whether there will be a strike rests with the employees concerned. First the union members vote on what action should be taken. In many cases, an agreement is reached and a contract is signed without any strike action. In only about 10 percent of contract negotiation situations is strike action considered necessary.

When a union does strike, employees usually picket their place of employment to draw attention to their problem. Some unions are required by law to provide essential services in the case of a strike, such as police protection and medical services. A strike means hardship for the employees, management, and the public: the employees need their wages, the company will lose money if operations are discontinued, and strikes always disadvantage the public in some way.

When a company hires non-union workers to replace the unionized workers during a strike, the replacements are sometimes referred to as scabs. Some provinces have anti-scab laws that prevent management from hiring non-union labour to fill union positions. In these cases, other members of the company (including management) are often forced to carry on operations by performing the tasks of the unionized workers, even if they're not fully qualified to do so.

Union members vote to strike or to end a strike at the local union level. Sometimes a strike is ended when management obtains an injunction, a court order that ends the strike. Any employees who continue to strike could be fined or lose seniority.

ACTIVITY 3 Report on Strikes

Are union employees currently on strike in your area? Why did the employees decide to strike? If a strike is not occurring in your area now, read the newspapers to see if one is underway elsewhere and write a report about it. If all else fails, do research and a report on past strikes. Your local library or newspaper office could be a source of information.

grievances

Employment contracts are intended to provide an orderly plan for dealing with most labour-management interactions. One of the most important sections of the contract is the one that specifies methods for the settlement of grievances, which are employee complaints that their rights are not being respected.

While every province has legislation that protects the rights of employees (see Chapter 9 regarding prohibited grounds of discrimination in employment, for example) and specifies minimum wages and working condition standards, many issues arise that don't fit precisely into certain legal categories. When this is the case, members can turn to their unions for assistance.

Grievances can concern a number of matters: safety of working conditions, appropriate rates of pay, changes in job description (meaning that an employee might be expected to do tasks that were not specified when that employee was hired), unfair dismissal, etc. An employee who has a complaint about a matter that's a violation of the terms of the contract, has the right to file a grievance with the union.

When a grievance is filed, steps are usually taken first to settle it within the department where the worker is employed. Key people in the settlement effort might be the supervisor of the department and the union shop steward, the person who is usually the head of the local union. The shop steward is one of the employees who has been chosen by co-workers, through the union, to represent the interests of those who work in his or her section.

If a settlement is not reached at this stage, the matter is taken to a higher level involving more senior union officers and company officials. If after this process no agreement is reached, the matter can be placed before a third party from the outside called an *arbitrator* or before several people on an arbitration board. Sometimes a case is heard by a judge from Human Resources Development Canada. The decision given is then binding on the company, the employee, and the representative union.

union membership dues

Whether all employees are required to join the union depends on the terms agreed on by the employees who are already members of the union. The term *closed shop* refers to a company that hires only union members. In a *union shop*, employees are required to join a union after a specified period of time. Even part-time employees such as summer employees are required to pay dues if they work in a union shop, although they might not be required to join the union. In an *open shop*, employees aren't required to be or to become union members.

The term *Rand Formula* refers to a provision whereby the employer deducts a portion of the salaries of *all* employees in a bargaining unit, even if they are not union members, to be given to the union as union dues. This is called *checkoff*. It was named for a decision handed down in 1946 by Mr. Justice Ivan Rand of the Supreme Court of Canada while he was arbitrating the first strike after World War II, which took place at the Ford Motor Company in Windsor, Ontario. The major issue in this strike was for union recognition, and Rand's decision marked a significant step forward in union–management negotiations.

Under the Rand Formula, employees aren't required to actually join the union but they are required to pay union dues. This plan is based on the philosophy that all employees benefit from the activities of the union and should, therefore, contribute to its maintenance. It should be remembered that, with reference to all of these plans, the union is required to obtain and prove the support of a majority of the workers before it can attain a position to gain such provisions.

Formation of Local 18 of the Canadian Union of Delivery Workers

After work one day, four drivers of the ABC Courier Company met for coffee and, in the course of their conversation, decided that something had to be done about the way they were being treated at work. The drivers' wages varied but it seemed that wages averaged a measly $6.95/h (for those who talked about it). It also seemed that the boss's favourite drivers got much higher wages.

Another problem seemed to be the company's expectation that, with last-minute notification, the employees would willingly work overtime. This happened frequently and inconvenienced many of the drivers and dispatchers. Many of the employees were single parents and others who had to get home to handle family responsibilities. Also unfair was the requirement that the dispatchers be on the job half an hour prior to their shifts when they were not paid for this time. To top it all off, employee benefits were non-existent.

Employees who complained or frequently refused to work late or come in early were notified that they were "redundant" or "not flexible enough"—and fired. Jobs were hard to come by, so the employees grudgingly accepted the situation.

The issue of favouritism also aroused great resentment. Unless you played up to the boss or supervisors, you didn't get anywhere. The boss's favourites got better pay and the best delivery routes.

Eventually the situation became intolerable. The employees were tired of being treated unfairly and taken for granted. Over coffee, the four drivers decided to seek the help of a union organizer. They called the offices of the Canadian Union of Delivery Workers and arranged to meet with a union official in secret the next night.

After that meeting, a committee of ABC Courier Company employees was formed. The committee had to go to all employees' homes—also secretly—to ask them to sign union cards and pay a small fee. Many employees were nervous about signing up, but the organizing drive was very successful and 43 out of 60 employees signed.

The union made an application to the government for certification as the bargaining agent for all of the employees of the ABC Courier Company. ABC's management were not happy. They tried to correct some past wrongs and even increased all of the employees' wages, but the damage had already been done. The government received the application and issued a vote order at the workplace. Weeks later the government sent a representative to the ABC office and set up a polling station. The employees voted in secret to determine if they wanted a union. The union won certification because 70 percent of the employees voted to join the union.

Questions

1. List five complaints of the drivers and dispatchers of the ABC Courier Company.
2. Which drivers and dispatchers do you think would not want to have a union? Explain your answer.
3. List some of the ways in which a union could help the drivers and dispatchers of the ABC Courier Company.
4. Why were ABC management unhappy about the union applying for certification? What did they try to do? Why did they not succeed?

ACTIVITY 4

Understanding Union Functions

1. In terms of the workplace, what is a union? How does your dictionary define the word union?
2. Explain what a grievance is and give examples of the types of grievances you think employees might have.
3. Name some company policies and benefits that might be particularly important to female employees.
4. Explain the process of collective bargaining.
5. Do you think that employees who provide essential services should have the right to strike? Explain your answer. Name two essential services and explain the effects of each going on strike.
6. Would you like to belong to a union? Why or why not?

Chapter Summary Exercises

In your notebook, write each statement below and fill in the word or phrase from the following list that best fits.

a) grievance
b) shop steward
c) COLA
d) negotiating
e) injunction

f) strike
g) employee benefits
h) seniority
i) certification
j) closed shop

k) picket
1) collective bargaining
m) checkoff
n) collective agreement
o) conciliation

1. A refusal to work because a satisfactory contract cannot be negotiated is called a/an ____.
2. An employer and employees who are trying to come to an agreement are ____.
3. A legal step that can be used by an employer to end a strike is called a/an ____.
4. A/an ____ lists the agreements between an employer and a union relating to wages, working conditions, fringe benefits, etc.
5. The ____ is the union worker elected by co-workers to represent them in dealings with management.
6. Dental plans, pension plans, sick-leave plans, etc., are called ____.

7. A company that won't hire non-union workers is called a/an ____.
8. The method of settling a dispute between an employer and employees by bringing in a third party is known as ____.
9. One method of collecting union dues is ____.
10. ____ is a legal requirement for a group to become a union.
11. Workers on strike usually ____ their place of work.
12. A unionized employee has the right to file a ____ if some part of her or his contract is not honoured.
13. In a unionized organization, ____ is taken into account when promotions are being considered.
14. A method of determining wages, hours, etc., through direct negotiation between the union and the employer is called ____.
15. ____ is the short form for "cost of living allowance."

Adapted from Ontario Ministry of Education. *Work and Employability Skills Program*, 1982, p. 94.

Reflective Journal

1. Do the workers at your placement workplace have a union? How does belonging to a union affect the worker?
2. How do you feel about unions? Has your opinion of unions changed while studying this chapter?
3. How do you feel about the issue of equal pay for work of equal value for women and men? Contact your member of the provincial government for his or her response to this issue, and describe your conversation.
4. Have you ever been aware of any stereotypes, biases, and discriminatory behaviours, that may affect opportunities for people in certain occupations?

Internet Activity

Using Internet information sources, list ten occupations that have a high *percentage* of union membership and five occupations that have large *numbers* of union members.